dX -STAT

WRITTEN BY

Mark C. MacKinnon

ADDITIONAL WRITING BY

Adam Jury, Stephen Kenson, Jeff Mackintosh, David L. Pulver, Jesse Scoble

ART DIRECTION AND GRAPHIC PRODUCTION BY

Jeff Mackintosh

EDITING BY

Jeff Mackintosh , Jesse Scoble

SPECIAL THANKS

To the hundreds of Tri-Stat playtesters that contributed to the system since GUARDIANS OF ORDER hit the scene in 1997.

MEMBER OF

THE GAME
MANUFACTURERS
ASSOCIATION

© 2003 GUARDIANS OF ORDER, INC. All Rights Reserved.

All images © 2003 of their respective copyright holders and used with permission.

GUARDIANS OF ORDER, and TRI-STAT SYSTEM are trademarks of GUARDIANS OF ORDER, INC.

First Printing — June 2003 Printed in Canada

ISBN 1-894525-81-7 • Production Number 18-001

GUARDIANS OF ORDER, INC. • P.O. Box 25016, 370 Stone Road, Guelph, Ontario, CANADA, N1G 4T4

Phone: (519) 821-7174 • Fax: (519) 821-7635 • info@guardiansorder.com • http://www.guardiansorder.com

Core System Role-Playing Game

Role-Playing Game Manifesto

These rules are written on paper, not etched in stone tablets.

Rules are suggested guidelines, not required edicts.

If the rules don't say you can't do something, you can.

There are no official answers, only official opinions.

When dice conflict with the story, the story always wins.

Min/Maxing and munchkinism aren't problems with the game; they're problems with the player.

The Game Master has full discretionary power over the game.

The Game Master always works with, not against, the players.

A game that is not fun is no longer a game — it's a chore.

This book contains the answers to all things.

When the above does not apply, make it up.

TABLE OF CONTENTS

WELCOME TO TRI-STAT dX

The quest for the perfect role-playing system. Endless ... tireless ... it constantly eludes your grasp. You cross your fingers and take a deep breath as you open the first page of this book. Is Tri-Stat dX the answer you've been waiting for?

Sorry, but probably not. It may come damn close, though.

Everyone has a preference concerning the elements they like in an RPG. Rules-light vs. rules-heavy. Point-based vs. class-based. Effects-based vs. power-based. Three stats vs. six stats vs. nine stats. Multi-genre vs. campaign specific. Roll low vs. roll high. Modular vs. integrated. Bell curve vs. linear. d6 vs. d10 vs. d20. Independent rolls vs. opposed rolls. Role-playing intensive vs. combat intensive. The list is endless.

Our Role-Playing Game Manifesto on page 2 gives you insight into our design philosophy at GUARDIANS OF ORDER. If you want a few more hints into what Tri-Stat dX has in store, you can consider it a rules-light, point-based, effects-based, three-stat, multi-genre, roll-low, modular, bell-curved, independent-rolling, role-playing-intensive game system that uses any sized dice.

So is this the game for you?

Read on. We'll let Tri-Stat dX speak for itself.

HISTORY OF THE TRI-STAT SYSTEM

The Tri-Stat System premiered at GenCon 1997 in our first publication, *Big Eyes, Small Mouth*. It used two six-sided dice to resolve all tasks, didn't include a skill system, and had very few rules. The little 96-page anime RPG was an instant success, selling through its first print run very quickly and earning an Origins Award nomination for the Best RPG.

Over a year later, Tri-Stat was expanded in the *Sailor Moon RPG and Resource Book* to include more options and game mechanics. From 1999 to 2002, new mechanics and options were added to each RPG that we published to customise the game to suit our goals. The core elements remained the same, but the details were refined.

- *Dominion Tank Police RPG and Resource Book* included a mecha creation system and Skills.
- *Demon City Shinjuku RPG and Resource Book* added new magical/occult-related powers.
- *Tenchi Muyo! RPG and Resource Book* added new powers, including Duplicate and Summon/Control Servant.
- *Big Eyes, Small Mouth* Second Edition compiled the previously published Tri-Stat System material, added new combat options, and expanded on the genre-dependent costs for Skills.
- *Ghost Dog RPG and Resource Book* introduced grittier game mechanics, including Shock Value, for more realistic games.
- *Heaven & Earth* Second Edition changed dice rolling to drawing from a deck of playing cards, and featured an innovative destiny and fate mechanic.
- *El-Hazard RPG and Resource Book* incorporated mystery game points through a GM-driven Unknown Superpowers Attribute.
- *Hong Kong Action Theatre!* Second Edition changed the Stat costs to staged values and modified the all-or-nothing damage to all, nothing, or 50%.

In mid-2002, the Tri-Stat System changed substantially in the release of our *Silver Age Sentinels* superhero RPG. To reflect the awesome power characters have in comics, the scope of Tri-Stat powers expanded from 6 Levels to 10 Levels, Stats grew from 12 to 20 values, and average Point totals increased from 30-60 to 100-300. Additionally, 10-sided dice were used instead of 6-sided dice and Attributes became more customisable — adding area, duration, range, and target options — through the inclusion of Power Modifier Values. This wasn't the Tri-Stat System you used to play.

To further address superhero power levels, *Silver Age Sentinels* included a sidebar about scaling the Tri-Stat System. Of the three options presented, the one that suggested changing the game dice from d10s to another dice size struck a chord with us.

We had discovered our grand unification theory ... and it was right in front of us the entire time. The evolution of the Tri-Stat System moved beyond d6 (*BESM*) and d10 (*SAS*) to the new standard — dX.

APPLICATIONS OF TRI-STAT dX

Tri-Stat dX is the ideal game for running any adventure you can imagine — any genre, setting, theme, mood, time period, or power level. You can create characters for any nationality, race, occupation, archetype, class, or background. In short, Tri-Stat dX can handle anything you can throw at it ... and then some.

The flexibility of Tri-Stat dX is a result of its scalability. By changing the dice type used in games of different power levels — low-powered games use dice with fewer sides, while high-powered games use dice with a greater number of sides — Tri-Stat is easily customised for your campaign.

DICE AND NOTATIONS

Tri-Stat dX uses polyhedral (multi-sided) dice during game play, though usually only a single die type in each adventure or campaign. This typically includes dice with the following number of sides: 4, 6, 8, 10, 12, or (rarely) 20. When you need to generate a random number with a dice roll, always roll two dice with the appropriate number of sides, known as rolling 2dX, where:

- d represents the word "dice"
- X is the type of dice rolled (number of sides)

For example, 2dX in a street-level detective game would likely indicate 2d6 (roll two 6-sided dice), while 2dX in a superhero game could instead mean 2d10. The values showing on each die after the roll are added together to generate a random number between 2 and 2X. If your roll of 2dX generates a 4 on one die and a 6 on another, for instance, the final result is 10.

Sometimes X, called the "game dice," is used by itself in the text to suggest an upper limit for a specific game mechanic. For example, the game Attributes (page 9) available to characters typically range from Level 1 through Level X. Consequently, up to Level 8 is available in a posthuman game (8-sided dice); up to Level 12 is available in an inhuman game (12-sided dice).

The character power levels and associated game dice are explained further on page 7.

WHY CHANGE THE DICE?

The dice size needs to change to alter the probabilities of achieving success for the range of character aptitudes. For example, a Stat of 4 represents the adult human average. In Tri-Stat dX, to succeed in a Stat-related task, the player must roll his or her character's Stat or lower on two dice (task resolution is explained in Chapter 7: Game Mechanics; page 58). In a superhero game that uses d10, the probability of rolling 4 or less is only 6% — not very likely. This is a desired result, though, since average humans shouldn't often succeed in tasks that are considered normal for a superhero game.

In a human-level game that uses d6, though, the probability increases to 17%. Again, this percentage matches the desired result since an average human should have a reasonable, not miniscule, chance of succeeding in a game where above-average humans are the normal player characters.

Changing the size of the dice is an easy way to scale the game to the correct power level (and thus success frequency) for the players characters.

SAMPLE GENRES/SETTINGS/ PERIODS/THEMES

Included herein is a small sample of 30 different campaign types that are ideal for use with Tri-Stat dX, along with the most commonly associated game dice.

MULTI-GENRE

Any Campaign

Perhaps time-travel is in the plans, or maybe you're just not sure where your campaign will be going. If you need flexibility, the Multi-Genre campaign is what you need! Game Dice: d6 or d10.

MODERN DAY

Action Adventure

Like an adrenalin-pumping movie, Action Adventure campaigns thrust the heroes into the thick of things right from the get-go. While moral and ethical dilemmas will be present, the tempo should always pounding — play hard or go home! Game Dice: d8.

Animal Adventures

Animals speak their own languages and have their own adventures, independent, in spite, or because of humans. You may be avoiding slavery, saving your relatives, finding a new home, or all of the above and more! Game Dice: d4.

Conspiracy

They know something that they won't tell you — or you know something that they won't believe. The military and government cover-up aliens, mutants, and more in this genre, which mixes action and investigation in near equal parts. Game Dice: d6.

Law Enforcement

Organized and disorganized crime owns the streets, while the boys in blue try to keep the peace. Corrupt cops, mafia dons, FBI agents, CIA special ops, lawmakers, and judges — all players in the tangled webs of a law enforcement campaign. Game Dice: d6.

Loony Cartoons

Crazy capers in worlds where reality does not apply! Characters must foil the crew of bad guys time after time, because they just don't know when to quit! Game Dice: d4 or d6.

Occult / Horror

Horror can take many forms, from ghosts exerting night-time influence on the impressionable to cults seeking ultimate power for themselves. However the horror is created, the characters must be kept on their toes; one wrong move could be the ultimate end for them. Game Dice: d8.

Pulp

Travel the world in search of artefacts — many not meant for man's eye — thought to be lost forever. High action and heroism mixed with grave-robbing and evil masterminds. Game Dice: d6.

Reality TV

Some people will do anything for fifteen minutes of fame and Reality TV proves that! Daring and disgusting stunts, social drama, and physical hardships all play a role when your future lies in the hands of those you compete against — or with the watching public. Game Dice: d6.

Romantic Comedy

How many ways can love and lust go wrong in a single session? Bad blind dates, falling for your best friend, saying the wrong name at the altar ... love hurts! Game Dice: d6.

Soap Opera

Love. Hate. Marriage. Divorce. Bitter custody battles. Hospitals — what is so interesting about hospitals? Anything can happen in a soap opera, and backstabbing melodrama is certainly in the cards! Game Dice: d6.

Superhero

Uphold the values of liberty, justice, security, and peace ... or flip the coin and terrorize the world with your diabolical plans! Hey, why don't you play *Silver Age Sentinels*? Game Dice: d10 or d12.

Urban Fantasy

Myths are no longer just that; vampires, faeries, spirits, and magic all exist in the modern world, often forced to conceal their true nature for fear of persecution. Secret societies, sects, political intrigue, and backstabbing are cause for a tense and dramatic campaign. Game Dice: d6.

HISTORICAL

20th Century War

From the earliest days of World War I to the many Middle Eastern conflicts in the 90s, technology and tactics have changed a great deal. Jungles to Desert; General to Grunt; Land to Air — the scope of modern war offers a wide variety of campaigns. Game Dice: d6.

Age of Pirates

Arrrr! Set sail for far-away ports and mysterious bounty. Along the way you'll face the unforgiving ocean, potential mutiny, and other pirates. Will the treasure still be there when you arrive? Game Dice: d6.

Ancient China / Japan

Explore ancient dynasties while battling for and against feuding warlords. An honourable *samurai* can turn *ronin*, masterless and outcast, with one mistake. Game Dice: d6.

Ancient Egypt

The sands of time obscure some of the most amazing human creations and a very advanced civilization. Religion and worship dominated Egyptian life, and the afterlife was seen as very important. Game Dice: d6.

Ancient Rome / Greece

Greece was the founding point of democracy, city-states, and the site of the Trojan War. Political and military campaigns will be the focus — or go back to 700 BC and relive the first Olympics. Game Dice: d6.

Middle Ages

Feudal times were tough on everyone, especially the lower classes. Survive the plague, live through the wars, and raise your political influence. Game Dice: d6.

Old West

Seek out fortune and fame, but don't lose it all in a game of poker. Gold hunters, outlaws, Native Americans, sheriffs, gamblers and vigilantes roam the wild United States from east to west. Game Dice: d6.

Stone Age

Be the first to invent the wheel! In the Stone Age, the necessities — shelter, food, fire — take centre stage as you forge ahead and create basic tools and technology. Game Dice: d4.

Victorian

Elegant beauty and sophisticated tastes collide with overwhelming poverty and despair. The distance between the rich and poor is insurmountable, and a life of crime is the only way for some to get ahead. Game Dice: d6.

FANTASY

Low Fantasy

Wage war, explore mysterious new lands, and research the arcane arts. Monarchies rule the lands while gallant knights defend Queen and Country against outside threats. Game Dice: d6.

High Fantasy

The fate of civilisation is balanced on the edge of your sword. Globe-trot (or take a handy airship) to enchanted places, each one more fiercely guarded than the last, in search of the one way to destroy true evil. Game Dice: d8.

FUTURISTIC

Cyberpunk / Biopunk

The dark streets of the near future are home to street *samurai*, gangers, fixers, deckers, and all types of counter-culture. Country-owning megacorps, embittered police forces, and powerful syndicates employ them as deniable assets in a world of technological evolution. Game Dice: d8.

Hard SF

Science and exploration are the keys to this genre, which focuses on the realistic extrapolation of technology and society. Politics and sciences, both physical and social, drive you toward a better future. Game Dice: d8.

Mecha

Giant robots are an amazing combat tool — and great for picking up dates! With space travel common and new territory being fought over all the time, both politics and combat are of utmost importance. Game Dice: d8.

Post Apocalyptic

Following the largest disaster in recorded history, humankind struggles to regain what it has lost. Compounding the problem is the mundane (no clean water, hospitals, or electricity) and the insane (mutants, power-mad warlords, and strange geological shifts). Game Dice: d6 or d8.

Soft SF

Travel through far-away solar systems in search of new planets, life forms, and intelligence. Your discoveries may be routine or humbling — new plants, or an entire race of A.I.s. Game Dice: d8 or d10.

Space Opera

Galaxy-wide political and physical struggles between good and evil are never-ending. Faster-than-light starships, living planets, sentient robots, forbidden romances, and unstoppable dictators will keep the heroes in excitement and peril until the very end! Game Dice: d6 or d8.

WHY IS TRI-STAT dX ONLY $10?

With ever-increasing production and printing costs, you may wonder why we are offering our core rules for an unbelievably low price. This book is even available as a free PDF download from our website. Clearly, there has to be a catch ... right?

Right. Here's the catch: we want you to use Tri-Stat dX for all your role-playing campaigns. We hope that by offering an inexpensive alternative to other RPGs on the market, we will accomplish several goals:

- Expose gamers to Tri-Stat who would not otherwise see it because they are not interested in our anime (*Big Eyes, Small Mouth*) or superhero (*Silver Age Sentinels*) games.

- Encourage the Game Master and all players to own a copy of the core rules, rather than just the GM and one or two players in a gaming group.

- Foster growth of the Tri-Stat player network, which will make it easier for players to find local gamers with Tri-Stat experience.

- Add more companies to our creator-owned publishing imprint, Magnum Opus, by increasing the potential sales of their products to a wider audience (see page 91 for more information).

- Streamline future game products by focusing the game material on setting, theme, and player options, rather than republishing the core rules repeatedly.

- Establish a viable and inexpensive/free alternative to the industry behemoth, the d20 System.

Core System Role-Playing Game

CHARACTER CREATION

The design of a new character for the *Tri-Stat dX: Core System Role-Playing Game* should involve a thoughtful collaboration between the player and the GM. Your objective is to create a character who is fun to play, has plenty of reason to undertake adventures, and who fits into the GM's campaign. With Tri-Stat dX, you can choose to spend as little as ten minutes or upwards of an hour designing a character. The difference lies in the amount of detail and individuality given to your character. At no time during an RPG campaign do you have more control over the destiny of your character than during the creation process. If you have any questions about game mechanics or specific character abilities, talk to the GM before you begin character creation.

Step 1: GM Discussion

Talk to the GM about the nature of the upcoming game. Issues that should be addressed include the duration of the game, scheduled playtime, the setting and related timeline, and the thematic intensity level. Based on this, the GM should set the power level of the campaign, which will determine the number of Character Points that you may use to design you character and game dice. See below.

Step 2: Develop Character Outline

Use the game boundaries established through your talk with the GM to develop a rough character outline. See page right column.

Step 3: Assign Stats

Use Character Points to give your character Body, Mind, and Soul Stats, making sure each Stat is not lower than 1 nor higher than twice the size of the game dice. See page 8.

Step 4: Select Attributes

Any remaining Character Points may be used to acquire Attributes, which are rated in Levels from 1 to X. See page 9.

Step 5: Select Skills

Your character receives a number starting Skill Points determined by the game's power level, plus additional Points if you assigned the Highly Skilled Attribute or fewer if you will assign the Unskilled Defect (Step 6). Use the Skill Points to acquire Skills and Specialisations relevant to your character outline. Skill Levels range from 1 to one-half X. See page 41.

Step 6: Select Defects

You are encouraged to take Defects appropriate to your character outline. These Defects will provide you with more role-playing opportunities and give you Bonus Points you can use to raise Stats or acquire additional Character Attributes. See page 50.

Step 7: Calculate Derived Values

After you have modified your character's Stats through Attributes and Defects, you can calculate his or her derived values — Combat Value (both Attack and Defence) and Health Points. Additionally, if the GM is using rules for Energy Points or Shock Value, these Derived Values are also calculated now. See page 57.

Step 8: Earn Background Points

You can earn up to one-half X extra Character Points by giving the GM a background history of your character, an important character story, or a character drawing. See page 58.

STEP 1: GM DISCUSSION

You and the other players should discuss the nature of the upcoming game with the GM. Before any characters are created, the GM should outline such details as genre, setting, campaign duration, story boundaries, and expected time commitment. As a player, you should listen closely to the GM's descriptions since it will directly influence the character you wish to create.

Ask for clarification of any rule modifications the GM plans to use as well as any background restrictions on your character. If you have any game preferences involving issues such as combat intensity, maturity level, or drama versus comedy ratio, let the GM know about them. Help the GM create the game that you all want to play.

One of the most important things that the Game Master should discuss with his or her players is the power level of the game, which determines the Character Point total and game dice (Table 2-1: Character Power Levels). Character Points are a measure of the relative capability of characters. The power level of the game will determined how many Character Points are available to each player, though NPCs may be given widely varying Character Point totals depending on their roles in the game.

If the scope of the game will involve players and NPCs covering a wide range of Character Point values, the game dice should be set at the low or middle scale of these Points, rather than the upper end. For example, in a campaign featuring major NPCs and characters ranging from 75 to 150 Character Points, using d8s would be a better choice than d10s.

Table 2-1: Character Power Levels

POWER LEVEL	CHARACTER POINT VALUE	GAME DICE (dX)
Subhuman	25- 50 Points	Four-sided (d4)
Human	50-75 Points	Six-sided (d6)
Posthuman	75-125 Points	Eight-sided (d8)
Superhuman	125-200 Points	Ten-sided (d10)
Inhuman	200-300 Points	Twelve-sided (d12)
Godlike	300+ Points	Twenty-sided (d20)

STEP 2: DEVELOP CHARACTER OUTLINE

A character outline is a broad concept that provides you with a frame on which to build your character. It is not fully detailed; there is no need for you to concern yourself with the character's specific skills, powers, or background details at this stage. Use the game boundaries established in your discussion with the GM as the starting point for your character and build your outline on that foundation. Discuss your character ideas with the GM to ensure your character will work with those of the other players and with the overall themes and focus of the campaign. Here are some issues to consider:

IS THE CHARACTER HUMAN?

In many game settings, non-human or part-human characters may exist. Examples include: aliens, androids, cyborgs, fantasy races (for example, elves, ogres, or centaurs), genetic constructs (clones, genetically-enhanced people, or human-animal hybrids), ghosts and spirits, gods and goddesses, monsters (for example, demons, shapechangers, or vampires), and robots.

WHAT ARE THE CHARACTER'S STRENGTHS?

In some campaigns, the players may want to create complimentary characters with distinct sets of abilities. A degree of specialisation helps players enjoy their characters by giving them a unique identity. At the same time, it is equally important that the characters are not too specialised, or the group will lack cohesion and other players will sit around bored while each specialist has his or her own little adventure within the game.

WHAT ARE THE CHARACTER'S WEAKNESSES?

Game characters may be larger than life — figures of myth and legend — but usually still have weaknesses. Is the character vulnerable to magic? Does it take a while for the character's powers to activate or can they be negated by some special substance? Does the character have an Achilles Heel? Does the character struggle with an addiction? Providing weaknesses to a character adds greater depth and potential for role-playing.

WHAT HELPS DEFINE THE CHARACTER?

You should decide on the character's age and sex, determine a broad archetype for his or her personality, and sketch an idea of ethnic and social background. On the other hand, it is equally important that a character have room to grow beyond your initial concept. A character that you have spent hours perfecting and detailing may quickly become stagnant and uninteresting once play begins. A good character outline usually focuses on one or two main personality traits and leaves plenty of room for you to explore and develop the character into a fully rounded personality over time. Although the starting archetype should be an integral part of the character, it should not rule all of his or her actions. At some point during the game, your pacifistic martial artist may be driven to an act of vengeance, or your angst-ridden vigilante may finally discover a cause in which to believe. As long as these developments proceed naturally from events in the game, they should be a welcome part of the role-playing experience.

STEP 3: ASSIGN STATS

Stats (or Statistics) are numerical assignments that reflect your character's basic capabilities. Higher Stat values indicate an advanced level of accomplishment or achievement. Tri-Stat dX uses three Stats to represent your character's abilities: Body, Mind, and Soul.

BODY STAT

This Stat measures the physical aspects of your character. This includes overall health, strength, endurance, quickness, rate of healing, manual dexterity, and ability to withstand trauma. A character with a high Body is in good physical shape.

MIND STAT

The Mind Stat represents a character's mental abilities. High values indicate intelligent, witty, and quick-learning characters.

SOUL STAT

The Soul Stat represents luck, willpower, determination, and spirit and can sometimes represent psychic ability, empathy, and unity with nature. A high rating in the Soul Stat helps a character focus his or her personal energies or life force to go beyond his or her normal limits and to fuel special abilities.

Increasing Stat Costs (Optional Rule)

Some GMs may prefer to have the cost for increasing a Stat by one value more expensive than 2 Character Points as the character approaches his or her maximum value. Using this optional rule, Stat values range in cost from 1 Character Point to 5 Character Points (see Table 2-2: Variable Stat Costs). Using this rule will result in a narrower range of Stat values, since few players will assign very high or very low Stats to their characters.

For example, in a posthuman game (d8), a Stat of 9 would cost 19 Character Points: 1 Point each for values 1 and 2, 2 Points each for values 3 through 6, and 3 Points each for values 7 through 9. Conversely, in an inhuman game (d12), a Stat of 9 would cost 16 Character Points: 1 Point each for values 1 through 3, 2 Points each for values 4 through 8, and 3 Points values 9.

Table 2-2: Variable Stat Costs

| | STAT VALUE RANGE | | | | | |
COST/VALUE	d4	d6	d8	d10	d12	d20
1	1	1	1-2	1-3	1-3	1-5
2	2-3	2-4	3-6	4-6	4-8	6-11
3	4-5	5-7	7-10	7-11	9-13	12-18
4	6-7	8-10	11-14	12-15	14-17	18-30
5	8	11-12	15-16	16-18	18-20	30-40

STAT COST

Raising a Stat by one value costs 2 Character Points.

STAT VALUES

For most games, Stats range from 1 to 20, although the maximum Stat values available to your character are determined by the game dice (see Table 2-4: Maximum Stat Values). A value of 4 in a Stat is the adult human average with ratings under 4 indicating decreasing competency and ratings over 4 designating increasing superiority. Although 4 may represent the human average, characters in a role-playing game are often significantly better than average. For more details, see Table 2-3: Stat Value Descriptions. Thus, a person of average build, high intelligence, and above average determination might have Body 4, Mind 7, and Soul 5.

Your starting Character Points (page 7) are used to purchase Stats. You must decide how many of them you will spend on Stats and then divide these Points amongst the character's Body, Mind, and Soul. At least 2 Character Points must be assigned to each Stat.

GMs are encouraged to require a solid character concept before allowing Stats values to exceed the "Talent Threshold," since these represent values beyond typical capacity for characters of a specific power level (see Table 2-4: Maximum Stat Values). Otherwise, it is up to you to decide how many Character Points you will use for Stats and what each Stat's value will be. Any Character Points not spent on Stats will be used to acquire various useful talents and abilities called Attributes (page 9). The GM may set an absolute ceiling or floor on the number of Character Points that can be allocated to Stats to ensure characters have a balance between Stats and Attributes.

LESS CAPABLE [STAT] DEFECT

With only three Stats, the Tri-Stat dX is obviously slanted towards well-rounded, balanced characters. But what if your character is weak in a particular area of a Stat? For example, your character might be strong, healthy, and durable, but not dextrous. Similarly, he or she could be intelligent and witty, but forgetful, or strong-willed and composed, but unlucky. On page 53, you will find the Less Capable [Stat] Defect, which was designed specifically to further divide the Stats. Although you do not normally assign Defects until Step 6, become familiar with Less Capable [Stat] at this point if you need to define your character with more precision.

Table 2-3: Stat Value Descriptions

STAT VALUE	DESCRIPTION
1	Inept; infant
2	Significantly below adult human average; child
3	Below adult human average; teenager
4	Adult human average
5	Above adult human average
6	Significantly above human average
7	Highly capable
8	Extremely capable
9	Best in the region
10	Best in the country
11	World-class ability
12	Maximum human potential
13	Above human achievement
14	Significantly above human achievement
15	Moderately powerful superhuman ability
16	Powerful superhuman ability
17-18	Extremely powerful superhuman ability
19-20	Legendary ability
21-24	Maximum achievement in the galaxy
25-30	Maximum achievement in the universe
31-40	Godlike achievement

Table 2-4: Maximum Stat Values

GAME DICE	TALENT THRESHOLD	MAXIMUM VALUE
Four-sided (d4)	6	8
Six-sided (d6)	8	12
Eight-sided (d8)	10	16
Ten-sided (d10)	12	18
Twelve-sided (d12)	14	20
Twenty-sided (d20)	18	40

Maximum Human Potential

A Stat Value of 12 is regarded as the maximum human potential. Can a normal human have Stats higher than 12? Yes, when "maximum human potential" is defined as the greatest achievement possible using currently living humans as the standard.

Consider the events surrounding the four-minute mile. Since ancient Greece, athletes have tried to run a mile in under four minutes. For millennia, it was an impossible task. Experts claimed it was physiologically impossible for a human to run a mile that quickly. It could never be done.

In May of 1954, Sir Roger Bannister of Britain proved millions of people wrong by running a mile in 3 minutes 59.4 seconds. The impossible became possible. In 1955, a total of 37 runners across the world broke the four-minute mile. In 1956, over 300 athletes did the same. "Maximum human potential" had changed.

Presently, there are probably a dozen or so people on Earth that have a 12 Mind Stat; they represent the brightest minds the world has to offer — "maximum human potential." Your human character could be better than all of them by a wide margin, representing what humanity may eventually achieve. What might have been considered a Stat of 12 in the early 20th century, for example, may only be a Stat of 10 or 11 in the early 21st century.

In short, a Stat of 12 represents the greatest possible achievement for a real human being. Role-playing game characters can surpass this limit and remain quite human.

Designer's Note

Why Not Have More Stats?

Since the Tri-Stat System first appeared in our *Big Eyes, Small Mouth* anime RPG in 1997, people have asked us why we only have three Stats. The simple answer is design philosophy: we only needed three Stats to create the game we desired. Yes, Body, Mind, and Soul could each be subdivided into smaller categories, but this begs the question: where do we stop the division? Body could be divided into strength and agility ... but what about endurance, dexterity, constitution, damage resistance, running speed, immune system, etc., etc., etc. Where do we stop? Every player has his or her own preference and we still couldn't please everyone no matter how the Stats were divided. Since we want the Tri-Stat System to put equal emphasis on the physical, mental, and spiritual development of a character, we need to maintain balance among the Stats as well; if we subdivide Body into five sub-Stats, then Mind and Soul each require five as well.

One solution that will please everyone is the Less Capable [Stat] Defect (page 53), which allows you to subdivide each Stat into the categories that you believe best suit your character. We don't tell you what physical Stat aspects you must use to create your character — that decision is yours to make. If you want a well-rounded hero, just use the three Stats as provided. If you want to define your creation more specifically, assign as many Less Capable [Stat] Defects as you require. Agile but weak? No problem. Perceptive but unintelligent? Easy. Charismatic but unlucky? Again, Tri-Stat dX can handle it.

We have given you the tools, but you decide how to use them.

STEP 4: ASSIGN ATTRIBUTES

The three Stats represent your character's basic abilities, but his or her more specific acquired or innate talents and abilities are known as Attributes. Any Character Points remaining after you have purchased Stats are available to acquire Attributes.

There are many different Character Attributes, each representing a particular talent or special ability. Most Attributes are rated with a Level from 1 to X, though Attributes can be extended beyond Level X with the GM's permission. A few Attributes are restricted to only a specific number of Levels. Acquiring an Attribute or increasing it in Level requires the expenditure of one or more Character Points depending on the Attribute's Character Point cost per Level.

The selection of Attributes is one of the most important steps during character creation. Through Attributes, you define your character's unique capabilities compared to other individuals. Think carefully about the balance between a few high-Level Attributes and a large number of low-Level Attributes.

If you find yourself needing more Character Points than you have been assigned, consider burdening your character with one or more Defects (Step 6: Defects, page 50). Each Defect can provide you with additional Character Points, which can be used to acquire more Attributes or higher Stats.

MODIFYING ATTRIBUTES AND ADJUSTING POINT COSTS

Players may occasionally find that an Attribute does not exactly match their concepts of how a particular power or capability should function. The GM (and, with GM permission, the players) may redefine the effects of existing Attributes to better suit particular character concepts. If the GM feels a changed effect makes the Attribute significantly more or less powerful, he or she may alter its Point cost to reflect this.

Additionally, the value of Attributes assumes the setting of the game gives them a good chance of actually being useful in play. If a character is given an Attribute that the GM decides is unlikely to have much, if any, utility in the campaign, he or she can reduce its Character Point Cost or even give the Attribute away for free. If circumstances change and the Attribute becomes useful on a regular basis, the character should pay for the Attribute with Character Points granted through advancement (page 73).

POWER MODIFIER VALUES (PMVS)

Several Attributes can be modified by a variety of factors known as PMVs, referring to Table 3-1: Power Modifier Values. These modifiers allow players to customise their characters' Attributes, making each Attribute unique to the character. The description for each Attribute lists which PMVs are required, and which are optional. Required PMVs must be assigned at a minimum of Rank 1.

PMV COST

Each Rank in a PMV costs 1 Character Point.

AREA

Area modifies the radius of influence of the Attribute, centred on either the character (for Attributes with a Range of zero) or on a specific location (for Range Rank 1 or higher).

DURATION

Duration determines the maximum period of time that the Attribute's effect will influence a target (requires no concentration to maintain after it is activated). In most cases (with the exception of Mimic Powers; page 26), this only applies when the character is using an Attribute to affect someone or something else. Duration does not normally apply when using the Attribute to affect him or herself, since the character can simply reactivate the Attribute at will. At the end of an Attribute's Duration, its effects will cease.

RANGE

Range determines the distance at which the Attribute may be used. Range is a measure of how far away the centre of an Attribute can be manifested; it does not determine the area or number of targets affected (see Area and Targets). Attributes with the Range PMV at Rank 0 can only be used through contact with the target. Alternatively, if the Attribute has the Area PMV above Rank 0, characters may centre the effect upon themselves (or any other location within the Range).

TARGETS

Targets determines the maximum mass of objects and/or number of people, as is appropriate, that the Attribute can affect. A Rank of zero indicates that only the character can be affected; a Rank of 1 means that any single individual (including the character) or appropriate mass can be targeted. It should be noted that the target objects or people must still be within the Attribute's Area and Range to have an affect. For rules on using an Attribute against unwilling targets, see Using Attributes Against Opponents, page 71.

ZERO RANK PMVS

What does it mean when an Attribute has an optional PMV at Rank zero? Can the Attribute still work? How does it function?

For Area, it means the Attribute affects a pinpoint area even smaller than a grain of sand. Unless the character is using the Attribute on him or herself or on an incredibly small target, its effect is virtually insignificant, unnoticed to almost everyone. It is appropriate to take the Area PMV at Rank zero if the character will only use the power to affect him or herself.

Duration of zero means the Attribute has an instantaneous effect. Since the effect of the Attribute vanishes instantly, nobody but the most perceptive people will be aware that anything happened. Consequently, most Attributes that list Duration as a PMV require it to be assigned, or the Attribute is virtually useless.

A Range of zero means that the Attribute can only be used on him or herself, or when touching a target. This restriction is appropriate for many Attributes that require contact to activate.

Targets at Rank zero means that the character can only affect him or herself with the Attribute — it cannot be used on other targets. Many Attributes have Rank zero Targets that only affect the character directly.

Consequently, if the character wishes to use his or her Attribute to affect other people than just him or herself, assigning PMVs at Ranks 1 or higher is necessary. If, however, the character simply wishes to affect him or herself, PMVs may not be required for the Attribute at all.

Table 3-1: Power Modifier Values

RANK	AREA	DURATION	RANGE	TARGETS
0	pinpoint	instantaneous	touch	self
1	10 cm	1 round	10 m	1 Person/50 kg
2	1 m	5 rounds	100 m	5 People/100 kg
3	10 m	1 min	1 km	10 People/500 kg
4	100 m	10 min	10 km	50 People/1 tonne
5	1 km	1 hr	100 km	100 People/5 tonne
6	10 km	12 hr	1,000 km	1,000 People/10 tonne
7	100 km	1 day	10 k km	10 k People/100 tonne
8	1,000 km	1 week	100 k km	100 k People/1,000 tonne
9	10 k km	1 month	1 M km	1 M People/10 k tonne
10	100 k km	6 month	10 M km	10 M People/100 k tonne

ATTRIBUTE PROGRESSION

The effects of each Attribute improve as its Level increases. Most Attribute description indicates which column of Table 3-2: Progression Charts you should reference when determining the game effect of the Attribute. For example, Animal Summon/Control (page 13) has a Progression of "Medium Progression Chart, starting at 1 animal." When determining the game effect of Animal Summon/Control, the player looks at the Medium column of Table 3-2: Progression Charts and cross-references it with the Rank equal to his or her character's Level in

How do PMVs Work?

The Power Modifier Value Chart allows players to create distinct applications of the same Attribute. By assigning a certain Rank in a PMV to an Attribute, you will create different variations of the base use. Take Teleport, for example. Each Level of Teleport dictates how far your character can teleport, starting at 10 metres at Level 1. Without PMVs, every character with Teleport will use it in the same way, on him or herself only. By using the PMVs for Area, Range, and Targets, however, you can create a specific version of the Attribute that works very differently than another character's. If one character possessed Teleport at Level 4, he could Teleport himself up to 10 km away. Another character, however, takes Teleport (also at Level 4) but assigns Area Rank 3, Range Rank 2, and Targets Rank 4. She is able to teleport herself up to 10 km away, but she is also capable of teleporting up to 50 people or 1 tonne in mass (Targets Rank 4) within a 10-metre radius (Area Rank 3) that is 100 metres away from herself (Range Rank 2), up to 10 km away. Thus, she could teleport a car (under 1 tonne in mass and under 10-metres in radius) located at the other end of a football field (under 100 metres away) to the other side of the city (within 10 km teleport). The first character can only use his Attribute to teleport himself while the second character can use her Attribute to teleport people and objects around her as well.

In short, the PMVs allow you to push Attributes beyond their base, standard mechanics and use them in new and innovative ways.

the Attribute. Thus, if his or her character had Animal Summon/Control at Level 6, the character would be able to affect up to 500 animals with the Attribute.

Some Attributes begin the progression at a higher Rank on the Chart. For example, Flight (page 19) has a Progression of "Medium Progression Chart, starting at 10 kph." Thus, the Level 1 effect of Flight (10 kph) is equal to Rank 3, or two ranks higher than the Level of the Attribute. Therefore, if a character had Flight at Level 6, the player would reference Rank 8 on the Medium Progression Chart and see that his or her character could fly at speeds up to 5,000 kph.

SLIDING UP AND DOWN THE METRIC SCALE

Since Tri-Stat dX uses the metric scale, converting between units of measure is easy. For example, Computer Scanning has a Progression of "Fast Progression Chart, starting at 10 cm." Following Table 3-2, the Attribute at Level 2 would function at

Table 3-2: Progression Charts

RANK	FAST	MEDIUM	SLOW	TIME
1	1	1	1	10 Initiative
2	10	5	2	1 round
3	100	10	4	5 rounds
4	1 k	50	8	1 min
5	10 k	100	15	10 min
6	100 k	500	30	1 hr
7	1 M	1 k	60	12 hr
8	10 M	5 k	125	1 day
9	100 M	10 k	250	1 week
10	1 B	50 k	500	1 month
11	10 B	100 k	1,000	6 month
12	100 B	500 k	2,000	1 year
13	1 T	1 M	4,000	10 year
14	10 T	5 M	8,000	100 years
15	100 T	10 M	15,000	1 k years
16	1 Q	50 M	30,000	10 k years
17	10 Q	100 M	60,000	100 k years
18	100 Q	500 M	125,000	1 M years
19	1 Quint	1 B	250,000	10 M years
20	10 Quint	5 B	500,000	100 M years

k = Thousand   M = Million   B = Billion

T = Trillion   Q = Quadrillion   Quint = Quintillion

Table 3-3: Attributes

Attribute Name	Cost per Level	Progression	Required PMVs	Optional PMVs	Relevant Stat	Page	Attribute Name	Cost per Level	Progression	Required PMVs	Optional PMVs	Relevant Stat	Page
Adaptation	1	Linear	None	None	Body	12	Insubstantial	4	Descriptive	None	None	Body	24
Agents	5	Slow	None	None	Soul	12	Invisibility	2 or 3	Linear	None	A,T	Body	24
Alternate Form	2, 3, or 9	Linear	None	None	Body	12	Item of Power	3 or 4	Linear	None	None	Soul	24
Animal Summon/Control	1, 3, 5	Medium	D	A	Soul	13	Jumping	1	Medium	None	None	Body	24
Armour	1 or 3	Linear	None	None	Body	13	Mass Increase	8	Variable	None	None	Body	25
Attack Combat Mastery	3	Linear	None	None	None	13	Massive Damage	2 or 5	Linear	None	None	None	25
Block Power	1 or 6	Linear	None	A,D,T	Soul	14	Metamorphosis	5	Linear	D,T	A,R	Mind/Soul	25
Combat Technique	1	Linear	None	None	None	14	Mimic Powers	7 or 10	Linear	None	D,R	Mind	26
Combination Attack	2	Linear	None	None	None	15	Mind Control	2, 3, 4, 5	Variable	D,T	A,R	Mind	26
Computer Scanning	2	Fast	None	None	Mind	15	Mind Shield	1	Linear	None	A,R,T	Mind/Soul	26
Contamination	2 or 4	Time Rev	T	A,R	Body	15	Natural Weapons	1	Linear	None	None	None	27
Creation	2 or 3	Medium	D	R	Mind/Soul	16	Nullify	7 or 12	Linear	T	A,D,R	Soul	27
Damage Absorption	8 or 10	Linear	None	None	Body	16	Organisational Ties	1, 2, 3	Descriptive	None	None	Soul	27
Damage Conversion	6 or 8	Linear	None	None	Body	16	Own a Big Mecha (OBM)	8	Descriptive	None	None	None	28
Defence Combat Mastery	2	Linear	None	None	None	17	Plant Control	2	Fast	D	None	Mind/Soul	28
Divine Relationship	1	Linear	None	None	None	17	Pocket Dimension	2, 3, 4	Fast	Special	A,D,R,T	Mind/Soul	29
Duplicate	6 or 8	Linear	D	None	Body	17	Power Flux	5, 10, 15, 20	Linear	Special	None	Variable	29
Dynamic Powers	10, 15, 20	Linear	Special	A,D,R,T	Variable	17	Projection	3	Medium	A	D,R	Mind	30
Elasticity	2	Descriptive	None	None	Body	18	Regeneration	6	Linear	None	None	Body	30
Energy Bonus	2	Linear	None	None	None	18	Reincarnation	2 or 4	Time Rev	None	None	Soul	30
Enhanced [Stat]	2	Linear	None	None	None	18	Sensory Block	1	Linear	A,D	R	Mind	30
Environmental Influence	1	Linear	A,D	R	Soul	18	Servant	2 or 6	Linear	None	None	Soul	31
Exorcism	2	Linear	T	A,R	Soul	18	Shrink	1	Variable	None	A,D,R,T	Body	31
Extra Arms	1	Slow	None	None	None	19	Sixth Sense	1	Linear	A	None	Soul	31
Extra Attacks	8	Linear	None	None	None	19	Special Attack	1 or 4	Linear	None	None	None	32
Extra Defences	3	Linear	None	None	None	19	Special Defence	1	Linear	None	None	Variable	36
Features	1	Linear	None	None	None	19	Special Movement	1	Linear	None	None	Body	37
Flight	2, 3, 4	Medium	None	None	Body	19	Speed	6	Medium	None	None	Body	37
Force Field	4	Linear	A	D,R	Mind	19	Superstrength	4	Slow	None	None	Body	37
Gadgeteer	2	Slow	None	None	Mind	20	Swarm	2	Linear	None	None	Body	38
Gadgets	2	Linear	None	None	None	21	Telekinesis	2 or 4	Fast	None	A,R	Mind	38
Grow	10	Variable	None	None	Body	21	Telepathy	1, 2, 3	Descriptive	T	A,R	Mind	39
Healing	4	Linear	T	A,R	Body/Soul	21	Teleport	5	Fast	None	A,R,T	Mind	39
Heightened Awareness	1	Linear	None	None	Body/Mind	22	Tough	2	Linear	None	None	None	39
Heightened Senses	1	Linear	None	None	Body/Mind	22	Transfer	5 or 10	Linear	D	R	Soul	40
Henchmen	1 or 2	Slow	None	None	Soul	22	Transmutation	3, 4, 5	Medium	D	R	Mind/Soul	40
Highly Skilled	1	Linear	None	None	None	22	Tunnelling	2	Medium	None	None	Body	40
Hyperflight	1	Fast	None	None	Body	22	Unique Attribute	1-10	Variable	Variable	Variable	Variable	40
Illusion	1, 2, 3, 4	Fast	A,D,T	R	Mind	22	Unknown Superhuman Power	Variable	Special	Variable	Variable	Variable	40
Immovable	1	Linear	None	None	Body	23	Water Speed	2	Medium	None	None	Body	40
Immunity	5	Descriptive	None	None	Body	23	Wealth	3	Medium	None	None	None	41

100 cm, Level 3 at 1,000 cm, and Level 4 at 10,000 cm. Of course, 100 centimetres equals 1 metre, so the progression is effortlessly converted to metres: Level 2 is 1 m, Level 3 is 10 m, and Level 4 is 100 m.

DESCRIPTIVE OR SPECIAL PROGRESSION

If the Attribute indicates a descriptive progression, read the Attribute entry for more information.

LINEAR PROGRESSION

If an Attribute follows a linear progression, the advancement per Level is indicated clearly. For example, the entry for Tough reads, "Linear; +20 Health Points each Level."

REVERSED PROGRESSION

A few rare Attributes require a reversed progression as the Level of the Attribute increases. Contamination, for instance, has a Progression of "Time Progression Chart Reversed, starting at 6 months." Thus, the Level 1 effect for Contamination is equal to Rank 11 on the Time Progression Chart. For each additional Level of the Attribute, the Rank decreases by one.

ATTRIBUTE RESTRICTIONS

Players may wish to assign the Restriction Defect (page 55) to one or more of their characters' Attributes, thereby reducing the Attribute's total cost by 1 to 3 Points (or sometimes more). The description of each Attribute lists some example Restrictions that are appropriate for the Attribute. GMs, however, are always the final arbiter of whether or not a Restriction is acceptable for an Attribute.

ATTRIBUTE REDUCTIONS

In addition, players can assign the Reduction Defect (page 55). Reductions decrease the Attribute's cost per Level by a number of Character Points, determined by the severity of the Reduction.

ATTRIBUTE ENTRIES

The Attribute entries in the following section indicate: the Character Point cost; the Stat most often relevant to the Attribute's use should a check be needed (page 58); the associated required and optional Power Modifier Values; the Attribute's Level progression; several suggested limitations to the Attribute (for the Restriction and Reduction Defects); and finally the Attribute's game effects.

ADAPTATION

COST: 1 Point/Level
RELEVANT STAT: Body
REQUIRED PMVS: None
OPTIONAL PMVS: None
PROGRESSION: Linear; +1 environment each Level
REDUCTION: None
RESTRICTIONS: Time limit; no Armour; naked form only

The character can adapt to survive in a number of environments hostile to ordinary humans equal to his or her Adaptation Level. Examples of hostile environments include: acidic/basic liquids, extra dimensional, extreme pressure, intense cold, intense heat, noxious gases, radiation, underwater (the ability to "breathe" water), and vacuum (low pressure, not the absence of air). Adaptation does not apply to non-human characters whose natural environment is not the Earth's atmosphere (such as a mermaid living in the ocean). In these cases, the character must assign Adaptation (Earth Atmosphere) to survive in normal human environments. Surviving in low- or no-oxygen environments is a Special Defence Attribute (page 36), not Adaptation.

The Attribute also provides 5 points of Armour against environmental conditions and attacks similar to the adapted environment. For example, Adaptation (Heat) provides Armour while in the desert heat and against fiery blasts, while Adaptation (Pressure) provides Armour while deep-sea diving and against a crushing gravity attack. In most natural Earth environments, this Armour provides complete protection against the elements. Adaptation can thus be viewed as a very limited form of the Armour Attribute in many situations. A character with even Level 1 Armour gains the benefits of Adaptation against damage due to environmental conditions. Armour does not protect against specific hostile environments that have less tangible damaging effects, such as extra dimensional, noxious gases, and underwater.

AGENTS

COST: 5 Points/Level
RELEVANT STAT: Soul
REQUIRED PMVS: None
OPTIONAL PMVS: None
PROGRESSION: Slow Progression Chart, starting at 1 Agent
REDUCTION: Built on fewer Character Points
RESTRICTION: Agents have further limited Stats/Attributes/Defects/Skills

The Agent Attribute represents mercenary employees, hired guns, researchers, or fanatical followers. Unlike Henchmen, Agents are often well trained, and can become reasonably dangerous. Agents fill the gap between Henchmen and Servants, allowing for a squad of effective, capable followers.

Individual Agents are NPCs. All of the character's Agents normally have identical Stats and Attributes, although Skills may vary. A character may have followers with varied Stats or Attributes, but each one counts as two Agents. Agents are built on 30 Character Points, and have 10 Skill Points. For every additional +2 Points spent, however, they all gain X Character Points (X is the game dice). It is recommended that the Character Point total for the Agents not exceed one-quarter to one-half the character's Point total.

Agents will fight for the character, although they need not be soldiers. Many advisors, scientists, or even lawyers fall under this Attribute. Agents, due to their secondary nature to the story, should usually not have the following Attributes: Agents, Henchmen, Servant, Special Attack, or Transfer.

ALTERNATE FORM

COSTS: 2, 3, or 9 Points/Level
RELEVANT STAT: Body
REQUIRED PMVS: None
OPTIONAL PMVS: None
PROGRESSION: Linear; +10 Character Points for the Alternate Form each Level
REDUCTION: Fewer Character Points awarded
RESTRICTIONS: Under certain conditions, time limit, requires special equipment

A character with Alternate Form can instantaneously transform into one other specific form that is determined during character creation and approved by the Game Master. Once selected, the form cannot be altered. Alternate Form allows the character to possess a radically different body shape than his or her normal human form, and exhibit exotic physical features as well.

If a character only has a single, permanent, non-human form, this Attribute should not be applied. Instead, the character must acquire the relevant Attributes and Defects that best represent the form's capabilities. A character with several different Alternate Forms should assign this Attribute multiple times. The Attributes gained in the character's Alternate Form obviously cannot be Dependent (page 52) upon the Alternate Form Attribute. Different Alternate Forms can be built with different Attribute Levels as well. To create a character with unlimited additional forms, see the Dynamic Powers Attribute (page 17) with a Shapeshifting speciality.

PARTIAL-POWERED FORM (3 POINTS/LEVEL)

The form is built from 10 Character Points for each Alternate Form Level, which can be used to acquire Stats, Attributes, and Defects. The character's Stats all drop to zero and thus must be raised with the Alternate Form's new Character Points; Derived Values also must be recalculated. Additionally, the character's regular Attributes, Skills, and Defects no longer function in the Alternate Form, though the GM may decide that some Attributes (such as Gadgets, Henchmen, Organisational Ties, Wealth, and others) and some Defects (such as Achilles Heel, Bane, and others) still retain their effects. Defects can also be assigned to the new Form to provide additional Character Points. Unless the GM indicates otherwise, normal clothing becomes part of the Alternate Form as well.

FULL-POWERED FORM (9 POINTS/LEVEL)

The form is built from 10 Character Points for each Alternate Form Level, which can be used to acquire Attributes and Defects. The character retains all the Stat Values, Attribute Levels, Skill Levels, and Defect Bonus Points associated with his or her regular form. The newly acquired Attributes and Defects add to the character's normal form. If the character's Stats are modified by the Enhanced [Stat] Attribute or Less Capable [Stat] Defect, the Derived Values should be recalculated as necessary. Unless the GM indicates otherwise, normal clothing becomes part of the Alternate Form as well.

COSMETIC CHANGES (2 POINTS)

A "Level 0" option of the Alternate Form Attribute is also available at the cost of 2 Character Points. This Level allows a character to undergo cosmetic changes that confer no additional abilities on the target. This includes: a 10% size increase or decrease, change of gender, 50% age increase or decrease, colour changes (eye, skin, or hair), and minor physical changes (shape of ears, facial features, or bodily proportions). This can also add the Features (Appearance) Attribute or Unappealing Defect.

SAMPLE ALTERNATE FORMS

The examples given below suggest some Attributes that may be appropriate for the Alternate Forms, but the GM can modify them if desired. Other types of alternate forms can include electricity, radiation, light, emotion, data, dream, sound, and many others.

Animal Forms

Many nature-based shapeshifters have one or more Partial-Powered animal forms. Suggested Attributes: any that are relevant to the specific animal form, such as Armour, Attack Combat Mastery, Features, Flight, Heightened Senses, Jumping, Natural Weapons, Special Movement, Tough, Tunnelling, etc.

Elemental/Chemical Forms

This option covers a wide range of possible forms, including: acid, base, gold, granite, ice, mercury, water, sulphur, synthetic drugs, etc. Suggested Attributes: Adaptation, Armour, Elasticity, Enhanced [Stat], Extra Arms, Immunity, Insubstantial, Mass Increase, Massive Damage, Regeneration, Special Attack, Special Defence, Special Movement, Superstrength, Swarm, Tough, Water Speed.

Flame Form

The character is composed of fire, and can ignite flammable objects on contact. Any person near the character may suffer burn damage as well. Suggested

Attributes: Adaptation (Heat), Armour (Optimised to heat), Damage Conversion (Heat), Environmental Influence (Heat), Flight, Force Field, Special Attack (Aura).

Gaseous Form

This form is less substantial than a liquid form. The character cannot pick up solid objects and can only exert the pushing force of a gentle wind. Suggested Attributes: Adaptation, Creation, Extra Attacks, Flight, Heightened Awareness, Insubstantial (Level 2), Invisibility, Projection, Regeneration, Shrink, Sixth Sense, Special Attack, Special Defence, Speed.

Incorporeal Form

An Incorporeal form is without physical substance (for example, a ghost or living shadow). The character can pass through walls, walk on air or water, and perform similar ghost-like feats. Suggested Attributes: Adaptation, Flight, Insubstantial, Invisibility, Special Defence.

Melding Form

The character can meld into any inanimate object, and still perceive nearby events as though he or she is still human. Once merged, the character cannot be harmed unless the object is damaged. Suggested Attributes: Adaptation, Insubstantial, Teleport (Within melded object), Tunnelling.

Superhuman Form

Some characters maintain dual human/super identities and do not have access to all of their Attributes until transformed into superheroes or supervillains. Suggested Attributes: any that are relevant to character's superhuman form.

Two-Dimensional Form

A 2-D character has height and width, but not depth. He or she can squeeze through the spaces between atoms, and is completely invisible when viewed from the side. An entire new two-dimensional universe may be waiting to be explored by such a character. Suggested Attributes: Adaptation, Immunity, Insubstantial, Pocket Dimension, Special Defence, Special Movement, Speed.

ANIMAL SUMMON/CONTROL

COST:	1, 3, or 5 Points/Level
RELEVANT STAT:	Soul
REQUIRED PMVS:	Duration
OPTIONAL PMVS:	Area
PROGRESSION:	Medium Progression Chart, starting at 1 animal
REDUCTION:	Can only give limited commands
RESTRICTIONS:	Check needed to maintain control; animals aggressive towards Summoner once released; demons require gift/offering

Characters with this Attribute (at 1 Point/Level) can summon animals from the surrounding area (as determined by the Area PMV Rank), and command them to perform a variety of simple activities: attack, confuse, hunt, defend, track, etc. Human control is covered by the Mind Control Attribute (page 26). The Attribute Level determines the maximum number of animals that can be summoned. If fewer animals are in the area of effect, only those will obey the summons. Additionally, the animals do not appear magically; they must find a way to travel to the character. After the Duration PMV has expired, the animals will return to their normal activities and habitats. Any animals still travelling to the summoning character will cease their journeys at that time.

If the character limits the Summon/Control to a single broad group of animals, the Attribute functions at one Level higher. Broad animal groups include: mammals, insects, reptiles, amphibians, fish, avians, etc. If limited to a single specific group, the Attribute functions at two Levels higher. Specific animal groups include: dogs, cats, rodents, ants, bees, large reptiles, frogs, sharks, birds of prey, etc. If limited to a specific type of animal, the Attribute functions at three Levels higher. Examples of animal types include: poodles, tigers, rats, fire ants, crocodiles, tree frogs, hammerhead sharks, eagles, etc.

For 3 Points/Level, the animals are summoned through supernatural means. The character can always summon the maximum number of allowable animals (as determined by Level), and the animals arrive within a single round. When the Duration expires, the animals instantly return to their original location.

An alternate 5 Points/Level version of this Attribute — Demonic Summon/Control — allows the character to summon creatures from other dimensions or planes of existence. The creatures arrive within a single round. The creatures are built using 5 Character Points for each Level of Area PMV assigned. When the Duration expires, the creatures instantly return to their original location.

ARMOUR

COST:	1 or 3 Points/Level
RELEVANT STAT:	Body
REQUIRED PMVS:	None
OPTIONAL PMVS:	None
PROGRESSION:	Linear; +10 damage reduction each Level
REDUCTION:	Reduced Armour values
RESTRICTIONS:	Needs repairs; cumbersome and restricts movement; under certain conditions

The Armour Attribute represents actual armoured plates, or simply skin or clothing that is highly resistant to damage. It is most often found on combat vehicles, cyborgs, androids, giant monsters, and powerful beings.

Armour reduces the damage that is inflicted on the character or structure (see Chapter 8: Combat for how damage works; page 68). Armour reduces the damage of each attack by 10/Level (20/Level for Shield). The base cost for Armour is 3 Points/Level, or 1 Point/Level for Shield.

A number of options are available for the Armour Attribute, which alter the Attribute's Point cost or modify the Armour's effectiveness. The minimum Point cost of Armour, regardless of options, is 1 Character Point.

PARTIAL

The Armour has a small thin area (half Armour value, -1 to Point cost) or an unarmoured area (no Armour value, -2 to Point cost) that can be targeted using a Called Shot (page 63). Point cost reductions apply to the total cost of Armour, not the cost per Level.

OPTIMISED ARMOUR

The Armour is focused against a particular uncommon attack form. Eligible attack forms include electricity, cold, laser beams, fire/heat, energy blasts, etc. Armour cannot be optimised against broad categories such as blunt impacts or piercing weapons, however. Optimised Armour provides doubled protection against the chosen attack form only, and no protection against other forms. A character can acquire both Optimised Armour and ordinary Armour by assigning the Armour Attribute twice.

SHIELD ONLY

The Armour does not cover the character's entire body. Instead, it is a Shield that the user must deliberately interpose in front of a melee or unarmed attack using a Block Defence (page 67). The character must also possess the Combat Technique (Block Ranged Attacks) Attribute to use the Shield in a Block Defence against ranged attacks. If the character successfully defends, the Shield's Armour can protect against 20 damage each Level (rather than 10). This option reduces the cost of Armour to 1 Point/Level (rather than 3 Points/Level).

ATTACK COMBAT MASTERY

COST:	3 Points/Level
RELEVANT STAT:	None (uses Combat Value)
REQUIRED PMVS:	None
OPTIONAL PMVS:	None
PROGRESSION:	Linear; +1 Attack Combat Value each Level
REDUCTION:	None
RESTRICTIONS:	None

Attack Combat Mastery denotes either an innate "killer instinct" or the character's intimate knowledge of a wide range of offensive combat techniques covering all aspects of armed and unarmed encounters (including Special Attacks and ranged weapons). Individual Combat Skills (page 49) let a character specialise with particular weapons or specific styles, but Attack Combat Mastery allows a character to pick up any weapon (or use none at all) and be dangerously proficient. See page 57 for more information on the Attack Combat Value.

BLOCK POWER

COST: 1 or 6 Points/Level
RELEVANT STAT: Soul
REQUIRED PMVS: None
OPTIONAL PMVS: Area, Duration, Targets
PROGRESSION: Linear; -1 Check Value penalty to effect character using +1 specific Attribute each Level
REDUCTION: More than one but less than all
RESTRICTIONS: Under certain conditions; against broad or specific group of people; weak against an Attribute

Opponents have difficulty affecting the character with specific Attributes because the Attributes' effects are blocked. For 1 Point/Level the character can block one Attribute at each Level, which must be determined during character creation (or when Block Power is assigned as advancement). In the case of the Special Attack Attribute, only another character's single, specific attack is blocked (which reduces an enemies chance to hit the character). For 6 Points/Level, the character can block all Attributes, including all Special Attacks (they suffer a penalty to hit the character but if they do hit, they have full effect). The Duration PMV only applies when the character is using Block Power to stop specific Attributes from affecting a willing or unwilling target, rather than him or herself. Targets cannot be blocked from the effects of their own Attributes, however.

When an opponent targets the character, he or she must make a successful Stat check at a -1 penalty for every Level of the target character's Block Power Attribute. If the check fails, the Attribute does not affect the character (although a multi-target Attribute may still affect the other targets). The base Check Value is determined by the "Relevant Stat" of the Attribute used. If no Stat is indicated, the Soul Stat is used as a default. If the check succeeds, the target character is affected by the Attribute as normal.

COMBAT TECHNIQUE

COST: 1 Point/Level
RELEVANT STAT: None (uses Combat Value)
REQUIRED PMVS: None
OPTIONAL PMVS: None
PROGRESSION: Linear; +1 technique each Level
REDUCTION: None
RESTRICTIONS: Under certain conditions; against broad or specific group of opponents; with specific weapons or weapon groups

The Combat Technique Attribute allows a character to perform astounding feats with a wide variety of melee or ranged weapons, or special attacks. For a listing of penalties associated with some special combat manoeuvres, see page 66. Each Level gives the character one combat technique; the Game Master will determine if a specific manoeuvre can be assigned multiple times. The GM and players are encouraged to develop their own combat techniques as well.

ACCURACY

The character suffers reduced dice penalties when attempting an accurate attack, such as striking at partial Armour, weak points, or vital spots, shooting at longer-than-usual ranges. Accuracy is also used when attempting a special trick shot, such as carving an initial on someone's body or ricocheting an arrow off a wall to shoot a target around a corner, and when using the Deflection or Reflection techniques (explained later in this section). Each difficulty penalty is reduced by 2 (to a minimum of 0). For example, attacking a vital spot (-8 penalty) would become a -6 penalty, while firing at double range (-4 penalty) would receive -2 penalty.

ACV KNOCKBACK

This technique is only available in campaigns that use Knockback rules (page 70). The character is proficient at maximizing the distance that he or she knocks opponents back after a successful hit. The character adds his Attack Combat Value, in metres, to the knockback distance inflicted upon the target of a successful hit.

BLIND FIGHTING

The character does not suffer penalties associated with attacking or defending with melee weapons or while unarmed in poor light, absolute darkness, or against an invisible opponent.

BLIND SHOOTING

The character suffers half penalties associated with attacking with ranged weapons in poor light, absolute darkness, or against an invisible opponent. This technique can be assigned twice to reduce the penalty to zero. The character must be capable of detecting the general presence of the target, however, through one of his or her senses (smell, hearing, sixth sense, etc.).

BLOCK RANGED ATTACKS

Under normal circumstances, a character cannot use a Block Defence (page 67) against a ranged attack. With this technique, a character gains this defensive option.

CONCEALMENT

The character has an unearthly ability to conceal weapons about his or her person. As long as the character has something to hide the weapons (even if it only long hair or a light robe) the character's weapons will not be noticed by anything short of an actual physical search, and such a search is conducted at a -8 Check Value penalty. A Special Attack weapon with the Concealable Ability (page 33) is even harder to find: searches suffer a -12 Check Value penalty.

DEFLECTION

If the character makes a successful Block Defence, he or she can deflect a standard melee or ranged attack away harmlessly without damaging the blocking object. The GM may decide that some types of attacks cannot be deflected. When trying to deflect a Special Attack (page 32), the Block Defence roll is penalised: -2 for each Level of the Special Attack.

JUDGE OPPONENT

The character can judge his or her opponent's approximate Combat Value and weapon Skill Levels from the foe's attitude and posture even without actually seeing him or her fight. Additionally, the character can accurately estimate the opponent's remaining Health Points. For both of these advantages, the GM may decide to provide descriptive indications such as "your enemy is much better than you with a sword, but if you connect a few times with your eye blast, it will drop him", rather than saying "the enemy's ACV is 12, with a Melee Attack (Sword) Skill of 2, and he has 60 Health Points remaining."

LEAP ATTACK

The character can make leaping attacks with his or her melee weapon, delivering additional damage due to momentum. Any time the character has a higher Initiative than his or her opponent, he or she may attempt a leaping attack. If the strike is successful (it hits and the target fails a defence) the character gets an extra +5 bonus to damage and may additionally add his or her Acrobatics Skill Level (if any) to the damage. If the character fails to hit, however, or the opponent succeeds with his or her defence, the character is off balance and receives a -2 penalty to any further defence checks until his or her turn to act in the following round.

LIGHTNING REFLEXES

The character reacts quickly in combat and frequently outmanoeuvres opponents. Each time this technique is selected, the character gains +5 to all his or her Initiative rolls.

ONE SHOT LEFT

The character will always have at least one projectile remaining for his or her ranged weapon, even after an extended combat. This might be a final bullet in a gun, arrow in a quiver, plasma unit in a wrist blaster, or stone in a sling. This option does not remove the need to reload weapons in a game that uses realistic ammunition rules, but rather assures that the character will not be forced to reload at a critical moment. One Shot Left does not affect weapons or attacks built using the Limited Shots Disability (page 35).

PORTABLE ARMOURY

The character will always have easy access to any weapon required for a particular task, including illegal weapons and accessories not available to the general public. The actual weapons and accessories must still be acquired via the Gadgets Attribute (page 21), but remarkably, the character can access them whenever he or she needs them instead of being forced to return to where they are normally stored. Characters with Portable Armoury may also make field modifications on their weapons, switching options such as laser sights or scopes in a single round.

REFLECTION

If the character has the Deflection Combat Technique (see earlier) and makes both a successful Deflection defence and a successful attack roll (which uses an attack action), he or she can reflect a standard melee or ranged attack towards any target within range (including the attacker) without damaging the blocking object. This Reflection is treated as a normal attack against the target using standard attack rules (page 63). The GM may decide that some types of attacks cannot be reflected.

STEADY HAND

This is the ability to use Attack Combat Skills with ease while the character is moving quickly (running at full speed, flying at high speeds, riding in a vehicle, etc.) or otherwise engaged in complex stunts. This greatly reduces the penalties a character normally suffers for attacking while in motion. Each penalty is reduced by 2 (to a minimum of 0). A character with this ability may also use weapons in conjunction with the Acrobatics Skill, and may aim while they are moving.

TWO WEAPONS

The character can effectively fight with two melee or ranged weapons at once against the same or different targets, provided both weapons are designed for one-handed use. When using two weapons, the character can attack twice using the normal Two Weapons rules (page 63), but the penalty for doing so is reduced by 2 (to a minimum of 0). Alternatively, the character can attack with one weapon and defend with another receiving a -2 penalty to attack checks he or she makes but adding a +2 bonus to his or her defence checks vs. melee or unarmed attacks. This bonus lasts until the character's turn in the following round.

WEAPONS ENCYCLOPAEDIA

A character has the ability to recall the vital statistics and important quirks of practically all known commercially available weapons. This includes, but is not limited to, its general level of reliability as well as all vital statistics — material composition, manufacturer, ammunition capacity, calibre, model year, possible outfitted accessories, etc. Characters without this ability will only have such information on weapons they actually own or use regularly and will need to successfully roll a Mind-based Military Science (Hardware Recognition) Skill check to recall important details. In addition, Weapons Encyclopaedia also includes knowledge on acquiring weapons, so characters will have a +4 bonus on any Street Sense or Business Management Skill checks needed to locate or buy legal or illegal weapons.

COMBINATION ATTACK

COST:	2 Points/Level
RELEVANT STAT:	None
REQUIRED PMVS:	None
OPTIONAL PMVS:	None
PROGRESSION:	Linear; the character can combine attacks with +2 other characters each Level
REDUCTION:	Attribute always used in same way
RESTRICTIONS:	Under certain conditions; specific targets; Initiative penalty to use

With training, individual characters can learn to combine their Special Attack Attribute into awesome displays of power. In order to do this, all the characters must have both the Combination Attack Attribute and the Special Attack Attribute. The number of characters that can combine at once is dependant on the Level of Combination Attack; a character can combine with up to 2 other characters for each Level. If the campaign uses the optional Energy Points (page 57), there is also an Energy Point cost associated with Combination Attack: 2 Energy Points per person involved in the attack. Each character must pay this cost separately. For example, if four characters are combining, they each must pay 8 Energy Points.

The attack takes place on the Initiative of the character with the lowest Initiative. The character with the lowest Attack Combat Value makes a single attack roll for the entire group (combat Skills do not apply to the attack roll). The target has a defence penalty of -1 per character involved in the attack. If the attack succeeds and defender fails his or her defence (or does not attempt a defence), the attack inflicts double damage. For example, if two character combine, one with a 20 damage Special Attack and one with a 60 damage Special Attack, the total damage inflicted would be 160 — double the sum of the attack damages.

Note that characters with the Combination Attack Attribute are not subject to the same restrictions as normal characters that perform a similar action (see Combined Attacks, page 64).

COMPUTER SCANNING

COST:	2 Points/Level
RELEVANT STAT:	Mind
REQUIRED PMVS:	None
OPTIONAL PMVS:	None
PROGRESSION:	Fast Progression Chart, starting at 10 cm radius area
REDUCTION:	Access but cannot understand
RESTRICTIONS:	Under certain conditions; in particular regions; specific types of computers or data

With a successful Mind Stat check, characters with this Attribute can access, read, and understand data from all computers or "Silicon Age" technology in the surrounding area. When attempting to access a computer built as an Item of Power, the character suffers a penalty to the Mind Stat check of -2 for each Level of the Item of Power. The Attribute Level determines the maximum area in which the computers can be scanned. To read multiple computers over a network, the area Level must be high enough to encompass the target computers. Since this Attribute can be a very powerful tool in a campaign, the GM and players should ensure it is used appropriately.

Characters who can control and manipulate computer data should acquire the Dynamic Powers Attribute with a computer data specialisation. Alternatively, characters who can control machine technology such as automobiles and construction equipment might instead possess the Telekinesis Attribute (page 38), with a specific restriction.

CONTAMINATION

COST:	2 or 4 Points/Level
RELEVANT STAT:	Body
REQUIRED PMVS:	Targets
OPTIONAL PMVS:	Area, Range
PROGRESSION:	Time Progression Chart Reversed, starting at 6 months
REDUCTION:	Partial effectiveness
RESTRICTIONS:	Under certain conditions; specific targets; temporary change

This Attribute represents the character's ability to transform other people (or animals, or objects) into entities like him or herself. Frequently, this victim can then contaminate even more people. The method should be specified when the character is created. It might be similar to myths behind the vampire legend — the character's blood carries a "plague" that, when ingested, mutates the person over a matter of hours or days. Alternatively, the character might lay an egg or seed (real or metaphorical) in the body of his or her prey, which will later hatch within the victim, killing him or her as a new monster is born. The character might even need to perform some special ritual that alters the victim. Whatever the case, the conditions under which the victim can become "contaminated" must be specified.

For 2 Points/Level, contamination is "difficult" — the victim must be willing, unconscious, or restrained for deliberate contagion to occur, or the target must perform an unusual activity (such as eating a morsel of the character's flesh).

For 4 Points/Level contamination is "easy" — the contagion might be similar to a traditional werewolf attack, where a scratch or bite results in a victim becoming a werewolf. The GM can add special conditions, limitations, or effects to ensure that becoming a monster is a curse and not a blessing.

The higher the Level of Contamination, the faster the transformation occurs. There should always be some means of curing or delaying the eventual mutation, however. Possible cures include the death of the creature that inflicted the contaminant, radical surgery, blood transfusion, or a successful mystical healing.

The GM will decide whether a player character who is turned into a monster remains in the player's control or is reclassified as an NPC. Any retention (dreams, memories, etc.) of the victim's former existence depends on the nature of the contamination and whether the victim has been "transformed," "devoured," or "reborn" in the process. A person who has been successfully contaminated will usually gain a certain number of Attributes "paid for" with the Bonus Points acquired by assigning new character Defects (often including Cursed, Ism, Marked, Permanent, and Owned, the last one representing servitude to his or her new master). Usually the mutation will result in a monstrous form similar to that of the character responsible. Thus, a spider alien that laid an egg in its victim may produce another spider alien, the victim of a vampire will grow fangs, etc. The GM should be wary of potentially undesirable possibilities such as a werewolf character infecting the entire group of characters.

The Contamination Attribute usually allows the creator or mother some measure of control over the newly transformed character. In these instances, the Level of Contamination is added as a favourable modifier to any Mind Control attempts performed against the subject.

A variation to Contamination inflicts the target with some sort of curse or disease, rather than transforming him or her into a different type of creature. Examples of these afflictions include rapid ageing, debilitating diseases, sensitivity to specific elements, etc.

CREATION

COST: 2 or 3 Points/Level
RELEVANT STAT: Mind or Soul
REQUIRED PMVs: Duration
OPTIONAL PMVs: Range
PROGRESSION: Medium Progression Chart, starting at 1 kg
REDUCTION: Very specific utility
RESTRICTIONS: Under certain conditions; creation is visually flawed; limited control over actual object created

This Attribute allows a character to create a non-living object (or set of connected objects, like clothing or a gun and its ammunition). Creation costs 3 Points/Level if the character can create anything (within the limits of his or her Level). It costs 2 Points/Level if the creation is limited to a general class of objects such as "metal," "weapons," "clothing," or "food."

The character cannot create new objects outside his or her experience. The character could create a book, painting or videotape, but the content must be something with which he or she was already familiar. Likewise, a character who had no familiarity with guns could not create one using Creation. The GM may choose to require a Mind Stat check (or relevant Skill check) if the character attempts a particularly complex creation. Failure may indicate the created object does not function properly, or is otherwise flawed; this is especially applicable when creating complex technological devices. Unless the GM decides otherwise, Creation is only able to make objects that could be classified as Gadgets; it cannot create Items of Power.

The created object will remain in existence for a period of time indicated by the Duration PMV. The ability to change one object into another is covered by the Transmutation Attribute (page 40).

DAMAGE ABSORPTION

COST: 8 or 10 Points/Level
RELEVANT STAT: Body
REQUIRED PMVs: None
OPTIONAL PMVs: None
PROGRESSION: Linear; +10 damage converted into Health Points each Level
REDUCTION: Partial effectiveness
RESTRICTIONS: Under certain conditions; against specific attack types; when battling specific opponents

A character with this Attribute can absorb up to 10 damage received from physical attacks (such as guns, swords, punches, or energy blasts) each Level, and change them into a corresponding number of Health Points before damage is inflicted. The new Health Points are added to the character's current total immediately, which may temporarily raise the total above its normal maximum. Damage that is blocked by the character's Armour or Force Field Attributes cannot be absorbed. For 8 Points/Level, the character's Health Point total can never rise above his or her normal maximum (extra points are lost). For 10 Points/Level, the character's Health Points total can be raised as high as twice their normal maximum value (for a duration of one hour). Damage can both be absorbed and converted (by the Damage Conversion Attribute; below) at the same time.

Damage Absorption does not convert damage from non-physical or complex attacks, including Special Attacks with the following Abilities: Burning, Drain (Any), Flare, Incapacitating, Irritant, Mind or Soul Attack, Stun, Tangle.

DAMAGE CONVERSION

COST: 6 or 8 Points/Level
RELEVANT STAT: Body
REQUIRED PMVs: None
OPTIONAL PMVs: None
PROGRESSION: Linear; +1 Character Point for every 20 damage received each Level
REDUCTION: Partial effectiveness
RESTRICTIONS: Apply Character Points to specific Attributes; against specific attack types; when battling specific opponents

A character with this Attribute suffers damage from physical attacks (such as guns, swords, punches, or energy blasts) as normal, but receiving damage grants additional Character Points he or she can assign to Attributes temporarily. Points can be accumulated between attacks or combat rounds. Additionally, Character Points can only be assigned to Attributes the character already possesses at Level 1 or higher. Damage can both be converted and absorbed (by the Damage Absorption Attribute; above) at the same time. Damage Conversion does not convert damage from non-physical or complex attacks, including Special Attacks with the following Abilities: Burning, Drain (Any), Flare, Incapacitating, Irritant, Mind or Soul Attack, Stun, Tangle. The extra Character Points gained through combat dissipate very shortly after the battle has finished, or before the next dramatic scene (GM's discretion).

For 6 Points/Level, damage that is blocked by the character's Armour Attribute cannot be converted. For 8 Points/Level, damage that is blocked by the character's Armour Attribute can be converted. Damage blocked by the Force Field Attribute can never be converted.

At each Level, the character gains 1 Character Point for every 20 damage received from each single attack (round down). Most often, characters use these Points to enhance the following Attributes: Armour, Extra Attacks, Extra Defences, Massive Damage, Regeneration, Special Attack, and Superstrength. Damage Conversion cannot be used to increase Tough — to increase the character's Health Points see Damage Absorption, above.

For example, a character with Level 5 Damage Conversion gains 5 Character Points for every 20 damage received. If an enemy blasted the character with a weapon that inflicts 87 damage, the character's Health Point total would reduce by 87 points, but he or she would gain 20 temporary Character Points (87 ÷ 20 = 4.35, rounded down to 4; 4 x 5 = 20). If the character possessed Superstrength at a minimum of Level 1, he or she could raise it by 5 Levels immediately (since 20 Character Points ÷ 4 Points/Level = 5 Levels). Alternatively, the character could raise his or her Stats by a total of 10 Stat Values through the Enhanced [Stat] Attribute (since 20 Character Points ÷ 2 Points/Level = 10 Levels).

With GM permission, Damage Conversion may be designed to convert forms of energy into Character Points, rather than converting damage. Examples of energy include: sound, light, radiation, mass, heat, and others. The progression of the Attribute under these conditions must be discussed with the GM.

DEFENCE COMBAT MASTERY

COST:	2 Points/Level
RELEVANT STAT:	None (uses Combat Value)
REQUIRED PMVs:	None
OPTIONAL PMVs:	None
PROGRESSION:	Linear; +1 Defence Combat Value each Level
REDUCTION:	None
RESTRICTIONS:	None

Defence Combat Mastery denotes either an innate "danger instinct," or the character's intimate knowledge of a wide range of defensive combat techniques covering all aspects of armed and unarmed encounters (including Special Attacks and ranged weapons). Individual Defence Combat Skills (page 49) let a character specialise with particular weapons or specific styles, but Defence Combat Mastery allows a character to pick up any weapon (or use none at all) and still proficiently defend. See page 57 for more information on the Defence Combat Value.

DIVINE RELATIONSHIP

COST:	1 Point/Level
RELEVANT STAT:	None
REQUIRED PMVs:	None
OPTIONAL PMVs:	None
PROGRESSION:	Linear; +1 dice re-roll per game session each Level
REDUCTION:	None
RESTRICTIONS:	Time limitation; combat checks; Stat/Skill checks

A character possessing a Divine Relationship may have powerful forces acting as his or her guardian, which can beneficially influence the outcome of important events. Alternatively, the character may be really lucky, have great karma, or can subtly influence his or her surroundings with thought alone. This relationship is represented through the re-rolling of undesirable dice rolls (this includes undesirable re-rolls as well). The player may choose to use the original roll, or any of the re-rolls, when determining the success of the action. The Level dictates the number of times dice can be re-rolled in a single role-playing session, though the GM can alter this time frame as desired.

DUPLICATE

COST:	6 or 8 Points/Level
RELEVANT STAT:	Body
REQUIRED PMVs:	Duration
OPTIONAL PMVs:	None
PROGRESSION:	Linear; +10 Character Points to build duplicates each Level
REDUCTION:	Fewer Character Points awarded
RESTRICTIONS:	Under certain conditions; only certain Attributes are duplicated; shorter duration

A character with this ability can create one or more independent, self-aware duplicates of him or herself, each of which have a maximum number of Character Points dictated by the Attribute Level. The duplicate is not under the character's control, but will act in a manner consistent with the original character. Multiple duplicates can be in existence at any time, but creating a duplicate requires one non-combat action.

Duplicates only remain in existence for a limited time, usually for a single scene or long enough to complete a single task (Duration PMV is typically 1-5). Since this Attribute can have tremendous impact on a campaign if used too frequently, the GM should impose restrictions on its use as necessary. The player should consider what consequences, if any, will arise should an enemy kill the duplicate.

There are two different types of Duplicate: Customised (8 Points/Level) and Proportionate (6 Points/Level).

CUSTOMISED DUPLICATE

The character can assign the duplicate's Character Points as desired when this Attribute is first acquired, provided the duplicate does not gain any Attributes or Defects the original character does not possess. Additionally, Attributes and Defects cannot be raised to Levels that would exceed the original character's Levels. The GM may waive this restriction if it seems appropriate. Once the Character Points are allocated to the duplicate in a specific pattern during character creation, the distribution cannot be changed; all duplicates ever made will be identical.

PROPORTIONATE DUPLICATE

If the Duplicate Level is not sufficiently high to create a duplicate with the exact same number of Character Points as the original, a less-powerful duplicate is created. In these cases, the reduced Character Points are distributed over the duplicate's Stats, and Attributes, Skills, and Defects proportionately with the original character. The one exception to this rule involves the Duplicate Attribute; the character may decide that his or her twin does not have the Duplicate Attribute.

DYNAMIC POWERS

COST:	10, 15, or 20 Points/Level
RELEVANT STAT:	Variable
REQUIRED PMVs:	Special
OPTIONAL PMVs:	Area, Duration, Range, Targets
PROGRESSION:	Descriptive
REDUCTION:	One aspect of category
RESTRICTIONS:	Under certain conditions; use weakens character, specific targets

Dynamic Powers represents extensive control over an element, ideology, natural phenomenon, or sphere of influence. At low Levels, the character is an initiate, and can only effect minor changes in the Attribute. At high Levels, the character holds mastery over a Realm, and has an intimate understanding of all things relating to the Attribute. This is a very open-ended Attribute and should be discussed with the GM at length to determine the effects and limitations in his or her game. Proper use of Dynamic Powers will not unbalance the game, but rather can provide many opportunities for character innovation. As an alternative option to Dynamic Powers, see the Power Flux Attribute (page 29).

Minor or small categories cost 10 Points/Level. Examples include: a classical element (water, fire, wind, earth), a limited concept or idea (lust, protection, charm, pride), a minor aspect of nature (temperature, friction, insects, sunlight, clouds, orbits, sea creatures), or a limited sphere of influence (keys, silence, cats, writing, guns, a small locality, nutrition).

Major or large categories cost 15 Points/Level. Examples include: a broad concept or idea (love, communication, travel, strength), a major aspect of nature (weather, magnetism, gravity, electricity, animals), or a broad sphere of influence (cities, computer data, health, truth, manufacturing, fertility, weapons, drugs, shapeshifting).

Primal or universal categories cost 20 Points/Level. Examples include core concepts and primary spheres of influence: Time, War, Death, Life, Earth, Stars, Thought, Magic, Force, Math, Self, Law, Chaos, Creation, Heaven, Hell, Dimensions, Dreams, and others.

If the character makes a successful Stat check (the relevant Stat is determined by the GM), he or she can manipulate aspects of the chosen area of influence. The extent of control is determined by the Dynamic Powers Attribute Level and any relevant PMVs. Since this is a story-driven Attribute, there are few definitive rules regarding what a character can and cannot do with a particular Attribute Level.

For those players and Game Masters who desire a more rigid outline, the recommended guideline is as follows: characters can influence their area with maximum control approximating the abilities listed for other Attributes, with total Levels corresponding to twice the Dynamic Powers Level. No single effect can exceed a Level equal to the Dynamic Powers Level, however. The PMVs available to the character while creating effects is limited by the Dynamic Power PMV Ranks. Under normal circumstances, Dynamic Powers cannot imitate the Transfer Attribute; additionally, the GM may wish to restrict some Attributes such as Agents, Henchment, Organisational Ties, Servant, and Wealth.

For example, a character with Level 4 Dynamic Powers (Weather) can initiate effects similar in scope to a total of 8 Levels of other Attributes at once; the maximum single effect is limited to Level 4 abilities, though. This means that the character could activate weather-associated abilities approximating: 8 Level 1

Attributes; or 2 Level 4 Attributes; or 1 Level 4, and 2 Level 2 Attributes; or 1 Level 3, 2 Level 2, and 1 Level 1 Attributes; or any other combination of Levels that adds to 8 Levels total, provided no effect exceeds a Level 4 ability. Likewise, a character with Level 10 Dynamic Powers can initiate effects similar in scope to a total of 20 Levels of other Attributes at once, provided no effect exceeds a Level 10 ability. Each ability must operate within the PMV Ranks assigned to Dynamic Powers.

In addition, any effect that is an attack on another entity (one that is best represented by the Special Attacks Attribute, page 32) also requires a successful attack check to hit; the target will normally be allowed a defence check to avoid it. If the controlled area produces something that has a more indirect effect, the target should be allowed to attempt an appropriate Stat Check to resist its influence.

ELASTICITY

COST:	2 Points/Level
RELEVANT STAT:	Body
REQUIRED PMVS:	None
OPTIONAL PMVS:	None
PROGRESSION:	Descriptive
REDUCTION:	Attribute always used in same way
RESTRICTIONS:	Time limit; naked form only; stretching inflicts pain

The character can stretch or contort his or her limbs and/or body to a superhuman degree. Increased Levels not only provide greater flexibility, but also the control over fine manipulation (such as using a stretched finger to move specific tumbling mechanisms on a key lock). At high Levels, characters can squeeze under doors and through small holes, as well as mimic crude shapes. While stretched, the character receives +1 Unarmed Attack/Defence (Grappling) Skill bonuses for each Level of Elasticity. Extremely malleable characters — who can contort their bodies into a virtually unlimited number of shapes to gain the benefits of other Attributes — should acquire the Dynamic Powers Attribute (page 17), rather than Elasticity.

LEVEL 1-3 The character can stretch 1 (L1), 2 (L2), or 3 (L3) body parts up to 5x their regular dimensions.

LEVEL 4+ The character can stretch his or her entire body. The length the body can be stretched follows the Medium Progression Chart, starting at 10 metres (Level 4).

ENERGY BONUS

COST:	2 Points/Level
RELEVANT STAT:	None
REQUIRED PMVS:	None
OPTIONAL PMVS:	None
PROGRESSION:	Linear; +20 Energy Points each Level
REDUCTION:	None
RESTRICTIONS:	None

This Attribute is only available in campaigns where Energy Points are used. Possessing this Attribute increases the Energy Points of the character, allowing him or her to draw on a greater pool of energy reserves in times of need. See page 57 for information on Energy Points and their uses.

ENHANCED [STAT]

COST:	2 Points/Level
RELEVANT STAT:	None
REQUIRED PMVS:	None
OPTIONAL PMVS:	None
PROGRESSION:	Linear; +1 Stat Value each Level
REDUCTION:	None
RESTRICTIONS:	Only under certain conditions, time limit, does not apply to all dice rolls

This Attribute is useful when a character should have one or more high Stat Values, but the player wants to indicate that the elevated Stats were gained after a supernatural event occurred. For most instances, assigning Character Points to the Enhanced [Stat] Attribute or to the Stat directly results in the same benefit: a character with a Body of 15 or a Body of 7 with Enhanced [Body] at Level 8 both have a Body of 15.

ENVIRONMENTAL INFLUENCE

COST:	1 Point/Level
RELEVANT STAT:	Soul
REQUIRED PMVS:	Area, Duration
OPTIONAL PMVS:	Range
PROGRESSION:	Linear; influence over +1 environment each Level
REDUCTION:	None
RESTRICTIONS:	Very specific influence effect, only under certain conditions, easy to counteract

The character can initiate minor influence over environmental conditions such as light, darkness, heat, cold, sound, specific weather conditions, etc., as determined by the GM. The control is not sufficient to inflict significant damage on individuals or objects within the Area PMV of influence unless the target is particularly susceptible to damage from that environment (such as delicate plants dying from cold air, or a vampire with a Bane Defect to bright light). For damaging environmental effects, the character should acquire the Special Attack Attribute (page 32) with the Dependent Defect (page 52). For enhanced influence over the environment (such as weather control), see the Dynamic Powers Attribute (page 17).

EXORCISM

COST:	2 Points/Level
RELEVANT STAT:	Soul
REQUIRED PMVS:	Targets
OPTIONAL PMVS:	Area, Range
PROGRESSION:	Linear; -1 Soul Stat each Level
REDUCTION:	Fewer Stat Values drained
RESTRICTIONS:	Under certain conditions; usage inflicts pain; against specific opponents

A character with this Attribute knows how to perform or create rituals, charms or spells capable of driving out, binding, or banishing supernatural entities. Exactly what entities qualify will depend on the nature of the game world; in some settings, undead, such as zombies or ghosts, may be vulnerable to Exorcism. Using this Attribute on other "normal" targets has no effect.

Each attempt at Exorcism counts as an attack and requires a Soul Stat check with a -1 bonus per Level of the Attribute. A ritual action is also necessary in most cases, such as a chant or mystical gestures, or use of particular objects, such as holy water or spirit wards. During the Exorcism attempt, the character is completely focused on the Exorcism and cannot defend against other attacks. In addition, the targets entities must fail a Soul Stat check, with a -1 penalty for each Level of the Exorcism Attribute.

If the attack succeeds (the Exorcist makes his or her Soul Stat check and the entities fails their own Soul Stat checks) the entities will be affected. They cannot attack the exorcist (and any companions sheltered behind him or her) for one round. In addition, the entities each loses one Soul Stat value for every Exorcism Attribute Level. Although prevented from attacking the exorcist for one round, the entities may choose to take other actions, such as taunting or threatening the exorcist, fleeing, or even vanishing.

Exorcism may be repeated each round with successes draining additional Soul Stat values from the targets, and failures having no effect (and leaving the entities free to attack the character). If the entities are ever reduced to a Soul Stat of 0 or lower as a result of the spiritual attack, they are either banished to their own dimension (if normally extra-dimensional), turned to dust, or permanently "sealed" in an object or in a mystic location (an Item or Place of Power may be ideal) until a specific action is taken that breaks the seal (GM's option).

If the campaign uses Energy Points (page 57), Exorcism may instead reduce the entities' Energy Points by 5 for each Attribute Level, rather than reduce their Soul Stats (GM's discretion). If the entities are ever reduced to a 0 Energy Points (or lower), they are banished as noted earlier.

EXTRA ARMS

COST:	1 Point/Level
RELEVANT STAT:	None
REQUIRED PMVS:	None
OPTIONAL PMVS:	None
PROGRESSION:	Slow Progression Chart, starting at 1 extra arm
REDUCTION:	None
RESTRICTIONS:	Extra arms are cumbersome; arms only function sometimes; arms are awkwardly placed

Unless indicated otherwise, all characters possess two arms and hands. By assigning this Characteristic Attribute, the character can acquire more. An "arm" is defined loosely as an appendage that can reach out and manipulate objects. A trunk, tentacle, or prehensile tail is an arm; an appendage that simply ends in a gun-barrel, melee weapon, stump, or tool mount is not. Legs with paws or feet are not usually considered to be "arms" unless the character has good manipulation ability when using them (such as the way chimpanzees can use their feet to grasp objects). Extra arms are useful for holding onto several things at once, but do not give extra attacks (for that ability, see Extra Attacks Attribute, below).

Possessing only one arm or no arms is reflected by the Physical Impairment Defect (page 55).

EXTRA ATTACKS

COST:	8 Points/Level
RELEVANT STAT:	None
REQUIRED PMVS:	None
OPTIONAL PMVS:	None
PROGRESSION:	Linear; +1 attack per round each Level
REDUCTION:	Less often than each round
RESTRICTIONS:	Extra attacks must all be similar in nature; only extra melee attacks; only extra ranged attacks

This Attribute reflects the character's ability to use every offensive combat situation to his or her benefit. Each round, the character may make one or more additional offensive or non-combat actions. In addition, unless two or more opponents are very close together, armed or unarmed hand-to-hand attacks must target the same person.

The GM must decide when the character can use his or her extra attacks. The suggested method spreads the actions roughly evenly over the character's Initiative range. For example, if a character had three attacks and rolled an Initiative of 18, he or she would attack on Initiative numbers 18, 12, and 6. If the enemy rolls an Initiative of 35 and has 5 attacks, he or she can attack on Initiative numbers 35, 28, 21, 14, and 7. This option has the advantage that it spreads actions over the entire combat round, but it involves the player paying closer attention to the Initiative numbers. Alternatively, the attacks may be carried out at the same time during the character's single Initiative.

EXTRA DEFENCES

COST:	3 Points/Level
RELEVANT STAT:	None
REQUIRED PMVS:	None
OPTIONAL PMVS:	None
PROGRESSION:	Linear; +1 defence per round each Level
REDUCTION:	Less often than each round
RESTRICTIONS:	Extra defences must all be similar in nature; only extra melee defences; only extra ranged defences

This Attribute reflects the character's ability to use every defensive combat situation to his or her benefit. Each round, the character may make one or more additional defensive or non-combat actions. Additionally, penalties for performing more than one defensive action each round (page 67) only apply after the extra defences are used. For example, a -4 penalty is applied to the fifth defence for a character with Level 3 Extra Defences.

FEATURES

COST:	1 Point/Level
RELEVANT STAT:	None
REQUIRED PMVS:	None
OPTIONAL PMVS:	None
PROGRESSION:	Linear; +1 feature each Level
REDUCTION:	None
RESTRICTIONS:	None

The character possesses various secondary abilities that grant useful, but minor, advantages. Features are typically possessed by non-humans and reflect various, minor biological or technological advantages. Examples of racial features include homing instinct, secondary eyelids, longevity, a pouch, feathers, soft fur, moulting ability, scent glands, diagnostic equipment, gyrocompass, etc. A wide range of other Attributes covers other more useful features such as gills, wings, fangs, and enhanced senses.

One additional Feature is appearance, representing beauty, cuteness, or good looks. Assigning appearance multiple times indicates heightened levels of extreme beauty.

FLIGHT

COST:	2, 3, or 4 Points/Level
RELEVANT STAT:	Body
REQUIRED PMVS:	None
OPTIONAL PMVS:	None
PROGRESSION:	Medium Progression Chart, starting at 10 kph
REDUCTION:	Limited control
RESTRICTIONS:	Under certain conditions; time limit; Stat/Skill check required to fly safely

A character with Flight can fly through an atmosphere or in space. The method used to achieve flight can vary greatly: wings, paranormal power, rotors, rockets, anti-gravity, psionic levitation, magic, or some other technique.

Depending on the speed at which the character is moving, opponents may suffer a penalty to hit the character (see Attacking Moving Targets, page 66). A fast-moving character may have an attack penalty as well.

Flight costs 4 Points/Level if the character can hover and fly at variable speeds, take off and land vertically, or stop in mid-air. This is the most common type of flight possessed by characters.

Flight costs 3 Points/Level if the flyer cannot hover, but instead flies like a normal airplane. Thus, the character needs a smooth surface or running start for landing and take off, and must maintain a minimum speed (at least 1/10 of his or her maximum speed) once airborne to avoid crashing.

Flight costs 2 Points/Level if the flyer is either a Skimmer/Hovercraft or a Glider:

SKIMMER / HOVERCRAFT

The character is limited to skimming no more than a metre or two off the ground or water. He or she may be riding on a cushion of air, magnetic lines of force, or even travelling along a magical weave.

GLIDER

The flyer can only become airborne if he or she launches from a high place (like a tree or rooftop) or from a fast-moving vehicle. Additionally, he or she can only gain speed by diving, or gain altitude by riding thermals.

FORCE FIELD

COST:	4 Points/Level
RELEVANT STAT:	Mind
REQUIRED PMVS:	Area
OPTIONAL PMVS:	Duration, Range
PROGRESSION:	Linear; -20 damage reduction each Level
REDUCTION:	Lower damage reduction
RESTRICTIONS:	None (see Limited Disability, below)

A Force Field is an energy field around the character that protects against incoming attacks. Force Fields can represent magical barriers, telekinetic shields, or technological "screens." The Area PMV is essential for the Force Field; Area Level 2 is required to make it a form-fitting Force Field for a character. Additionally, Duration is only required if the character wishes to create a Force Field that remains unattended. In this case, the Duration indicates how long the Force Field will remain in place before vanishing. Force Fields created in this way cannot move — they are static structures.

A typical Force Field is different from Armour, since it can be battered down by a sufficiently powerful attack. A Force Field can be "up" or "down." When down, it does not stop any damage. Unless the Detectable Defect (page 52) is assigned, an up Force Field is invisible. Force Field status must be determined at the start of the character's actions for the round and cannot be changed until his or her turn to act in the next round.

Attack damage is first applied to the Force Field, with any additional penetrating damage applied against Armour (if any). Thus, if a weapon hit successfully penetrates a Force Field, the Armour Attribute can still protect against it. A Force Field can be reduced or even knocked down by a sufficiently powerful attack. If an attack does more damage than the Force Field prevents (even if the rest of the damage is absorbed by Armour), the Force Field temporarily loses one Level of effectiveness. The character can only regain Levels if the field is down and regenerating, unless the Regenerating Ability is assigned. A Force Field recovers one Level every round it is turned off and not in operation ("down"). A Force Field that is knocked down to zero Levels automatically shuts off to regenerate.

A Force Field can be given additional customised Abilities or Disabilities. Each Ability taken reduces the protection provided by the Field by 20 points, but gives it some special capability. Each Disability taken increases the protection of the Field by 20 points but adds some sort of weakness.

FORCE FIELD ABILITIES
Air-Tight

The field prevents the passage of gas molecules. While this is a beneficial defence against toxic gas attacks, a character in the field will eventually deplete all breathable oxygen.

Blocks Incorporeal

The field prevents the passage of astral, ethereal, or otherwise incorporeal characters through it.

Blocks Teleport

A character cannot teleport into or out of the field. This Ability cannot be used with the Shield Only Disability.

Field-Penetrating

The Force Field can be used to interpenetrate other Force Fields while making attacks (or moving through them). If the character's Force Field is in direct contact with an enemy Force Field, and can stop more damage than the foe's, the enemy's field offers no protection against the character's attack, but it is still up. In this case, the character may actually move through the neutralised field.

Offensive

The field delivers a powerful electric or energy shock to anyone who touches it. The damage equal 10 for every 20 damage that the Force Field currently stops. Consequently, the damage delivered by an Offensive Force Field decreases as the Field becomes damaged and is knocked down in levels of effectiveness.

Regenerating

If the character uses one non-combat action to regenerate the Force Field, it regains one lost Level of effectiveness. A character with the Extra Attacks Attribute (page 19) can regenerate multiples Levels each round.

FORCE FIELD DISABILITIES
Both Directions

The Force Field blocks attacks moving in any direction, both inwards and outwards, thereby virtually preventing the user from attacking when the Force Field is up. This means that when the Force Field is active and the user makes an attack, the Force Field will affect their attack as it would an outside attacker's (reducing the

damage inflicted and going down in Level if its protection value is exceeded). This Disability cannot be used with the Shield Only Disability.

Full Impact

This Disability is only available in campaigns that use Knockback rules (page 70). Whenever the character is hit with an impacting physical attack, he or she can feel the force of the attack though he or she may not receive any damage. Consequently, the character is affected by the attack's full Knockback value, before the damage is reduced by the Force Field.

Internal

The field is only usable inside a specific building or other structure. This can be used to represent a Force Field that protects a vital part of a building's interior such as the power plant or dungeon cells, or a character who draws personal Force Field energy from some sort of power source inside his or her headquarters.

Limited

The field has a major or minor limitation. An example of a minor limitation would be a Force Field that is effective against ranged attacks but not melee or one that offers full-strength frontal and rear protection but only half-strength protection from above. An example of a major limitation would be a Force Field that prevents the character from making any attacks during operation, one that is unstable in certain types of environments (such as sub-zero temperatures or near water), or one that only works against a very specific type of weapon (such as lasers). A minor limitation counts as one Disability, a major limitation as two Disabilities.

Shield Only

This option is only available for Force Fields with Area PMV of Level 1 or 2. The Field does not entirely surround the character's body. Instead, it is a shield that the user must deliberately interpose in front of an attack using a Block Defence (page 67). The character must also possess the Combat Technique (Block Ranged Attacks) Attribute to use the force shield in a Block Defence against ranged attacks. If the character successfully defends, the Force Shield can protect against damage associated with the Attribute Level. This Disability cannot be used with the Block Teleport Ability or Both Directions Disability. It counts as three Disabilities.

Static

The character cannot move when generating the field. He or she may still attack or otherwise act, but must stay in one place (or continue to drift if floating through space, continue to fall if falling, etc.).

GADGETEER

COST:	2 Points/Level
RELEVANT STAT:	Mind
REQUIRED PMVs:	None
OPTIONAL PMVs:	None
PROGRESSION:	Slow Progression Chart, starting at 2 times normal building rate
REDUCTION:	Very specific utility
RESTRICTIONS:	Under certain conditions; specific types of machines; requires expensive/consumable equipment

The character has an innate knack for creating, modifying, and working with complex machines. Unlike someone who is merely well trained in a particular technical skill, a Gadgeteer is a natural and is able to flip through a tech manual for an advanced technology in 30 seconds and figure out a way to repair the machine in an hour or so. Most Gadgeteers have high Levels in Electronics and Mechanical Skills as well.

A character with this Attribute can also build new and modify existing Gadgets at an astonishing rate, provided he or she has appropriate parts and facilities. In game terms, this means he or she can modify existing Gadgets or technology-based Items of Power by exchanging Attributes and Defects, as long as the overall Point total is unchanged. A Gadgeteer can also build Gadgets and Items of Power, but their creation requires the character to allocate the appropriate number of Character Points.

Alternatively, the GM may describe this Attribute as "Magical Gadgeteer," that allows a character to modify magical Items of Power by exchanging Attributes and Defects.

GADGETS

COST: 2 Points/Level
RELEVANT STAT: None
REQUIRED PMVs: None
OPTIONAL PMVs: None
PROGRESSION: Linear; +1 major and +4 minor Gadgets each Level
REDUCTION: Only major or minor Gadgets
RESTRICTIONS: Limited functioning; poor workmanship; consumable

The Gadgets Attribute represents a character's access to useful equipment. Characters do not need to spend Character Points for items that are legal, inexpensive, and mundane in the campaign setting (such as clothing, a backpack, a knife, or consumer goods), unless taken in quantity (GM's option). For example, "a complete tool box" could be a single minor Gadget; a single wrench is mundane. GMs may ask players to allot Points to this Attribute, however, if their characters will begin the game with numerous pieces of equipment to which the average person might not have easy access such as weapons, body armour, or specialised professional equipment.

Gadgets cannot include magic items, secret prototypes, or equipment that is significantly more technologically advanced than what is standard in the setting (instead, see Item of Power Attribute; page 24). It can include common civilian vehicles appropriate to the setting (for example, a car, truck, light airplane, or motorbike in the present day). Less common or more expensive vehicles should count as several items of gear. The GM always has the final say on whether or not an item is available to the characters. Some examples of Gadgets can be found in Chapter 9: Equipment (page 73); the GM can create the statistics of other items.

Although characters may have items that are owned by the organisations to which they belong, they still must acquire these items as Gadgets if they will make regular use of them (though the Conditional Ownership Defect may apply; page 51). Thus, a police officer would use Gadgets for a pistol, police car, or handcuffs, although these items are property of the police department. This rule is intended mainly for play balance and, naturally, the GM has final say on this issue.

Each Level in this Attribute permits the character to take one major and four minor Gadgets. Alternatively, the character can exchange one major Gadget with an extra four minor Gadgets (or vice-versa). Use the guidelines below to differentiate between major and minor Gadgets.

MINOR

The item is somewhat hard to get, or rather expensive. It is something available in a shop or store or from a skilled artisan, but it costs as much as an average person's weekly or monthly wage. Alternatively, the item can be less expensive but needs a license or black market contact to acquire. Non-standard items that modify or improve other items of gear, but are not functional by themselves (for example, a scope for a rifle, silencer for a pistol, or a supercharged engine for an automobile) are also minor Gadgets; for more information, see page 73 and 79.

Modern examples of minor Gadgets include: weapon and vehicle modifications, handguns, premium medical kits, night vision goggles, full camping gear, burglary tools, expensive tool kits, and personal computers. Ancient or medieval examples include quality weapons, light-weight armour (such as leather or a light mail shirt), lock picks, poisons, or a mule. Gadgets must be appropriate to the world setting — a pistol is a minor Gadget in a modern-day or future setting, but an Item of Power in a medieval fantasy game!

MAJOR

The gear is usually illegal for civilians, but it may be issued to an elite law enforcement agency, an average soldier, licensed superhero, or a government spy. Modern-day examples of major Gadgets include machine guns, tactical armour, and grenade launchers. Major gear can also include quite expensive but commercially available equipment such as a workshop, car, or motorbike. Very expensive items (such as an airplane, big rig truck, science lab, or medical facility) counts as two or more items (GM's discretion). Ancient or medieval examples of major Gadgets include a full suit of plate armour, a cavalry horse, a smith's forge, an alchemist's lab, or a wagon and team of draft animals.

GROW

COST: 10 Points/Level
RELEVANT STAT: Body
REQUIRED PMVs: None
OPTIONAL PMVs: None
PROGRESSION: Variable; see chart
REDUCTION: Associated Attributes not gained, or gained more slowly
RESTRICTIONS: Time limit on growth; naked form only, growth inflicts pain

This Attribute reflects the ability to increase the stature and mass of the character, giving him or her access to several other Attributes and effects (see chart). In addition to increased height and mass, the character gains a corresponding Level of the Armour, Immovable, and Superstrength Attributes. Also, the character's running speed, weapon range, and damage inflicted by physical attacks and Special Attacks (physical, not energy-based) increase as the character grows. The damage bonus of +5 per Grow Level is in addition to those bonuses gained by Superstrength for muscle-powered weapons (see Superstrength, page 37). Finally, opponents attacking the character gain a bonus to their attack checks equal to the character's current Grow Level size.

In campaigns that do not use Knockback (page 70), the cost of Grow should be reduced to 9 Points/Level instead of 10.

Table 3-4: Grow

Current Grow Level	Height Speed Range Multiplier	Mass Multiplier	Armour Immovable Superstrength Level	Damage Bonus	Enemy's Attack Bonus
1	2	10	1	+5	+1
2	3	30	2	+10	+2
3	4	60	3	+15	+3
4	5	100	4	+20	+4
5	6	200	5	+25	+5
6	7	400	6	+30	+6
7	10	1,000	7	+35	+7
8	20	10,000	8	+40	+8
9	40	50,000	9	+45	+9
10	80	500,000	10	+50	+10
+1	x2	x10	+1	+5	+1

HEALING

COST: 4 Points/Level
RELEVANT STAT: Body or Soul
REQUIRED PMVs: Targets
OPTIONAL PMVs: Area, Range
PROGRESSION: Linear; +20 restored Health Points each Level
REDUCTION: Fewer Health Points restored
RESTRICTIONS: Specific targets; specific wound types; character suffers damage when Healing others

This Attribute allows a character to heal a target's injuries (including him or herself; for continuous healing, see the Regeneration Attribute, page 30). At higher Healing Levels, the character can also revive someone who is "clinically" dead but not actually brain-dead (Level 3+), repair massive trauma such as lost limbs or organs (Level 5+), or restore a character who was cut in two (Level 7+). No healer can repair someone who was blown to bits, disintegrated, or dead for more than a few minutes, however.

The Attribute Level dictates the maximum number of Health Points that healers can restore to a particular target in a single day. This cannot be exceeded, even if multiple healers work on a subject; the combined Health Points restored cannot exceed the maximum Health Points that the character with the highest Level of Healing could restore. The subject must have at least a full day's rest before he or she can benefit from any additional healing.

HEIGHTENED AWARENESS

COST:	1 Point/Level
RELEVANT STAT:	Body or Mind
REQUIRED PMVS:	None
OPTIONAL PMVS:	None
PROGRESSION:	Linear; +2 Check Value bonus each Level
REDUCTION:	None
RESTRICTIONS:	Under certain conditions; situations detected by only one sense; specific situations

The character possesses a high degree of situational awareness. He or she is usually very alert and receives a Check Value bonus to notice nearby hidden things, such as concealed objects, ambushes, or anything else related to sensory awareness. The bonuses of Heightened Awareness are cumulative with those of Heightened Senses (below).

HEIGHTENED SENSES

COST:	1 Point/Level
RELEVANT STAT:	Body or Mind
REQUIRED PMVS:	None
OPTIONAL PMVS:	None
PROGRESSION:	Linear; +1 sense or technique each Level
REDUCTION:	None
RESTRICTIONS:	Under certain conditions; weakened technique; adverse effects upon detection

A character with Heightened Senses has one or more senses that have been sharpened to a superhuman level of acuity. It can represent either the preternatural sharpening of a specific sense honed by special training (such as a blind person's trained sense of touch) or the enhanced senses of a paranormal or technologically augmented character. Additionally, several Levels of Heightened Senses can reflect the capabilities of sensors built into spaceships and other commercial or military vehicles. For each Level of the Heightened Senses Attribute, the character will either gain one enhanced sense (Type I) or one sense technique (Type II). The character must make a successful Body Stat check to detect and pinpoint a specific target within a large area (for example, to listen to a specific conversation thought the background noise of the city).

The Heightened Awareness Attribute (above) allows for a lower Level of enhancement for all of a character's senses.

TYPE I

One of the character's five senses — hearing, smell, vision, taste, or touch — is enhanced, and can operate over an area of several city blocks. The character may take the same sense twice, which doubles the effect and extends the area of detection. A character using a Heightened Sense has a +4 bonus (+8 if the sense was heightened twice) on Stat checks that relate to using that sense to perceive things that someone with human-level senses might conceivably notice.

TYPE II

The character has one Heightened Sense technique, which extends beyond human capabilities. Examples of techniques include: electric current detection; infravision; magnetic field detection; microscopic vision; radar sense; radio reception; sonar detection; ultrasonic hearing; ultravision; vibration detection; X-ray vision. Most techniques only work at short range, often requiring line of sight.

HENCHMEN

COST:	1 or 2 Points/Level
RELEVANT STAT:	Soul
REQUIRED PMVS:	None
OPTIONAL PMVS:	None
PROGRESSION:	Slow Progression Chart, starting at 1 henchman
REDUCTION:	Fewer Henchmen available
RESTRICTIONS:	Limited to specific type of henchmen; henchmen consume the character's resources; henchmen have further limited Stats/Attributes/Defects/Skills

The Henchmen Attribute represents the extent of a character's loyal and dedicated human resources. Henchmen — sometimes known as groupies, stooges, toadies, or flunkies — are always eager to carry out the character's commands, and ask for very little in return. They always aim to please, even at their own expense.

For 1 Point/Level, the Henchmen are not warriors; they may get in the way of an enemy, or fight in self-defence, but will not attack. For 2 Points/Level, the Henchmen will take up arms at the request of their master. For specific talented and loyal battle-ready followers, see the Agents or Servant Attribute (pages 12 and 31). Mercenaries who the character hires for specific tasks are not Henchmen, since they have an agenda and expect compensation.

Individual Henchmen are NPCs. All of the character's Henchmen normally have identical Stats and Attributes, although Skills may vary. A character may have followers with varied Stats or Attributes, but each one counts as two Henchmen. Each Henchman should be built on 20 Character Points (plus any Defects) and 10 Skill Points. Clearly, most Henchmen have focused abilities and numerous Defects (often including Inept Attack, Inept Defence, Less Capable, Marked, Not So Tough, Owned, and Wanted) to raise their Stats and Attributes to competent levels. The 1 Point/Level Henchmen should not possess the Attack Combat Mastery, Massive Damage, or Special Attack Attributes, nor should they have Combat Skills.

HIGHLY SKILLED

COST:	1 Point/Level
RELEVANT STAT:	None
REQUIRED PMVS:	None
OPTIONAL PMVS:	None
PROGRESSION:	Linear; +10 Skill Points each Level
REDUCTION:	None
RESTRICTIONS:	None

A character with this Attribute is more experienced or better trained than an ordinary person, and as a result has more Skill Points (page 41) than an average adult. Acquiring several Levels of the Highly Skilled Attribute is the ideal method for creating a versatile character.

HYPERFLIGHT

COST:	1 Point/Level
RELEVANT STAT:	Body
REQUIRED PMVS:	None
OPTIONAL PMVS:	None
PROGRESSION:	Fast Progression Chart, starting at 1 times the speed of light
REDUCTION:	Very specific utility
RESTRICTIONS:	Restricted area of flight; character may suffer damage during flight; unpredictable relativistic time effects (GM's control)

This Attribute is intended for use in star-spanning campaigns, involving travel between solar systems or galaxies. A character with Hyperflight can fly in the vacuum of space (not in an atmosphere) between planets, stars, asteroids, solar systems, and galaxies, at speeds equal to or exceeding the speed of light. The player can determine whether this Attribute represents warp technology, jump point formation, or the breaking of known physical laws. The Flight Attribute (page 19) is required to escape from the atmosphere and gravity of a planet similar to Earth. Without Flight, the character can only achieve Hyperflight speeds by taking off when already in space.

ILLUSION

COST:	1-4 Points/Level
RELEVANT STAT:	Mind
REQUIRED PMVS:	Area, Duration, Targets
OPTIONAL PMVS:	Range
PROGRESSION:	Fast Progression Chart, starting at 10 cm radius area
REDUCTION:	Illusion always the same
RESTRICTIONS:	Under certain conditions; illusions are flawed in some way; usage inflicts pain

The character can create mental Illusions that fool one or more senses. An Illusion appears to be real to the targeted observers but is not really there; it has no physical substance, and characters who are not the target of the Illusion are unaffected. Comic book characters that can create Illusions are often sorcerers, demons, or people with psionic abilities. See the Projection Attribute (page 30) for the ability to create real images that anyone can detect, rather than mental illusions that target specific people.

An Illusion may be of a particular object or entity, or of a complete scene (such as a furnished room or crowd). It may also be created over an existing person, scene, or object to make it appear different than it really is. An Illusion that is untended is normally static, either remaining in one place or (if created over something) moving as the underlying object or entity moves. To give an Illusion the semblance of independent activity (such as an illusionary person or crowd that moves and speaks) the character must actively concentrate on manipulating the Illusion, and perform no other actions. The maximum amount of time an Illusion will remain in existence is dictated by the Duration PMV.

For 1 Point/Level the character can create Illusions that deceive one sense, usually sight (sense must be determined during character creation). For 2 Points/Level the Illusions can deceive two senses, usually sight and hearing. For 3 Points/Level they can deceive three senses, usually sight, hearing, and smell. For 4 Points/Level they can deceive all senses. No matter how realistic the Illusions, however, they can never cause physical sensations intense enough to inflict damage. An illusionary fire may feel hot, and a character may believe that he or she is burning, but the fire cannot actually deliver damage. To create Illusions capable of injuring targets, the character should possess a Special Attacks Attribute (page 32) which is tied to the Illusion Attribute through the Dependent Defect (page 52).

A character can normally maintain only a single Illusion at a time. The ability to maintain multiple Illusions at once costs the character an extra 1 Point for every distinct Illusion the character can sustain simultaneously after the first. Thus, "Illusion Level 3 (Sight only, four Illusions)" would cost six Points: three Points for Level 3 (one sense) and three more Points for being able to sustain four Illusions at a time. A group of objects or entities within the Area PMV, such as a furnished room, a swarm of insects, or a horde of charging warriors, counts as a single Illusion rather than several. If a character is already sustaining his or her maximum number of Illusions and wishes to create another one, an existing Illusion must first be dispelled.

An Illusion may have two types of areas: the Area PMV, and the area determined by the Attribute Level. The Area PMV reflects the maximum area in which the Illusion may be created, while the Level-related area dictates the actual size of the Illusionary image. Thus, an Area PMV of Rank 6 (10 km) with Attribute Level 3 (10 metres) means that any image up to 10 metres in radius (such as a school bus) can be created, and moved around within a location that has a 10 km radius (such as a medium-sized city).

In order for the character to create a convincing Illusion of something complex, the GM may require a Mind Stat check. The GM can add modifiers depending on how familiar or unfamiliar the character is with the scene that is being simulated. The GM may also give the character a +1 bonus for every Level he or she has in excess of the minimum Level needed to create an Illusion. For example, if a character with Illusion Level 5 decides to create an image with an area radius of one metre (a Level 2 effect), a +3 Check Value bonus applies (Level 5 — Level 2 = +3). If the check fails, the character's Illusion has some subtle flaw in it; the character creating it may not be aware of this until someone else points it out, however.

Whether or not an observer recognises an Illusion for what it actually is depends on the circumstances and should be adjudicated by the GM. For example, if a character creates a visual-only Illusion of a tiger, it may easily fool everyone if it is a few hundred metres away, but if it comes close to the characters, the fact that it is not making any sounds will be obvious. Its lack of a tiger's scent will probably only be a clue to someone who has Heightened Senses (Smell). The audio-only Illusion of a tiger roaring from behind a closed door, however, should fool just about anyone ... at least until they open the door and see that there is nothing actually there. If appropriate, the GM can require Body or Mind checks to "see through" an Illusion; if successful, the Illusion disappears.

IMMOVABLE

COST:	1 Point/Level
RELEVANT STAT:	Body
REQUIRED PMVS:	None
OPTIONAL PMVS:	None
PROGRESSION:	Linear; +20 metre Knockback reduction each Level
REDUCTION:	None
RESTRICTIONS:	Under certain conditions; against specific opponents; against one type of attack

This Attribute is only available in campaigns that use Knockback rules (page 70). Characters with this Attribute absorb physical impacts better than the average person, reducing the distance by which they are knocked back from impact attacks and forceful blows. If a Special Attack's or melee attack's Knockback distance is reduced to zero or below, the target has successfully absorbed the impact of the entire attack (but the attack still inflicts damage). For more information on Knockback, see page 70 (or page 34 for the Special Attack Knockback Ability).

IMMUNITY

COST:	5 Points/Level
RELEVANT STAT:	Body
REQUIRED PMVS:	None
OPTIONAL PMVS:	None
PROGRESSION:	Descriptive
REDUCTION:	None
RESTRICTIONS:	Under certain conditions; time limit; limitations on use

With this Attribute, the character is completely immune to damage and adverse effects that stem from a particular weapon, element, application, or event. For example, a character with Level 2 Immunity to silver cannot be hurt by silver weapons and perhaps will not feel pain if clubbed with a sack of silver dollars. Similarly, a character with Level 8 Immunity to fire/heat could walk into the most intensive firestorm possible and emerge unscathed.

Though only six Attribute Levels are described below, GMs can easily extrapolate intermediate or higher Levels as required.

LEVEL 2   The Immunity plays a small role in the game. Typical examples include: weapons made from a rare substance (such as gold, silver, or adamantine); attacks from a specific opponent (such as a brother, single animal type, or oneself); under specific conditions (such as in water, one hour during the day, or at home).

LEVEL 4   The Immunity plays a moderate role in the game. Typical examples include: weapons made from an uncommon substance (such as wood, bronze, or iron); attacks from a broad opponent group (such as blood relatives, demons, or animals); under broad conditions (such as during the night, on weekends, or in holy places).

LEVEL 6   The Immunity plays a large role in the game. Typical examples include: electricity; cold; a specific weapon type (such as daggers, arrows, or rapiers).

LEVEL 8   The Immunity plays a major role in the game. Typical examples include: fire/heat; a broad weapon type (such as swords or clubs); mental attacks.

LEVEL 10   The Immunity plays an extreme role in the game. Typical examples include: gunfire (including forms of artillery); bladed weapons; unarmed attacks.

LEVEL 12   The Immunity plays a primal role in the game. Typical examples include: weapons; energy; blunt trauma.

INSUBSTANTIAL

COST: 4 Points/Level
RELEVANT STAT: Body
REQUIRED PMVS: None
OPTIONAL PMVS: None
PROGRESSION: Descriptive
REDUCTION: Partial effectiveness
RESTRICTIONS: Under certain conditions, time limit, naked form only

Each Level reduces a character's density so much that he or she can pass through certain types of objects (including weapons) as though insubstantial. If a specific substance is not listed in the chart below, the GM should use the entry that it most closely resembles. The density of water, and thus the human body, for example, falls between Level 4 (Wood) and Level 6 (Concrete/Earth); consequently, a punch from an enemy would harmlessly pass through a character with Level 6 Insubstantial. Characters with Level 12 Insubstantial are effectively incorporeal and can pass through virtually anything, including most forms of energy.

Though only six Attribute Levels are described, GMs can easily extrapolate intermediate or higher Levels as required.

Table 3-5: Insubstantial

Attribute Level	Can Pass Through
2	Paper/Cloth
4	Wood
6	Concrete/Earth
8	Iron/Steel
10	Lead/Gold
12	Energy

INVISIBILITY

COST: 3 Points/Level
RELEVANT STAT: Body
REQUIRED PMVS: None
OPTIONAL PMVS: Area, Targets
PROGRESSION: Linear; invisibility to +1 sense or technique each Level
REDUCTION: Partial effectiveness
RESTRICTIONS: Time limit; invisible to certain types of characters; naked form only

This Attribute will completely hide the character from one or more senses or detection methods. The character may possess a supernatural concealment ability or a technological cloaking device, or have a psychic or magical talent that causes observers to overlook him or her. To represent partial invisibility, see the Sensory Block Attribute (page 30).

For each Invisibility Level, the player selects one sense or technique to which the character is "invisible." Senses include the human range for sight, hearing, taste, touch, or smell. Detection techniques include: astral; ethereal; infrared; mental; radar; radiation; sonar; spiritual; ultraviolet; vibration. The GM may decided that the most common forms of Invisibility — usually sight and hearing — cost 2 Attribute slots rather than only 1.

While the character may not be detected using specific methods, indirect evidence can still reveal the character's presence. For example, a character who is invisible to sight will still leave footprints in muddy ground. Similarly, a vase that is knocked from a table by a character who is invisible to sound will still make noise as it smashes on the floor.

In normal combat situations involving human or nearly human opponents, a character who is invisible to sight has a great advantage. Once the invisible character gives away his or her general position (for example, by firing a gun, attacking with a sword, or shouting) he or she can be attacked, but there is a -4 penalty for anyone within melee range and -8 for anyone at a greater distance. Heightened Awareness and Heightened Senses can reduce this penalty, as can the two Combat Techniques, Blind Fighting and Blind Shooting (page 14). This penalty is halved if using an Area or Spreading attack on the invisible character.

ITEM OF POWER

COST: 3 or 4 Points/Level
RELEVANT STAT: Soul
REQUIRED PMVS: None
OPTIONAL PMVS: None
PROGRESSION: Linear; +5 Character Points for item building each Level
REDUCTION: Fewer Character Points awarded
RESTRICTIONS: Under certain conditions; limited functioning; item's Attributes are only partially conferred

This Attribute describes any exotic, usually portable item that directly enhances a character in some way (perhaps by conferring Attributes), or one that serves as a useful tool or weapon. An Item of Power represents advanced technology or a relic with paranormal or magical powers. More ordinary but useful items (such as a car or gun) are covered by the Gadgets Attribute (page 21). Special weapons that others can use are often designed with Item of Power, with Points allocated to the Special Attack Attribute (page 32).

Each item is built using up to 5 Character Points per Level of the Item of Power Attribute, which can be used to assign Attributes. Assigning Defects to the item earns Bonus Points, which are used to acquire additional Attributes for the item. Defects that cannot usually be assigned include: Conditional Ownership, Famous, Ism, Marked, Nemesis, Owned, Red Tape, Significant Other, Skeleton in the Closet, and Wanted. Players selecting this Attribute must have a discussion with the GM to determine what abilities the Item of Power possesses and how it works. The player, with GM approval, may also create specific abilities for Items of Power using the Unique Attribute (page 40). An Item of Power may be combined with a mundane, minor, or major Gadget (such as a car that can fly, or a sword that can teleport people).

The item costs 4 Points/Level if it is difficult for the character to misplace or for an enemy to steal/knock away, or it is almost always with the character. Examples include jewellery, frequently worn clothing, or equipment the character carries with them always. The item costs 3 Points/Level if it is easier for the character to misplace or for an enemy to steal/knock away, or it is often distant from the character. Examples include thrown weapons, armour that is stored when not in use, and vehicles or equipment that stay at the character's home until needed.

Additionally, the total Point cost (not cost per Level) for the Item is increased by 1 if it can only be used by a small subset of individuals (Restricted Use). For example: only characters with a superhuman Body Stat, only magicians, only members of a specific native tribe, or only gods. The total Point cost is increased by 2 if the Item can only be used by the character (Personal Use); this restriction cannot be reconfigured by someone with the Gadgeteer Attribute.

Items that cannot be lost or stolen, such as objects that are implanted in or fused to the character's body, are not Items of Power. In these cases, the items are considered part of the character and thus the player should use Character Points to acquire the relevant Attributes directly. If a character requires a specific object, or group of objects, to act as a focus when using one or more of his or her innate Attributes, Item of Power does not apply; see the Special Requirement Defect (page 56).

JUMPING

COST: 1 Point/Level
RELEVANT STAT: Body
REQUIRED PMVS: None
OPTIONAL PMVS: None
PROGRESSION: Medium Progression Chart, starting at 5 times normal distance
REDUCTION: None
RESTRICTIONS: Under certain conditions; need running start; damage inflicted upon landing

With this Attribute, the character can jump great distances (and land without injury) but cannot actually fly. Jumping does not enable a character to exceed the character's normal maximum running speed (or swimming speed for aquatic characters capable of leaping). Consequently, unless the character also has the appropriate Level of the Speed Attribute (page 37), long-distance jumps may require several round, minutes, or hours to complete. For example, a character with a Body

Stat of 10 can sprint approximately 60 metres/round (page 65). If the character jumps a distance of 120 metres, he or she will be airborne for two rounds rather than finishing the jump in just one (120 ÷ 60 = 2). The advantage to jumping, rather than running, however, is the character can ignore terrain and is not fatigued as the character would be if he or she had to run the same distance. See Jumping (page 66) in Chapter 8: Combat for additional jumping rules.

MASS INCREASE

COST:	8 Points/Level
RELEVANT STAT:	Body
REQUIRED PMVS:	None
OPTIONAL PMVS:	None
PROGRESSION:	Variable; see chart
REDUCTION:	Associated Attributes not gained, or gained more slowly
RESTRICTIONS:	Under certain conditions, time limit, naked form only

This Attribute reflects the ability to increase the mass — and thus density — of the character. In addition to increased mass, the character gains a corresponding Level of the Armour, Immovable, and Superstrength Attributes. The chart entry indicates two columns (realistic and perceived) of substances that have a similar density to a character with increased mass. The realistic column matches the character's density (also know as specific gravity) with a close counterpart in the natural world. The perceived column matches the character's density with a substance that is commonly believed in fiction to have a corresponding strength. For example, the gemstone, diamond, has an actual density close to four times that of the human body (3.3 to 3.7, to be specific). Because it is one of the strongest substances on Earth, however, it is also perceived as one of the densest. GMs and players may use either column when determining density/strength values in their games.

In campaigns that do not use Knockback (page 70), the cost of Mass Increase should be reduced to 7 Points/Level instead of 8.

Table 3-6: Mass Increase

Attribute Level	Mass Multiplier	Similar Density (Realistic)	Similar Density (Perceived)	Armour Immovable Superstrength Level
1	2	Brick/Concrete/Rock	Hardwood	1
2	4	Gemstones	Aluminium	2
3	6	Iron	Concrete	3
4	8	Steel	Granite	4
5	10	Copper	Lead	5
6	12	Lead	Iron	6
7	14	Mercury	Steel	7
8	16	Uranium	Titanium	8
9	18	Gold	Diamond	9
10	20	Platinum	Adamantine	10

MASSIVE DAMAGE

COST:	2 or 5 Points/Level
RELEVANT STAT:	None
REQUIRED PMVS:	None
OPTIONAL PMVS:	None
PROGRESSION:	Linear; +10 damage each Level
REDUCTION:	Less damage delivered
RESTRICTIONS:	Under certain conditions; against specific opponents; one attack type is excluded

A character with the Massive Damage Attribute knows precisely how and where to hit any opponent in order to inflict incredible amounts of damage.

For 2 Points/Level, additional damage is only inflicted when the character uses one specific weapon type, Special Attack (page 32), or method of attack; this attack is defined during character creation. For example, it might represent a special talent with a weapon (such as guns, blades, blunt weapons), knowledge of a particular martial arts technique, or ability with a specific Special Attack.

For 5 Points/Level, this knowledge can be applied to all forms of physical combat including armed, unarmed, martial arts, and ranged weapons, as well as Special Attacks such as energy blasts, magical spells that inflict damage, or vehicle weapons.

Naturally, the character's attack must be successful to inflict any damage. Physical strength is not the key to delivering massive damage in an attack; the ability to sense a weakness is far more important. The capacity of Massive Damage to augment any kind of attack makes it a very useful Attribute for a combat-oriented character. For more information on physical combat and damage, see page 68.

METAMORPHOSIS

COST:	5 Points/Level
RELEVANT STAT:	Mind or Soul
REQUIRED PMVS:	Duration, Targets
OPTIONAL PMVS:	Area, Range
PROGRESSION:	Linear; adding +1 Character Point or adding/removing +3 Bonus Points each Level
REDUCTION:	Change fewer Character Points and/or Bonus Points
RESTRICTIONS:	Specific targets; limitations on Attributes/Defects that can be changed; limited to several distinct changes

The Metamorphosis Attribute allows a character to transform others into alternate forms by adding Attributes to, or adding/removing Defects from, the target character. The maximum duration of this change is dictated by the Duration PMV. Additionally, this Attribute requires a Targets PMV at Rank 1 minimum. If the target character successfully makes a Body or Soul Stat check (whichever is higher), the Metamorphosis attempt does not work. The GM may rule that Metamorphosis automatically fails if the subject's new form could not survive in the present environment. Consequently, a character could turn an enemy into a goldfish, but the attempt would only work if the target was currently in water. This prevents this ability from being used as a quick way to instantly kill an opponent. Again, GMs may waive this restriction where appropriate (such as for a villain in a supernatural horror campaign). In order to transform him or herself, the character needs the Alternate Form Attribute (page 12).

For each Level of Metamorphosis, the character can assign 1 Character Point to a target's Attributes (or PMV Rank). This can either raise the target's current Attribute Level, or result in the target gaining a new Attribute. Alternatively, for each Level the character can add 3 Defect Bonus Points to, or remove 3 Defect Bonus Points from, a target. To negate Attributes, see the Nullify Attribute (page 27). Cosmetic changes that confer no additional abilities on the target, but do not fall under the Marked Defect, are considered a 1 Bonus Point change total (for all changes). This includes: change of sex, 50% apparent age increase or decrease, colour changes (eye, skin, or hair), and minor physical changes (shape of ears, facial features, or bodily proportions).

Unless the GM indicates otherwise, Character Points gained through Metamorphosis can only be used to add Levels to the following Attributes: Adaptation, Armour, Elasticity, Extra Arms, Features, Flight, Heightened Senses, Immunity, Insubstantial, Jumping, Mass Increase, Natural Weapons, Regeneration, Special Defence, Special Movement, Speed, Superstrength, Tunnelling, and Water Speed. Additionally, only the following Defects can be changed: Awkward Size, Diminutive, Ism, Less Capable, Marked, Not So Tough, Physical Impairment, Sensory Impairment, and Unappealing. Metamorphosis is not intended for transforming people into stone or other forms where they would be effectively immobilised. In order to do that, use the Special Attack Attribute (page 32) with the Incapacitating Ability (page 34).

MIMIC POWERS

COST:	7 or 10 Points/Level
RELEVANT STAT:	Mind
REQUIRED PMVS:	None
OPTIONAL PMVS:	Duration, Range
PROGRESSION:	Linear; +1 Attribute each Level
REDUCTION:	More than one but less than all
RESTRICTIONS:	Trade Attribute with target; specific targets; limitation on Attributes/Defects that can be mimicked

Upon a successful Stat check, the character can temporarily mimic any Attribute, Stat, or Skill Level of any single target character within the Range PMV distance. The Mimic Powers Attribute Level determines the maximum Attribute or Skill Level that can be mimicked. Stats Values (at any rank) can be imitated when Mimic Powers reaches Level 5 or higher. The Level of a mimicked Attribute/Stat/Skill only replaces the character's corresponding Level (if applicable) if it is higher; the character's Attribute/Stat/Skill Level cannot decrease through Mimic unless a specific Restriction is assigned. The character gains the benefits of a mimicked Attribute as long as indicated by the Duration PMV; it is recommended that GMs not allow Duration past Level 6 for Mimic Powers.

For 7 Points/Level the character can only mimic one Attribute/Stat/Skill at any single time. For 10 Points/Level, the character can mimic all Attributes/Stats/Skills simultaneously at the appropriate Levels (as indicated above), from one character or many. To create a character that steals a target's Attributes for his or her own use, assign both the Mimic and Nullify (page 27) Attributes, linked through the Dependent Defect (page 52).

MIND CONTROL

COST:	2-5 Points/Level
RELEVANT STAT:	Mind
REQUIRED PMVS:	Duration, Targets
OPTIONAL PMVS:	Area, Range
PROGRESSION:	Variable; see below
REDUCTION:	One aspect of thought only
RESTRICTIONS:	Under certain conditions; usage inflicts pain; target remembers the control

This Attribute allows the character to mentally dominate other individuals. Sorcerers, some psionic adepts, and creatures with hypnotic powers (such as many demons or vampires) are among those likely to have Mind Control. The Duration PMV Rank cannot exceed the Attribute Level without GM permission.

Mind Control costs 5 Points/Level if it can be used on any human or alien with a Mind Stat of 2 or higher (animals are excluded). It costs 4 Points/Level if it works on broad categories of humans ("any American" or "any male," for example). It costs 3 Points/Level if the category is more specific and less useful ("priests" or "people obsessed with beauty"). Finally, it costs 2 Points/Level if the category is very specific (members of the character's family, or mutants with a specific gene). The effects of Mind Control should be role-played. If necessary, the GM can take over the character, although it is more fun if the player (with GM guidance) continues to play the character.

Initiating Mind Control requires a non-combat action (page 67). Rather than making an attack check, however, the character must successfully make a Mind Stat check (if attacking multiple targets, roll only once). If the Mind Stat check is successful, the target gets a defence check, but, instead of using Defence Combat Value (page 57), the base Check Value is his or her Mind or Soul Stat (whichever is greater). When controlling a large number of people, an estimated Mind and Soul Stat average for the entire group could be used. At every odd Level (1, 3, 5, etc.), the character receives a +1 bonus to his or her Check Value when attempting to Mind Control a target. At every even Level (2, 4, 6, etc.), the target also receives a -1 penalty to his or her Check Value when attempting to defend against Mind Control (or when trying to break established contact; see below). At Level 7, for instance, the character gains a +4 bonus while the target suffers a -3 penalty. A character needs to defeat an opponent in Mind Combat (page 71) to toy with his or her emotions (for example, giving the opponent new fears or a prejudice).

Once Mind Control is established, it remains in effect until either the Duration PMV expires, or until the target breaks free from the control. A target may attempt to break control under two circumstances: whenever he or she is given a command that conflicts with the nature of the character, and whenever the GM deems it appropriate for dramatic effect. To break control, the target must make a successful Mind or Soul Stat check (whichever is higher), modified appropriately by the Mind Control Level of the initiating character.

AGAINST TARGET'S NATURE

If a Mind Controlled target is commanded to perform an action that he or she would not willingly do under normal circumstances, the target can attempt to break control. Additionally, the target may receive a bonus if the action goes against his or her nature. The more distasteful the target finds the command, the greater the Check Value bonus. For mildly distasteful actions (such as licking an enemy's boots), no bonus is given. For highly distasteful or undesirable actions (such as stealing from an ally), a +4 bonus is given. Finally, for exceptionally distasteful or undesirable actions (such as attacking an ally), a +8 bonus is given. Note that these bonuses are cumulative with penalties associated with the controlling character's Mind Control Level.

WHEN THE GM DEEMS APPROPRIATE

If the character commands his or her target to perform a number of mundane activities (clean the house, fetching a drink of water, etc.), the GM may decide the target does not receive an opportunity to break established control. Even a seemingly inoffensive command such as "sit in the closet" or "go to sleep," however, may have a drastic impact on the lives of others if a bomb is about to explode in the train station or the target is piloting an airplane at the time. In these instances, the GM may give the target a chance to break free of the Mind Control even if the target does not regard a command as dangerous or distasteful (which would present an opportunity to end the control). This option puts the GM in direct control of the situation, which will benefit the campaign. Naturally, the GM can also apply modifiers to the Stat check that are cumulative with penalties associated with the controlling character's Mind Control Level.

A character need not control every thought and action of his or her victims but can allow them to live normal lives until they are needed; these targets are known as "sleepers." Additionally, people who have been Mind Controlled will not remember events that occurred during the time period they are controlled and will have a gap in their memories (unless a Restriction is assigned).

The GM may allow a character to temporarily boost his or her Mind Control Attribute by one or two Levels against a single individual who is his or her captive by "working" on the subject for a day or more. This bonus can represent concentrated brainwashing techniques or dedicated study of a subject.

Player Characters should only be placed under Mind Control for extended periods of time in exceptional circumstances.

MIND SHIELD

COST:	1 Point/Level
RELEVANT STAT:	Mind or Soul
REQUIRED PMVS:	None
OPTIONAL PMVS:	Area, Range, Targets
PROGRESSION:	Linear; effective increase of +1 to the Mind and Soul Stats each Level
REDUCTION:	None
RESTRICTIONS:	Time limit; against specific characters; against one type of intrusion

A character with Mind Shield is protected against psychic intrusion. This may be a reflection of his or her own psychic abilities, a protective spell, special training, or some innate ability. A character with Mind Shield can detect and gain Check Value bonuses to block attempts to read or control his or her mind by a character with the Telepathy or Mind Control Attributes (pages 39 and 26). The bonuses also apply during telepathic mind combat (page 71), and against a Special Attack with the Mind or Soul Attack Ability (page 34). Additionally, each Mind Shield Level provides 10 points of "Mind Armour" that are used for defence during mind combat or against attacks with the Mind or Soul Attack Special Attack Ability.

NATURAL WEAPONS

COST:	1 Point/Level
RELEVANT STAT:	None
REQUIRED PMVs:	None
OPTIONAL PMVs:	None
PROGRESSION:	Linear; +1 Natural Weapon each Level
REDUCTION:	None
RESTRICTIONS:	Against specific targets; less damage; slow to use (Initiative penalty)

The character has one or more relatively mundane natural weapons, such as sharp teeth, claws, tentacles, etc. Natural weapons are normally possessed by animals, monsters, and similar characters, but could also represent technological capabilities that mimic such abilities, such as an android or cyborg with retractable claws. More powerful Natural Weapons can be designed using the Special Attacks Attribute (page 32), with the Melee Disability.

The character possesses one Natural Weapon per Level. Possessing more than one such natural weapon gives the character a wider variety of attack forms. Normal damage inflicted by a successful attack is outlined in Chapter 8: Combat (page 61).

Hands, feet, a heavy tail, ordinary teeth, or hooves are not normally counted as Natural Weapons since they are (relatively) blunt, and thus only inflict normal unarmed damage (equal to the character's Attack Combat Value).

CLAWS OR SPIKES

The character possesses sharp talons or spikes on his or her fingers, paws, or feet. In addition to regular damage, the claws inflict 10 additional damage when used in melee combat. This attack uses the Unarmed Attack (Strikes) Skill.

FANGS, BEAK, OR MANDIBLES

The character has very sharp teeth, or alternatively, a beak or insect-like mandibles. This natural weapon inflicts only 5 damage above normal damage in melee combat, but a successful strike that penetrates Armour gives the character the option to maintain a biting grip and continue to inflict equivalent damage in subsequent rounds. These additional attacks are automatically successful, but the opponent can break the hold with a successful defence check. While the attacker is maintaining a biting grip, his or her own ability to defend is impeded: the attacker cannot use weapons to defend, and suffers a -4 defence check penalty against all attacks. This attack uses the Unarmed Attack (Bites) Skill.

HORNS

These are large horns on the head, used for butting or stabbing. Horns add 5 extra damage to normal damage in melee combat but are exceptionally effective if the character charges into battle. If the character wins Initiative against an opponent and has room for a running start, he or she can lower his or her head and charge. A successful attack will deliver normal attack damage, plus 20 (rather than 5) damage. If a charge fails to connect (the character fails the attack check or the opponent makes a successful defence check), the charging character will be off balance and suffers a -2 penalty on defence checks for the remainder of the round and a -4 Initiative roll penalty on the following combat round. This attack uses the Unarmed Attack (Strikes) Skill.

SPINES

The character is covered in nasty spikes, quills, or sharp scales. Anyone who wrestles with the character automatically takes damage equal to the character's Attack Combat Value each round. This damage is in addition to any attack damage delivered. During these struggles, the opponent's clothes will also be ripped and shredded unless they are armoured.

TAIL STRIKER

If the character has a combat-ready tail it can be equipped with spikes, a stinger, or other similarly nasty weapon. It is difficult to strike with a swinging tail (-2 attack check penalty), but, since it is flexible, it is usually harder to dodge (opponent suffers a -4 defence check penalty). The attack inflicts normal unarmed damage. This attack uses the Unarmed Attack (Strikes) Skill.

TENTACLES

One or more of the character's limbs — or possibly his or her hair — are actually tentacles. A character with tentacles gains a +2 bonus to his or her Unarmed Attack and Unarmed Defence Skill Level when engaged in a grappling attack or defending against one. Tentacles are also difficult to avoid in combat (opponent suffers a -2 defence check penalty).

NULLIFY

COST:	7 or 12 Points/Level
RELEVANT STAT:	Soul
REQUIRED PMVs:	Targets
OPTIONAL PMVs:	Area, Duration, Range
PROGRESSION:	Linear; +1 Attribute each Level
REDUCTION:	More than one but less than all
RESTRICTIONS:	Under certain conditions; against specific targets; against specific Attributes

With a successful Soul Stat check, the character can temporarily render the Attributes of other characters unusable within the Area PMV. The Nullify Attribute Level determines the maximum Attribute Level that can be nullified. The character can nullify an Attribute as long as indicated by the Duration PMV; it is recommended that Duration not extend past Level 6 for Nullify.

For 7 Points/Level the character can only nullify one Attribute each combat action. Thus, a character with Extra Attacks Level 3 can Nullify four Attributes each round. For 12 Points/Level, the character can nullify all Attributes simultaneously at the appropriate Levels (as indicated above).

NULLIFY (DRAIN)

For an additional 3 Points/Level, this Attribute can be specified as a Nullify (Drain). At each Attribute Level, the target's single Attribute (at 10 Points/Level) or multiple Attributes (at 15 Points/Level) are reduced by one Level, to a minimum of Level 0. For example, if a character with Level 5 Nullify (Drain) at 15 Points/Level targets a character who has Level 3 Armour, Level 8 Flight, and Level 10 Teleport, the target is reduced to Level 0 Armour (3-5=0), Level 3 Flight (8-5=3), and Level 5 Teleport (10-5=5). If, instead, the character only had regular Nullify, the Flight and Teleport Attributes would be unaffected since they are above Level 5 Attributes.

If the character uses Nullify (Drain) on the Special Attack Attribute, only damage is reduced (-20 damage for each Nullify Level). None of the Attack Abilities are affected directly, though the effectiveness of Abilities that depend on the amount of damage delivered will be reduced.

To create a character that steals a target's Attributes for his or her own use, assign both the Nullify and Mimic Powers (page 26) Attributes, linked through the Dependent Defect (page 52).

ORGANISATIONAL TIES

COST:	1-3 Points/Level
RELEVANT STAT:	Soul
REQUIRED PMVs:	None
OPTIONAL PMVs:	None
PROGRESSION:	Descriptive
REDUCTION:	Very specific utility
RESTRICTIONS:	Favourably connected with only part of the organisation; character's connection results in conflict; high price to pay

Organisational Ties represents a character's close relationship with a hierarchy of some sort that grants him or her access to respect and privileges. Monetary advantages are usually covered by the Wealth Attribute (page 41), while access to special equipment may be represented by the Gadgets Attribute (page 21). Examples of organisations include hero leagues, powerful corporations, organised crime rings, secret guilds and societies, governmental positions, and some religions. For campaigns in which all players belong to the same organised group, the GM may decide that Organisational Ties are not required. Consequently, this Attribute is optional; the GM may prefer to treat organisation membership as a background detail instead.

The value of Organisational Ties depends on its importance in the setting. An organisation that exerts moderate power within the setting is worth 1 Point/Level, one that has significant power costs 2 Points/Level, and one that has great power in the setting costs 3 Points/Level. Players should not assign this Attribute to represent organisations that have very little power. The GM determines the extent of the organisation's influence. In a high school comedy campaign, the school's autocratic Student Council might wield "significant power," while in most other settings it would be completely trivial and not worth any points. Similarly, a criminal organisation like the Mafia or Yakuza might count as "great power" (3 Points/Level) in a traditional cop game set in modern times, but merely as "moderate power" (1 Point/Level) in a high-powered conspiracy game.

Normal organisations should be limited to a geopolitical area, such as a single country. Global organisations, or those that span multiple geopolitical areas, function at 2 Levels lower. Multi-planetary organisations function at 4 Levels lower, while multi-galaxy organisations function at 6 Levels lower. For example, the president of a global megacorporation needs to assign Level 12 to gain access to the Controlling Rank category (2 Levels lower). Similarly, a character who has Senior Rank in a universe-wide organisation should have Level 14 Organisational Ties (6 Levels lower). Some organisations may be ostensibly limited to a single country, but the higher ranks still have global or multi-planetary influence. For example, the President of the United States is a Controlling Rank (Level 10). Since the US has great influence across the world, however, the position would be Level 12 (as if it was a global organisation).

These far-ranging organisation positions are only relevant, however, if the character can actually gain access to the resources of all branches of the group. If an Earth character is Connected to a multi-planetary organisation, for instance, but can only interact with and be influenced by the Earth chapter of the organisation, the group is only considered to be a global organisation (2 Levels lower) for that character. The group is not categorised as multi-planetary (4 Levels lower), since the extensive resource benefits normally associated with an organisation that size are not available to the character.

Though only five Attribute Levels are described below, GMs can easily extrapolate intermediate or higher Levels as required.

LEVEL 2   Connected. Examples include a powerful political supporter, an ally to a group, or a valued corporate employee.

LEVEL 4   Respected Status. Examples include a Mafia "Wise Guy," a junior executive in a corporation, a city council member, a member on a medical Board of Directors, or an enlisted army soldier.

LEVEL 6   Middle Rank. Examples include a Mafia "Captain," a departmental vice-president in a corporation, a junior congressional representative, or a low- to middle-ranking army officer.

LEVEL 8   Senior Rank. Examples include a senior vice-president in a corporation, a US senator, or a high-ranking army officer.

LEVEL 10   Controlling Rank. Examples include the boss of a crime syndicate, the president of a corporation, US state governor, president of a small nation, or leader of a superhero justice team.

OWN A BIG MECHA (OBM)

COST: 8 Points/Level
RELEVANT STAT: None
REQUIRED PMVs: None
OPTIONAL PMVs: None
PROGRESSION: Descriptive
REDUCTION: Significantly weaker mecha
RESTRICTIONS: Under certain conditions; limited functioning; not all capabilities present

A mecha is a vehicle or construct of some sort such as a giant robot, spaceship, tank, submarine, sports car, motorcycle, helicopter, powered armour suit. Piloting is usually done from a cockpit inside the mecha, though lower-technology or "retro" mecha may be operated from the outside or via remote control. The mecha's aptitude for combat is determined by the pilot character's ability. By default, all mecha have two arms.

Mecha often appear in modern or future settings, but they can also be pre-modern such as sailing ships or science-fantasy gear like magical clockwork golems. "Mecha" that characters do not ride, pilot, occupy, or wear, such as robot companions, are best acquired through the Agents (page 12), Henchmen (page 22), or Servant (page 31) Attributes.

The basic capabilities of the mecha are outlined in the Level progression chart below. The exact details regarding the mecha's form, function, storage, and design are up to the player. With GM permission, a player can modify his or her character's mecha from this baseline by assigning Attributes and Defects to the mecha rather than the character. The Character Points associated with Attributes, and Bonus Points associated with Defects, assigned in this way are divided by two to determine the actual cost. For example, adding a Force Field (4 Points/Level) to the mecha would cost only 2 Points/Level. Similarly, adding a 2 Bonus Point Defect to the mecha would only return 1 Bonus Point to the character. The GM has final approval over all mecha modifications.

Note that in Table 3-7, the unarmed damage reflects the bonus from the corresponding Superstrength Level (page 37).

Table 3-7: Own a Big Mecha

Attribute Level	Health Points	Armour Unarmed Damage	Top Speed	Special Attack Superstrength Level
1	20	10	30 kph	1
2	40	20	60 kph	2
3	60	30	125 kph	3
4	80	40	250 kph	4
5	100	50	500 kph	5
6	120	60	1,000 kph	6
7	140	70	2,000 kph	7
8	160	80	4,000 kph	8
9	180	90	8,000 kph	9
10	200	100	15,000 kph	10
+1	+20	+10	x 2 kph	+1

PLANT CONTROL

COST: 2 Points/Level
RELEVANT STAT: Mind or Soul
REQUIRED PMVs: None
OPTIONAL PMVs: None
PROGRESSION: Fast Progression Chart, starting at 10 cm radius area
REDUCTION: Very specific utility
RESTRICTIONS: Under certain conditions; in particular regions; no or lower additional growth (1x through 4x)

Characters with this Attribute can control the growth and movement of all plants in the surrounding area. The Attribute Level determines the maximum area in which the plants can be controlled. After the Duration PMV Rank has expired, the plants will return to their normal state and size before the control.

If the character limits the Control to a single broad group of plants, the Attribute functions at one Level higher. Broad plant groups include trees, grasses, weeds, bushes, flowers, mosses, vegetables, ferns, vines, seaweeds, etc. If limited to a specific type of plant, the Attribute functions at two Levels higher. Examples of plant types include oak trees, wheat, dandelions, raspberry bushes, sunflowers, club moss, carrots, etc.

Controlled plants can grow to a maximum size of 5 times their normal mature state. For 10x growth, the Attribute functions at one Level lower when determining area. For 50x growth, two Levels lower; for 100x growth, three Levels lower; for 500x growth, four Levels lower; and for 1,000x growth, five Levels lower.

To cause significant damage with controlled plants, the character should acquire the Special Attack Attribute (page 32) with the Dependent Defect (page 52).

POCKET DIMENSION

COST: 2, 3, or 4 Points/Level
RELEVANT STAT: Mind or Soul
REQUIRED PMVS: Duration, Targets (Offensive use only)
OPTIONAL PMVS: Area, Duration, Range, Targets
PROGRESSION: Fast Progression Chart, starting at a dimension with a 10 cm radius area
REDUCTION: Attribute always used in same way
RESTRICTIONS: Limited to specific types of dimensions; damage inflicted when passing through portal; opening portal weakens character

This Attribute allows the opening of a hole or doorway — a portal — into another dimension. A Pocket Dimension could also represent an object that is simply bigger on the inside than on the outside.

The Level of Pocket Dimension determines the maximum size of the dimension. The environment and furnishings of the dimension are up to the player within the GM's limitations; extensive furnishings should be acquired as Gadgets (page 21). A dimension could even be partially unexplored or dangerous territory, providing adventuring opportunities to the characters.

The cost of Pocket Dimension is 2 Points/Level if it is limited to a single fixed portal (such as a house closet), 3 Points/Level if the portal is in a mobile location (such as inside a vehicle, or attached to an item), or 4 Points/Level if the character can use a particular class of objects as a portal (such as "any mirror" or "any pool of water"). The Range PMV cannot apply to the 2 Points/Level option; additionally, the Area PMV only applies to the 4 Points/Level version, or characters who can use the Attribute offensively (see below).

A character with this ability at 2 or 3 Points/Level cannot create new portals leading out of the dimension; he or she may only leave by the one that was entered. A character can usually only have a single portal opened to his or her dimension at a time, but additional apertures to the same dimension may be possessed for 1 extra Character Point each. At the 4 Points/Level version, the character can leave the Pocket Dimension through any other appropriate exit within the Area PMV of the entrance portal; the character is not required to leave through the same one he or she entered. For example, a character with Area 6 can leave his or her Pocket Dimension by any appropriate portal within 10 km of the entry point.

Once opened, a portal can stay open for as long as the creator is in the dimension. The creator may also be able to "leave the door open" if he or she wishes to allow individuals to enter or leave while the creator is not present within the dimensional pocket.

Pocket Dimensions may optionally be designated as only one-way, restricting access in or out until the character or machine maintaining them is destroyed, or some other condition is fulfilled. This Attribute may be taken multiple times to give access to multiple different dimensions. If so, it may be taken at different Levels for each individual dimension.

USING POCKET DIMENSION OFFENSIVELY

Some characters may have the exotic ability of being able to suck or warp unwilling targets into their alternate dimension (at the 3 or 4 Points/Level version only). To indicate this, assign the Area, Duration, Range, and Targets PMV. Duration only applies when the character uses Pocket Dimension to trap an opponent in this way — a character can be held in a pocket dimension for a maximum amount of time indicated by the Duration PMV Rank. The character is released from the dimension once the Attribute's Duration ceases. See Using Attributes Against Opponents, page 71, for rules on affecting an unwilling opponent with a Pocket Dimension.

Characters who have an ability to travel between dimensions should possess either the Dimension Hop Special Movement ability (few dimensions; page 37) or the Dynamic Powers Attribute (many dimensions; page 17) with the Dimensions category, depending on his or her ability to travel through dimensions.

POWER FLUX

COST: 5, 10, 15, or 20 Points/Level
RELEVANT STAT: Variable
REQUIRED PMVS: Special (Duration reversed; see below)
OPTIONAL PMVS: None
PROGRESSION: Linear; +5 Flux Points each Level
REDUCTION: One aspect of category
RESTRICTIONS: Under certain conditions; only raise or lower existing Attributes, limitations on Levels exchanged

Power Flux represents extensive control over an element, ideology, natural phenomenon, or sphere of influence. This is a very open-ended Attribute and should be discussed with the GM at length to determine the effects and limitations in his or her game. Proper use of Power Flux will not unbalance the game, but rather can provide many opportunities for character innovation. As an alternative option to Power Flux, see the Dynamic Powers Attribute (page 17).

A character with this Attribute has a pool of reserve Character Points (called Flux Points) that can be allocated to different Attributes as needed, within the thematic category chosen by the player. This often represents a magical or psionic ability, but it can also reflect a character who has several different powered forms, or a character who has little control over his or her range of Attributes (in conjunction with the Unreliable Power Defect, page 56).

Power Flux uses a special PMV that follows the reverse of Duration, starting at 6 months (Rank 1) and decreasing to 1 round (Rank 10). The GM may limit the Duration PMV to Rank 8 (1 minute) to ensure that the flow of combat is not impeded by characters fluxing Attributes too frequently. This PMV represents how frequently a character can change the allocation of Flux Points from one group of Attributes to a different group, and not how long a character can use Power Flux. At low Ranks, the character will be forced to use the same group of Attributes for extended periods of time before he or she can use the Flux Points for alternates. At high Ranks, the character can gain a complete new set of Attributes almost at will. Stats and Defects cannot be raised or lowered with Power Flux (though the Enhanced [Stat] Attribute may be altered). Fluxing some Attributes may require GM permission.

Minor or small thematic categories cost 10 Points/Level. Examples include a classical element (water, fire, wind, earth), a limited concept or idea (lust, protection, charm, pride), a minor aspect of nature (temperature, insects, sunlight, clouds, orbits, sea creatures), or a limited sphere of influence (keys, silence, cats, writing, guns, a small locality, nutrition).

Major or large thematic categories cost 15 Points/Level. Examples include a broad concept or idea (love, travel, strength), a major aspect of nature (weather, magnetism, gravity, electricity, animals), or a broad sphere of influence (cities, computer data, health, truth, manufacturing, fertility, weapons, drugs).

Primal or universal thematic categories cost 20 Points/Level. Examples include core concepts and primary spheres of influence: Time, War, Death, Life, Earth, Thought, Magic, Force, Math, Self, Law, Chaos, Creation, Heaven, Hell, Dimensions, Dreams, and others.

If the character makes a successful Stat check (the relevant Stat is determined by the GM), he or she can assign Flux Points to one or more Attributes that grant powers that fit within the thematic category. A Flux Point is equal to one Character Point, which can be assigned to the cost of the Attribute directly, or to the cost of raising an Attribute's PMV Rank. Under normal circumstances, Power Flux cannot imitate the Transfer Attribute or the Dynamic Powers Attribute.

For example, a character with Level 6 Power Flux with a "cat theme" and Reversed Duration PMV of Rank 5 (12 hours) has assigned a total of 65 Character Points to the Attribute (6 Levels x 10 Points/Level + 5 Points for the Duration PMV). In return, he or she gains 30 Power Flux Points. At a minimum interval of 12 hours, the character can allocate the 30 Power Flux Points to any combination of Attributes that fit the cat theme. Perhaps in the morning, the character needs to prowl around the city on patrol and assigns the following Attributes: Armour Level 3 (9 Flux Points); Heightened Awareness Level 9 (9 Flux Points); Heightened Senses (Hearing, Smell, Vision) Level 3 (3 Flux Points); Jumping Level 5 (5 Flux Points); and Superstrength Level 1 (4 Flux

Points). Later in the evening (13 hours later), the character might need to track down and capture a specific target and thus reassigns all 30 Flux Points to different Attributes as follows: Animal Summon/Control (Cats) Level 4 with Area PMV Rank 4 and Duration PMV Rank 6 (14 Flux Points); Extra Attacks Level 1 (8 Flux Points); and Invisibility (Sound; Partial) Level 4 (8 Flux Points).

LIMITED POINT EXCHANGE

An alternate method of Power Flux only costs 5 Points/Level, but limits the character to a small assortment of Attributes among which Character Points can be exchanged. At Level 1, Character Points can be exchanged in any way between the Level cost and PMV cost of any two Attributes, which are determined during character creation. From Level 2 on, each Level adds one additional Attribute to the list of Attributes that can be fluxed. For instance, if a character with this Level 3 Power Flux and Rank 4 Duration (1 day) has allocated 47 Character Points to four fluxable Attributes (Armour, Flight, Special Attack, and Teleport), he or she can redistribute the 47 Points in any way over the four Attributes and their PMVs once every 24 hours.

PROJECTION

COST:	3 Points/Level
RELEVANT STAT:	Mind
REQUIRED PMVS:	Area
OPTIONAL PMVS:	Duration, Range
PROGRESSION:	Medium Progression Chart, starting at 10 cm radius area
REDUCTION:	Projection always the same
RESTRICTIONS:	Under certain conditions; projection is flawed in some way; usage inflicts pain

The character can create projected images that may have audible or visual components, or both. This Attribute may reflect holographic technology, magical ability, control over environmental conditions, or a completely different method of creation. The Projection cannot be touched because it is not substantial, nor does it have a taste or smell. Depending on the situation, and the nature of other individuals or animals viewing the Projection, the image may appear to be a real object. Closer inspection will usually reveal the Projection for what it is, but this will not cause the Projection to disappear as it would for an Illusion. If appropriate, the GM can require Body or Mind checks to "see through" a Projection. See the Illusion Attribute (page 22) for the ability to create mental illusions that target specific people, rather than real images that anyone (including technological devices, such as cameras) can detect.

A Projection may be of a particular object or entity, or of a complete scene (such as a furnished room or crowd). It may also be created over an existing person, scene, or object to make it appear different than it really is. A Projection that is untended is normally static, either remaining in one place or (if created over something) moving as the underlying object or entity moves. To give a Projection the semblance of independent activity (such as a projected image of a person who moves and speaks) the character must actively concentrate on manipulating the Projection, and perform no other actions.

A character can normally maintain only a single Projection at a time. The ability to maintain multiple Projections at once costs the character an extra 1 Point for every distinct Projection the character can sustain simultaneously after the first. Thus, "Projection Level 5 (six Projections)" would cost 20 Character Points: 15 Points for Level 5 and 5 more Points for being able to sustain six Projections at a time. A group of objects or entities within the Area PMV, such as a crowd of androids or a furnished office, counts as a single Projection rather than several. If a character is already sustaining his or her maximum number of Projections and wishes to create another one, an existing Projection must first be dispelled.

A Projection may have two types of areas: the Area PMV, and the area determined by the Attribute Level. The Area PMV reflects the maximum area in which the Projection may be created, while the Level-related area dictates the actual size of the projected image. Thus, an Area PMV of Rank 7 (100 km) with Attribute Level 7 (100 metres) means that any image up to 100 metres in radius (such as a huge advertising billboard) can be created, and moved around within a location that has a 100 km radius (such as a large county district).

In order for the character to create a convincing Projection of something complex, the GM may require a Mind Stat check. The GM can add modifiers depending on how familiar or unfamiliar the character is with the scene that is being simulated. The GM may also give the character a +1 bonus for every Level he or she has in excess of the minimum Level needed to create a Projection. For example, if a character with Projection Level 8 decides to create an image with an area radius of 50 metres (a Level 6 effect), a +2 Check Value bonus applies (Level 8 - Level 6 = +2). If the check fails, the character's Projection has some obvious flaw in it.

REGENERATION

COST:	6 Points/Level
RELEVANT STAT:	Body
REQUIRED PMVS:	None
OPTIONAL PMVS:	None
PROGRESSION:	Linear; restoration of +5 Health Points per round each Level
REDUCTION:	Fewer Health Points restored
RESTRICTIONS:	Under certain conditions; specific wound types; regeneration is not automatic

Characters with this Attribute automatically heal their own injuries, whether the characters are awake, asleep, or unconscious. The character's Health Points cannot exceed their original total. At higher Healing Levels, the character's body will revive itself if "clinically" dead but not actually brain-dead (Level 3+), repair massive trauma such as lost limbs or organs (Level 5+), or restore the character if cut into several pieces (Level 7+). The body cannot repair itself if it is blown to bits or disintegrated, however.

REINCARNATION

COST:	2 or 4 Points/Level
RELEVANT STAT:	Soul
REQUIRED PMVS:	None
OPTIONAL PMVS:	None
PROGRESSION:	Time Progression Chart Reversed, starting at 6 months
REDUCTION:	Very specific utility
RESTRICTIONS:	Reincarnate after injury from specific weapons; alive for a limited time; limited to a specific target group

If the character is destroyed, some of his or her essence may still survive. This may be in spiritual or digital form, or it may be something that must be retrieved from the corpse. A robot whose memory can be copied or uploaded, a creature that leaves an egg in its body upon death, or an undead monster that will reform a few minutes, hours, or days after its apparent death are all examples of this. If this remnant can be salvaged or otherwise recovered, in a matter of days or weeks and with proper care, it will develop a new body similar to the original. A reincarnated character usually starts with 1 Health Point.

Reincarnation can be prevented in some way. This may be as simple as burning, blowing up, or dismembering a body, or as obscure as requiring a special ritual. For 2 Points/Level, the Reincarnation is easy to stop; for 4 Points/Level, the Reincarnation is difficult to stop. The GM and player must work together to determine the parameters involved in preventing the rebirth.

SENSORY BLOCK

COST:	1 Point/Level
RELEVANT STAT:	Mind
REQUIRED PMVS:	Area, Duration
OPTIONAL PMVS:	Range
PROGRESSION:	Linear; +1 blocked sense or technique each Level
REDUCTION:	None
RESTRICTIONS:	Under certain conditions; against specific targets; time limit

A character with Sensory Block can cover the Area PMV with a field that blocks specific senses or detection techniques. This can represent a magical ability, technological enhancement, or paranormal effect. For each Level of the Sensory Block Attribute, the character can either block one sense or enhanced sense (Type I) or one detection technique (Type II), which is determined during character creation. The GM may allow multiple assignments to the same sense or technique, which results in cumulative penalties. To fully block a detection technique, see the Invisibility Attribute (page 24).

TYPE I

One of the five senses — hearing, smell, vision, taste, or touch — is partially blocked. This may mean that individuals within the Area PMV cannot see well (vision), cannot hear well (hearing), etc. Checks made by these individuals when pertaining to the specific senses suffer a -4 penalty, which is cumulative with any Heightened Senses bonus (page 22).

TYPE II

A detection technique is partially blocked. Examples of techniques include: electric current detection; homing weapons; infravision; magnetic field detection; microscopic vision; radar detection; radio reception; sonar detection; a specific Sixth Sense technique; ultrasonic hearing; ultravision; vibration detection; X-ray vision. Stat checks relating to these detection techniques suffer a -4 penalty.

SERVANT

COST: 2 or 6 Points/Level
RELEVANT STAT: Soul
REQUIRED PMVS: None
OPTIONAL PMVS: None
PROGRESSION: Linear; Servant built using +X Character Points each Level
REDUCTION: Fewer Character Points awarded
RESTRICTIONS: Servant leads active life and is not always available; Servant has conflicting agenda; communication barriers

The character has a sidekick or companion entity. It serves as a familiar, pet, companion, or bodyguard. Examples of Servants could include: a talking animal companion, a pet robot, a sorcerer's apprentice, a fierce wolf, a bound demon or ghost, a dedicated and talented henchman, a mage's familiar cat, or a vampire's enslaved thrall. Servants are NPCs controlled by the GM, but they will normally work toward the character's best interests. Nevertheless, they should have their own personalities and may occasionally get into trouble of their own. Low Levels of this Attribute best represent animal or mechanical Servants; high Levels are required to create competent human (and superhuman) Servants.

This Attribute costs 2 Points/Level if the character is limited to one particular Servant. If the character can dismiss the Servant and replace him or her with a different one between adventures or during an adventure with suitable effort (GM's option, such as casting a summoning spell, training a new recruit, or taming a new animal), then the Attribute costs 6 Points/Level. A character can take the Attribute several times to have multiple Servant.

Each Level of the Servant Attribute gives the player up to X Character Points and 10 Skill Points with which to design the Servant (X is the game dice). The Servant is created exactly as a character (page 7) with two exceptions. First, it may not possess the Servant Attribute. Second, some relationship-based Defects should not be assigned due to the Servant's innate role as a character's assistant. Thus, it is usually inappropriate for a Servant to have the following Defects: Famous, Involuntary Change, Owned, or Red Tape.

SHRINK

COST: 1 Point/Level
RELEVANT STAT: Body
REQUIRED PMVS: None
OPTIONAL PMVS: Area, Duration, Range, Targets
PROGRESSION: Variable; see chart
REDUCTION: None
RESTRICTIONS: Suffer pain/damage while shrinking; naked form only, double damage penalties

This Attribute reflects the ability to decrease the stature and mass of the character; while this can certainly be an advantage, it also creates many potential problems (see chart). In addition to decreased height and mass, the character who shrinks has reduced running speed and weapon range, and inflicts less damage through physical attacks and Special Attacks (physical, not energy-based; minimum

of 1 damage). Although the character also suffers additional damage from normal-sized opponents, the enemies have a harder time hitting him or her with ranged weapons. The Duration PMV is only relevant when affecting others; a character can Shrink him or herself for an indefinite period.

At Level 10, the character has shrunk to the cellular range; at this size, normal combat rules cannot apply since the character is simply too small. At Levels exceeding 10, the character can shrink to the molecular, atomic, or sub-atomic scale — a size that requires GM guidance and permission. If the GM and players wish to make characters that can shrink to a "micro-verse" where they interact within an entirely new world, the Pocket Dimension Attribute (page 29) may be more suitable.

A character who is permanently shrunk should assign the Diminutive Defect (page 52), rather than Shrinking and the Permanent Defect.

Though only five Attribute Levels are described below, GMs can easily extrapolate intermediate or higher Levels as required.

Table 3-8: Shrink

Current Shrink Level	Rough Size	Height Range Speed Multiplier	Mass Lifting Multiplier	Damage Penalty	Enemy Damage Bonus	Enemy's Range Attack Penalty
2	Child/Dog	1/2	1/10	-5	+5	-2
4	Cat	1/5	1/100	-10	+10	-4
6	Rodent	1/20	1/10,000	-15	+15	-6
8	Bug	1/200	ten millionth	-20	+20	-8
10	Cellular	1/20,000	ten trillionth	???	???	???

SIXTH SENSE

COST: 1 Point/Level
RELEVANT STAT: Soul
REQUIRED PMVS: Area
OPTIONAL PMVS: None
PROGRESSION: Linear; +1 Sixth Sense each Level
REDUCTION: None
RESTRICTIONS: Under certain conditions; must actively use Sixth Sense; vague or partial detection

Some characters have the ability to detect things that may be hidden to normal senses or technological sensors, while others have affinities for specific objects or people. Sixth Sense typically represents psychic or magical ability, but can also reflect trained and acute senses or divine intervention.

The character may sense one particular category of phenomenon per Level. The player should define the category with the GM's approval (Sixth Sense is very much a GM-defined ability). As a guideline, the character is automatically alerted when something his or her Sixth Sense detects is in close proximity (minimum of Area PMV 1 - 10 cm radius area). The GM may require a Soul Stat check to do this, with difficulty modifiers depending on the strength of the source of whatever emanations the character can sense. The GM should give a bonus (+2 modifier or more) if the character is touching the source.

A character who specifically concentrates on using his or her Sixth Sense may gain more precise information on a successful Soul Stat check. The exact content of this information is up to the GM. If the check succeeds, the GM may provide the character with a few extra clues about the source such as "the magic is coming from those buildings over there" or "you sense the evil presence feels otherworldly ... and hungry." If the check fails, the character will not gain any additional information unless something happens, such as the phenomena becoming stronger, or coming much closer. The GM should always try to use Sixth Sense to plant clues that make a story more exciting, but not allow it to circumvent the process of discovery in a mystery plot.

Examples of phenomena to which the character may be sensitive include astral/ethereal beings, danger, Pocket Dimensions, electricity, elements, emotions, evil, illusions, interpersonal dynamics, magic, magnetics, paranormal nexus points, particular objects, places of power, psionics, spirits, telepathy, truth, virtue, or the use of specific Attributes or Defects.

PRECOGNITION AND POSTCOGNITION

Alternatively, Sixth Sense can be assigned to represent precognition and postcognition — the ability to access visions of past and future events. This option is a GM-defined Attribute, however, which allows him or her limit its application and scope within the campaign. For precognition, the Attribute's Level reflects the difference in time between the present situation and the future event follow the Time Progression Chart, starting at 1 round. For postcognition, the character can see back an amount of time equal to double the Attribute's Level in Rank on the Time Progression Chart, starting at 1 round (Level 1). For example, a character with Level 5 Precognition can see 1 hour into the future, or 1 month into the past with Level 5 Postcognition.

SPECIAL ATTACK

COST:	1 or 4 Points/Level
RELEVANT STAT:	None
REQUIRED PMVs:	None
OPTIONAL PMVs:	None
PROGRESSION:	Linear; +20 attack damage each Level
REDUCTION:	Less damage delivered
RESTRICTIONS:	Under certain conditions; usage inflicts pain; against specific opponents

Many superhuman characters wield powerful offensive energies, such as electric zaps, magical fireballs, *ki*-powered martial arts strikes, or energy swords. Additionally, some characters, such as cyborgs or robots, may have guns, missiles, or beam weapons built into their bodies.

Special Attacks deliver a maximum of 20 damage per Level; actual damage inflicted is determined by a roll on Table 8-6: Damage Percentage (page 68). Assigning one or more attack Abilities from the list on pages 32-35 further customises a character's Special Attack. Each attack Ability taken reduces the damage by 20 but adds an additional capability. Attacks may also be assigned one or more attack Disabilities from the list on pages 35-36. Each attack Disability increases the damage by 20 but reduces the attack's utility by imposing some form of limitation.

The player must assign the Abilities and Disabilities when the Special Attack is designed. He or she may assign a combination of Abilities and Disabilities that reduces the attack's damage to a minimum of 20. For example, suppose a character has a special Attack at Level 2. He or she would only be able to purchase one Ability, which would reduce the attack's damage from 40 to 20. If the character wanted to purchase a second Ability, he or she must first assign a Disability, which would raise the attack's damage back to 40. The character could then purchase a second Ability, reducing the damage back to 20.

When designing a Special Attack, the player (with GM input) should determine what Skill and Specialisation is appropriate for its use. For most magical or supernatural ranged attacks, it will be Special Ranged Attacks. Any weapon with the Melee Disability uses the Melee Attack or Unarmed Attack Skills, depending on its description. For example, Melee Attack (Sword) is appropriate for an energy sword, while Unarmed Attack (Striking) would be suitable for a character that drained energy by touch or used a *ki*-energised martial arts strike.

ALTERNATE ATTACKS

Although a character often uses his or her highest-Level "primary" weapon, alternate or backup ones may also be possessed. The Point cost of these additional "secondary" attacks are one quarter the cost of the primary attack at 1 Point/Level. The primary attack — the attack with the highest Level — is the only one that costs the standard 4 Points/Level. Secondary attacks may each possess different damages, Abilities and Disabilities.

SPECIAL EFFECTS

The special effects of Area Effect, Drain (Any), Flare, Incapacitating, Irritant, Spreading, and Tangle are determined by the Level of the Special Attack only. Massive Damage, Superstrength, and critical hit multipliers are not included in the calculation. Additionally, Armour and Force Fields do not normally protect against Drain (Any), Flare, Incapacitating, Irritant, or Tangle. Before making an attack, a character can choose to inflict less damage than the normal 20/Level, or reduce the power of their special effects.

Effects Based on Damage Inflicted

The scope of the special effects for attacks with the Area Effect, Drain (Any), Flare, Incapacitating, Irritant, Linked, Spreading, or Tangle Abilities depend on the Level of the Special Attack. For example, Drain (Mind) reduced the target's Mind Stat by 1 for every Special Attack Level; similarly, Tangle creates restraints that have 10 Health Points for every Special Attack Level. To introduce randomness into these special effects, their scopes could instead be based on every 10 damage that the attack inflicts (or would have inflicted in the case of attacks with the No Damage Disability). For the above examples, Drain (Mind) would reduce a target's Mind Stat by 1 for every 10 damage, and Tangle would create restraints that have 10 Health Points for every 10 damage. If this alternate rule is used, damage must be rolled for all attacks — including ones with the No Damage Disability — to determine the special effect scope.

SPECIAL ATTACK ABILITIES

The following Abilities may be assigned to a Special Attack. The GM may disallow any inappropriate Ability combinations.

Table 3-9: Special Attack Abilities

Ability	# of Slots	Ability	# of Slots
Accurate	1	Irritant	1
Affects Incorporeal	1	Knockback	1
Area Effect	1	Linked (Attack)	2 or 4
Aura	2	Long Range	1
Auto-Fire	3	Mind or Soul Attack	5
Burning	1	Muscle-Powered	1
Concealable	1	No Healing	1
Contagious	2 or 4	Penetrating (Armour)	1
Drain Body	1	Penetrating (Force Field)	1
Drain Energy	1	Quake	1
Drain Mind	1	Spreading	1
Drain Soul	1	Stun	1
Enduring	1	Tangle	2
Flare	1	Targeted	1 or 2
Flexible	1	Trap	1
Homing	1 or 2	Undetectable	4
Incapacitating	3	Unique Ability	Variable
Incurable	4	Vampiric	2 - 4
Indirect	1		

Accurate

The attack is unusually accurate, giving a +2 bonus to attack checks (or Stat checks if the attack has the Mind or Soul Attack Ability). This ability can be assigned two or three times for a +4 or +6 bonus, but may not be combined with the Linked (Attack) Ability. This Ability is usually assigned to hand-held weapons created as Items of Power (page 24) only, since attack Skills (page 49) better represent a character who is adept at using his or her Special Attack.

Affects Incorporeal

This attack will affect characters who have very low densities — or are currently astral, ethereal, or incorporeal — as if they were solid.

Area Effect

This is an attack, like an explosive blast, that affects not only the direct target, but also anyone in the immediate area. The area of effect is a sphere with a radius of 1 metre for every Special Attack Level. All affected characters are allowed a defence check (diving for cover, swerving out of the way), but a successful defence check may not be enough to escape completely (GM's discretion; depends on how target avoids attack). The target of the attack (or anyone at the centre of the effect) can reduce the damage percentage by one rank when successfully defending. All other individuals caught in the area of effect can reduce the damage percentage by two ranks when successfully defending. Area Effect can be assigned multiple times; each Ability doubles the area radius.

Aura

Rather than having to make an actual attack, the character instead automatically damages anyone who touches his or her body. An example might be a character who was sheathed in flame or electrified. If this Ability is combined with the Area Effect Ability, it automatically damages anyone in the designated area around the character. Aura counts as two Abilities.

Auto-Fire

The attack consists of a burst of multiple shots like a machine gun or rapid sequence of energy bolts. Instead of scoring one hit when an attack is successful, the attacker scores hits (minimum of one, maximum of 10) equal to the difference between the attack check and his or her Check Value (Attack Combat Value plus relevant Combat Skill). For example, if a character's attack Combat Value is 6 and relevant Combat Skill at Level 1, and the player rolled 5 (after all modifications), he or she would score 2 hits. The defender's chance to avoid the attack is derived in a similar way, however: a successful defence check will defend against a number of hits equal to the difference between the defence check and Check Value (Defence Combat Value plus relevant Combat Skill), with a minimum one hit avoided on a successful defence. Each hit delivers separate damage (important when considering Armour and Force Fields). Bonuses from Combat Value, Massive Damage, Superstrength, and critical hit multipliers are only applied to the first hit in an Auto-Fire burst — all others only inflict the percentage of base damage of the Special Attack. Auto-Fire counts as three Abilities.

Burning

This represents acid, flaming liquid, or similar attacks that deliver continuing damage over several rounds. If the initial attack damage penetrates the opponent's Armour, the target will suffer an additional 1/10 of the base damage for five rounds or until the effect is somehow neutralised (GM's discretion; it should depend on the type of attack, and may require several rounds for full neutralization). Armour does not protect against the extra Burning damage in subsequent rounds. Alternatively, Burning can be defined as an "hourly burn," which inflicts 1/10 of the base damage each hour after the attack, or "slow burn," which inflicts 1/5 of the base damage each day (rather than round-by-round). This ability may best represent a disease or slow poison attack. Unlike a regular Burning attack, the hourly and slow burn damage will continue until the victim is dead or makes a successful check with at -4 penalty against the average of his or her Soul and Body (made on an hourly or daily basis).

Concealable

This option is only available for hand-held weapons. The weapon is small enough to be used with one hand and concealed under clothing. Most pistol-sized or knife-sized weapons are Concealable. For more cinematic games, larger weapons such as swords and machine guns can be designed as Concealable as well.

Contagious

Some or all of the attack's damage or other effects will be passed on to others who touch (or otherwise contact) a victim. If mildly contagious, not everyone will be infected; a prospective victim must fail a Stat check at a +4 bonus to be affected. If taken twice, it is highly contagious; someone must fail a Stat check (without modifiers) in order to be affected, or possibly contagion may be automated under some circumstances. The base Check Value is normally the Body Stat, but magical or cybernetic contagion may use Mind or Soul. The GM should adjudicate effects and countermeasures. The Ability is usually combined with the Toxic Disability. Contagious counts as two abilities if mildly contagious or four abilities if highly contagious.

Drain Body

The attack causes the victim to suffer weakness and/or loss of co-ordination. The victim's Body Stat is reduced by 1 for every Special Attack Level. The Body Stat drain is in addition to any Health Point losses from the attack. To design an attack that only drains the Body Stat, but inflicts no other punishment, the No Damage Disability should also be assigned. A character who is reduced to a 0 Body Stat is unable to move. Lost Body Stat Points are recovered at one Point per hour of rest. Losing Stat Levels will also lower the Combat Value, but Health Points will not be affected.

Drain Energy

This Ability is only available in campaigns that use Energy Points (page 57). The attack drains away the victim's personal energy supply, causing him or her to become fatigued and/or despondent. In addition to the damage delivered to the victim's Hit Points, the attack causes the same loss of Energy Points. To design an attack that only drains Energy Points, the No Damage Disability must also be assigned. Lost Energy Points recover at their normal rate.

Drain Mind

The attack causes the victim to lose his or her sanity. The attack may be a psionic attack, a tranquilliser or similar drug, or another form of attack. The victim's Mind Stat is reduced by 1 for every Special Attack Level. This Mind Stat drain is in addition to any Health Point losses from the attack. To design an attack that only drains the Mind Stat, the No Damage Disability should also be assigned. A character reduced to 0 Mind is "mindless" and will act in an illogical and animalistic fashion. The drained Points return at the rate of one every hour. Losing Stat Levels will also lower the Combat Value.

Drain Soul

The attack affects the victim's spirit. This attack may be a wave of fear, despair, or some other willpower-destroying emotion. The victim's Soul Stat is reduced by 1 for every Special Attack Level. This drainage is in addition to any Health Point losses from the attack. To design an attack that only drains the Soul Stat, the No Damage Disability should also be assigned. A character reduced to 0 Soul is "broken," and lacks all drive or volition. The drained Points return at the rate of one every hour. Losing Stat Levels will also lower the Combat Value, but Health Points will not be affected.

Enduring

Enduring can only be assigned in conjunction with Area Effect. The attack remains active within the affected area over multiple rounds. Examples of this type of attack include chemical clouds, sheets of fire, electrical charges, or supercooled vapours. Anyone entering or remaining in the area is immediately subject to the attack; defence checks are outlined under Area Effect. Each time Enduring is assigned, the Area Effect attack remains active for 1 additional round.

Flare

If the target is hit (or in the radius of an Area Effect weapon attack) the defending character may be blinded. Every target looking in the vicinity of the attack must roll a Body Stat check at a -1 penalty for every Special Attack Level, ignoring Armour. To design an attack that only blinds opponents, the No Damage Disability should also be assigned. If a target character rolls greater than his or her Body Stat, he or she is blinded for a number of combat rounds equal to the difference between the Check Value and the dice roll. Flare may be taken multiple times; each time it is taken, add an extra -2 penalty to the Stat check. Flare can also be generalised to cover other sense-overloading attacks. For example, an acoustic attack might cause deafness.

Flexible

This ability represents long, flexible, or extendible attacks such as a prehensile whip, energy-lash, razor-ribbon, or similar attack mode. The target defends at a -2 penalty. If the attacker is strong enough to physically lift the target, a successful attack can trip or disarm an opponent (snagging a hand-held weapon) in lieu of delivering damage. Such non-damaging attack stunts are made at a -2 penalty to the attack check since they require great skill to execute accurately.

Homing

The attack or weapon fires a projectile or energy bolt that can track and follow its target. The character receives a +4 bonus to his or her attack check, and if the attack misses or the target successfully defends, the weapon will return to try again (only one more time) in the next combat round. A Homing attack may be vulnerable to Sensory Block, however (page 30). In a setting where electronic Sensory Blocks are not common (such as fantasy world campaign) Homing counts as two Abilities, rather than one.

Incapacitating

This represents any form of attack that can instantly incapacitate a foe even if it does not inflict actual damage. This includes putting an opponent to sleep or turning him or her to stone. Regardless of whether the attack does physical damage, the victim must make a Stat check (Body, Mind, or Soul — decide when the attack is designed) to avoid being completely incapacitated. The check is made at a +4 bonus with a -1 penalty for every Special Attack Level. For example, a Level 4 Attack would require a Stat check at 0 penalty; a Level 1 Attack would be made at a +3 bonus. When designing the attack, specify the form the incapacitation takes: asleep, awake but paralyzed, turned to stone, transformed into an inert doll, etc. The effects will wear off in several minutes, unless the Incurable Ability is also taken. To design an attack that only incapacitates the target, the No Damage Disability should also be assigned. Incapacitating counts as three Abilities.

Incurable

The attack produces wounds or other effects that do not heal naturally, and are incurable by normal methods. Rather than recovering at a normal rate or being amenable to medical treatment, recovery cannot take place until some exotic event or treatment has occurred. This requirement must be specified when the attack is designed, subject to GM approval. Incurable counts as four Abilities.

Indirect

The weapon can fire shots in a high ballistic arc. Examples include grenade launchers and plasma artillery guns. This allows the attacker to shoot at targets hidden behind buildings, hills, or other obstacles (or even shoot over the horizon, if the Long Range Weapon Ability is also taken). Indirect fire is tricky, however. To effectively fire at an indirect location, the attacker must be able to "see" the target (sensors can be used), or someone else must spot the target and relay its position to the attacker. Indirect fire results in a -2 penalty to the attack check; firing at a target the attacker cannot "see" results in an additional -6 penalty (-8 total). A weapon with the Indirect Weapon Ability can be used under normal mid-range conditions without any penalty.

Irritant

This represents pepper spray, a skunk's musk, an itching spell, or similar effect. Whether or not damage penetrated Armour or Force Fields, the subject must make a Body Stat check at -1 penalty for every Special Attack Level. If the target fails, the character is partially blinded and distracted (-2 penalty on all checks to do anything) for a number of rounds equal to the amount by which he or she failed the check. Irritant is usually taken in conjunction with the Toxic Disability to simulate an attack against which a gas mask offers protection.

Knockback

This Ability is only available in campaigns that use Knockback rules (page 70). The attack impacts the target forcefully, knocking him or her back one metre for every point of damage delivered. Armour is ignored when determining Knockback distance; Force Fields without the Full Impact Disability do reduce Knockback, however. This Ability is for attacks that impact the character, and may not be appropriate for slashing or piercing attacks. The Knockback distance is doubled each time this Ability is assigned. Combat Value (for characters with the ACV Knockback Combat Technique), Massive Damage, Superstrength, and critical hit multipliers may be added to the attack damage when determining final Knockback distance; apply these after any doubling for multiple Knockback assignments.

Linked (Attack)

An attack with this Ability is "attached" to another (or "master") attack. The master attack may be an ordinary weapon (such as a Gadget, like a sword or a gun), a Natural Weapon or unarmed attack, or a different Special Attack. If that attack is successful, this "linked" attack automatically hits as well (no defence allowed), but if it misses or fails to penetrate Armour, the linked attack automatically fails too. If the master attack hits and delivers enough damage to successfully penetrate Armour, then the Armour does not protect at all against the damage of the second linked attack. Damage bonuses from Combat Value, Massive Damage, Superstrength, and critical hit multipliers only apply to the master attack, not to each attack. An attack with the Linked Ability may not be given the Accurate or Long Range Abilities or the

Inaccurate, Melee, or Short Range Disabilities; its range and accuracy are dependent on the attack to which it is linked. Linked (Attack) counts as two Abilities. If damage bonuses from Combat Value, Massive Damage, Superstrength, etc. are applied to both attacks, this counts as four Abilities.

Long Range

An ordinary attack has an effective range of about 500 metres (10 km in space). This Ability extends the range to 5 km (100 km in space). It can be assigned multiple times: each time it is taken after the first doubles the actual range. Since the Earth's horizon limits line-of-sight for characters standing on the ground, multiple Long Range Abilities are often combined with the Indirect Ability. The Long Range Ability is incompatible with the Melee or Short Range Disabilities.

Mind or Soul Attack

The attack is not a physical attack but rather is a mental assault (Mind Attack) or contest of spirit or will (Soul Attack). During character creation, the player must specify either Mind or Soul as the focus of the Ability. Instead of the attack requiring Attack or Defence Combat Value checks, the players must roll successful Mind or Soul Stat checks for their characters to attack or defend (though appropriate Skills can modify this). Mind or Soul Attack ignores Armour, Shields, and Force Fields, and affects Insubstantial or Astral characters normally. Both versions count as five Abilities.

Muscle-Powered

This ability normally is only appropriate for melee or thrown weapons. The character may add any damage bonus from the Superstrength Attribute (page 37) to the attack's basic damage.

No Healing

This is a lesser form of Incurable. The damage from the attack cannot be restored using the Healing or Regeneration Attributes but can otherwise recover or be repaired normally.

Penetrating (Armour)

The Armour Attribute does not stop damage from these attacks as efficiently as usual. Each time Penetrating (Armour) is assigned, the Armour stops 20 less damage than normal from the attack (up to the Armour's maximum rating). For example, assigning Penetrating (Armour) to a Special Attack 3 times reduces the amount of damage the target's Armour stops by 60.

Penetrating (Force Field)

The Force Field Attribute does not stop damage from these attacks as efficiently as usual. Each time Penetrating (Force Field) is assigned, the Force Field stops 20 less damage than normal from the attack (up to the Force Field's maximum rating). For example, assigning Penetrating (Force Field) to a Special Attack 5 times reduces the amount of damage the target's Force Field stops by 100.

Quake

This attack creates a linear shock wave in the ground, causing rumbling and fractures. The quake "fault" will only be large enough for one person to fall into its depths unless it is combined with the Area Effect Ability. A victim may fall into the crevasse if he or she fails a Body Stat check (the Acrobatics Skill will provide a bonus). The fissure will be approximately one metre deep for the first 20 points of damage inflicted and is doubled for every additional 20 damage points. Thus, a 40 damage point quake would create a fissure two metres deep, while an 80 damage point quake would create a crevice eight metres deep. Although the Massive Damage Attribute is not usually considered for determining fissure depth, this limitation may be ignored if the Quake is also Muscle-Powered (see above). Quake can only be used on a solid surface (which may be earth, sand, cement, or asphalt), and may not be combined with the Aura Ability.

Spreading

This type of attack spreads to cover an expanding area like a cone of energy or a spray of projectiles or energy bolts. The defender receives a -1 penalty to his or her defence check. Multiple adjacent targets in the attack path may also receive damage if they are lined up or in a dense formation, up to a maximum of one extra target for every Special Attack Level. The Spreading Ability can be acquired multiple times;

each one further penalises the target's defence check by -1 and doubles the number of possible adjacent targets. Spreading is often assigned in conjunction with the Short Range Disability.

Stun

An attack with this Ability inflicts temporary damage such as an electric shock that shorts out electronics and renders people unconscious. Lost Health Points are recovered at one Point every minute. Stun damage cannot kill. Although the attack does less damage than a regular attack of a comparable Level, it has the advantage that it may be used to incapacitate a foe without the risk of killing him or her.

Tangle

Attacks that can entangle the victim may include an assault that freezes the target in ice, or traps him or her in the branches of an animated plant, or simple webbing. The entanglement has 10 Health Points for every Special Attack Level. If a target does not successfully defend against a Tangle attack, he or she is trapped until sufficient damage is delivered to the entanglement to reduce its Health Points to zero or lower (at this point, it is destroyed). A trapped character has restricted movement and: attacks physically at a -4 penalty, cannot defend, and cannot perform actions that require complex gestures. The character is usually able to speak, however. A victim who has partially destroyed an entanglement may regain additional body movement, however (GM's discretion). A Tangle attack also inflicts damage as normal unless the No Damage disability is also assigned to the attack. An "Incurable" entanglement can only be damaged by some special means (such as fire or water), defined when the Tangle attack is created. Tangle counts as two Abilities.

Targeted

The attack inflicts double damage to a specific group of targets and normal or no damage to everyone else. Thus, an attack could be good energy (double damage to evil creatures), chaos energy (double damage to lawful creatures), life energy (double damage to undead creatures), or detrimental to a specific race. Targeted counts as one Ability if no damage is delivered to non-Targeted opponents, or two Abilities if normal damage is delivered.

Trap

The attack lays a mine, booby trap, or some other similar device, which "sits and waits" until someone triggers it. A successful Mind Stat check will reveal the trap's presence. The Trap Ability can be paired with the Melee Disability (page 36) to simulate a booby trap that must be carefully planted. Without the Melee Disability, the trap can be deployed at a range; a successful attack check indicates that the Trap was fired or tossed into the correct area.

Undetectable

Most Special Attacks have a visible component that makes it easy for targets to determine who is attacking them. An attack with the Undetectable Ability does not provide any indication that it is about to strike and cannot be traced back to the attacker using normal methods. This may result in the attacker gaining surprise, which prevents the victim from making a defence check (page 67). If the target knows he or she is under attack, however, a defence check can still be made at a -8 penalty (as though the attack were invisible; page 66). This Ability is most often associated with non-physical attacks such as ones with the Drain (Any), or Mind or Soul Attack Abilities. Undetectable counts as four Abilities.

Unique Ability

The attack has some other unspecified Ability that is not listed, and is subject to GM approval. Examples can include an attack that alters the target's memories, one that affects the appearance of the target, and many more. The number of Ability slots is determined by the GM based on the benefit the Unique Ability provides.

Vampiric

This Ability can be added to any attack that causes normal damage or one that drains Stat Points. Upon a successful attack, the lost Health Points or Stat Levels are transferred to the attacker. Vampiric counts as two Abilities if the attack can only restore lost Points or Levels (thus, the character could heal him or herself). It counts as three Abilities if the attack can increase the character's Health Points above their normal maximum value (no more than twice normal, however). Finally, it counts as four Abilities if it can increase the character's Stats above their normal maximum

value (though not beyond a value of twice X). Any values or Points in excess of the user's normal Level fade at a rate of 20 Health Points or one Stat Level per hour. This Ability may not be combined with the Area Effect or Spreading Abilities. Vampiric costs 2, 3, or 4 Ability slots.

ATTACK DISABILITIES

Some, none, or many of these Disabilities may be assigned to a Special Attack. The GM may disallow any combination that seems inappropriate.

Table 3-10: Special Attack Disabilities

Disability	# of Slots	Disability	# of Slots
Backblast	1 or 2	Self-Destruct	4
Drop Shields	1	Short Range	1
Hand-Held	1 or 0	Slow	1-5
Inaccurate	1	Static	2
Internal	1	Stoppable	1-5
Limited Shots	1-3	Toxic	1
Low Penetration	1	Unique Disability	1
Melee	2	Unreliable	1
No Damage	1	Uses Energy	1 or 2
Only In (Environment)	1 or 2		

Backblast

The attack produces some sort of backblast or other side effect that affects anyone or anything standing directly behind the attacker (within 1-2 metres). An example is a rocket launcher that produces a hazardous backblast to anyone standing behind the gunner, but some spells or supernatural abilities might have similar risks. The damage of the backblast is normally one-fifth the damage of the actual attack. If this Disability is taken twice, it affects everyone in a 1-2 metre radius around it, including the attacking character (unless he or she also has Immunity to one's own attacks; page 23). Backblast cannot be combined with the Area Effect and Aura Abilities at the same time.

Drop Shields

This Disability can only be taken if the character also has the Force Field Attribute. It requires the character to turn off all Force Fields before using the attack, and they must remain down until the character's turn to act on the following round.

Hand-Held

Attacks usually emanate from the character, but they may be designated as hand-held. A hand-held weapon can be lost or grabbed by an enemy, or loaned to an ally. The character using the weapon must have at least one hand free to hold it. Optionally, the GM may decide this Disability takes up zero slots (it's for description only).

Inaccurate

The attack is not accurate, suffering a -2 penalty to all attack checks (or Stat checks, if it is a Mind or Soul Attack). This ability can be taken two or three times for a -4 or -6 penalty.

Internal

The attack is only usable inside a specific structure. This may represent a headquarter's built-in internal security systems or an attack for which the character draws power from inside the building and channels it through his or her body.

Limited Shots

The attack is only usable for a few combat rounds, after which it either runs out of ammunition or power, or simply burns out. Assigning this Disability once means it can make up to six attacks; if taken twice, up to three attacks; if taken three times, only one attack. If the attack also has the Auto-Fire Ability (page 33), one "attack" means a single Auto-Fire burst.

The base number of Disability slots are for attacks that take several minutes or more to "reload." If the attack can be "reloaded" with one action, the number of Disability slots is reduced by 1 (minimum of 1 slot). If the attack can be "reloaded" instantly (an ammunition source is still required), the Disability is worth two fewer slots (minimum of 1 slot).

Low Penetration

The attack has an inferior ability to penetrate Armour and Force Fields relative to its damage. Examples include shotgun blasts, hollow-point bullets, or phased plasma guns. Any Armour or Force Field Attribute stops an additional 20 damage. This Disability is incompatible with either of the two Penetrating Abilities. GMs must approve Special Attacks with multiple assignments of Low Penetration.

Melee

The attack is only usable against adjacent opponents and may require physical contact. An example of a Melee attack is a physical or energy sword, or a touch that inflicts debilitating effects. Of course, many Melee weapons can be thrown as well in desperate situations, but the attack suffers a -4 attack penalty and the base damage is divided in half. The Melee Disability cannot be combined with the Long Range Ability or Short Range Disability. It is sufficiently limiting that it is equivalent to two Disabilities.

No Damage

The attack does not deliver ordinary physical damage; the attacker's Attack Combat Value and Massive Damage Attribute bonus do not add to damage either. This Disability is usually only taken if combined with Abilities such as Drain (Any), Flare, Incapacitating, Irritant, or Tangle that produce effects that do not rely on physical damage. The damage value of the attack is used only to rate the effectiveness of these special abilities — the greater the damage value, the more effective the attack. Characters that use Special Attacks with the No Damage Disability may still need to roll the damage percentage (page 68), however.

Only In (Environment)

The attack or weapon can only target objects that are on or in a particular limited environment, for example, "only in water" (representing a torpedo) or "only in space" (representing a powerful weapon that requires a vacuum to work). The environment should not be one that is ubiquitous in the campaign (for example, "only in air" is not valid unless a lot of the game action will take place in airless environments). If the environment is very rare in the campaign, the GM may allow this to count as two Disabilities.

Self-Destruct

Use of this attack destroys the weapon (characters obviously take this Disability very rarely). This Disability is often combined with Melee and Area-Effect to represent an explosive self-destruct system. It may not be combined with Limited Uses. It counts as four Disabilities.

Short Range

This attack is only usable at close range (effective range of about 50 meters). The Short Range Disability cannot be combined with the Long Range Ability or the Melee Disability.

Slow

The attacker must use one combat action to aim, charge, chant an incantation, load the weapon, or perform some other necessary activity before each attack. Someone with the Extra Attacks Attribute (page 19) can use one of his or her extra actions to prepare the attack rather than wasting the entire round. The Slow Disability can be taken more than once to represent an attack that takes even longer to initiate. Assigning it twice increases the time to three rounds; three assignments increase the time to 10 rounds (about a minute); four increases the time to two-six hours; five increases the preparation to days. This Disability may not be used with the Linked (Attack) Ability.

Static

The attack cannot be used while the character is moving. This could be due to a need for precise aim or total concentration. The weapon might also require all power to be diverted to its energy supply, or might be static because of recoil, or another reason. The character may not even make defence checks on the round a Static attack is used; if he or she has already made a defence check, the character cannot attack with a Static weapon until the following round. Static is worth two Disabilities.

Stoppable

The attack fires a projectile or energy bolt that is massive or slow enough to be shot down and does not reach the target until Initiative zero. Consequently, the attack can be stopped in mid-flight. A cannon shell would probably not qualify, but a missile or plasma-ball might. Anyone with an unused combat attack action during the same round may make a ranged or melee attack against the projectile. To stop the attack, a successful hit (or hits) must deliver 5 damage for every Special Attack Level. Stoppable may not be combined with the Melee Disability. Stoppable may be purchased more than once to reflect an attack that takes even longer to reach the target. Each additional Stoppable rating grants one additional round where characters may attempt to intercept or otherwise stop the attack. Weapons using the Indirect or Long Range Abilities can take minutes or hours to reach their targets; in these cases, the Stoppable Disability is assigned a maximum of five times.

Toxic

The attack is a gas, toxin, biological weapon, sound, radiation, or other harmful effect that only damages living things. Non-living material or characters who have the appropriate Adaptation or Special Defence Attributes are immune to its effects.

Unique Disability

The attack has some other unspecified limitation, which is subject to GM approval. Examples could include a weapon that fires in a random direction, one that is extremely costly to operate, an attack that drains Heath Points from the user, etc.

Unreliable

Any time this attack is used and the attack check provides an unmodified (or "natural") roll equal to twice X, the attack fails to take place and the weapon or ability burns out, jams, overheats, or otherwise malfunctions. The Special Attack will not work again until some condition is fulfilled. For example, repairing a technological weapon requires a skilled individual to make a successful Mind Stat check (one attempt each round), and while the character is making repairs, he or she cannot carry out other activities. The same could apply to a magical attack with a Mind Stat check needed to remember the correct words. Other remedies might be appropriate for recovering different attacks (for example, a supernatural monster whose breath weapon has "burned out" might have to eat a hearty meal first).

Uses Energy

This Ability is only available in campaigns that use Energy Points (page 57). The attack draws upon the user's personal energy, each attack draining 10 Energy Points. This Disability can be taken twice, and, if so, it uses 10 Energy Points per Level of the Special Attack.

SPECIAL DEFENCE

COST:	1 Point/Level
RELEVANT STAT:	Variable
REQUIRED PMVS:	None
OPTIONAL PMVS:	None
PROGRESSION:	Linear; +1 Special Defence slot each Level
REDUCTION:	None
RESTRICTIONS:	Under certain conditions; time limit; partial defence (for 2 Slots only)

A character with this Attribute is resistant or completely immune to a specific type of uncommon ailment or injury, normally one whose effects are otherwise insidious in nature. Special Defence can be acquired multiple times to represent a character who is resistant or immune to different kinds of attacks/events.

If a category is assigned one slot, the character is partially resistant; for two slots, the character has complete or enhanced resistance. For ability to survive under harsh physical conditions, see the Adaptation Attribute (page 12). For characters who have defences against particular Attributes, see the Block Power (page 14) or Immunity (page 23) Attributes.

Several examples of Special Defences and their effects are shown below. The GM and players are encouraged to develop their own as well.

Table 3-11: Special Defence

Condition	# of Slots	Effect
Ageing	1 Slot	Ages slowly
	2 Slots	Does not age
Air/Oxygen to Breathe	1 Slot	Survive in low-oxygen environment
	2 Slots	Does not breathe
Hunger	1 Slot	Need to eat once every 2-4 days
	2 Slots	Never need to eat
One Type of Magic	1 Slot	+3 Stat/Stat checks
	2 Slots	+6 Stat/Stat checks
Pain	1 Slot	Unwanted sensation is reduced
	2 Slots	No pain is felt
Sleep	1 Slot	Sleep once every 3-7 days
	2 Slots	Never need to sleep
Specific Attack Ability	1 Slot	+3 Stat/Stat checks
	2 Slots	+6 Stat/Stat checks

SPECIAL MOVEMENT

COST:	1 Point/Level
RELEVANT STAT:	Body
REQUIRED PMVs:	None
OPTIONAL PMVs:	None
PROGRESSION:	Linear; +1 type of movement each Level
REDUCTION:	None
RESTRICTIONS:	Under certain conditions; movement is exhausting to the character; involving particular surfaces

The movement abilities may be the result of genetics, mystical forces, supernatural talents, or intense training. The character may select one Special Movement Ability for every Level of this Attribute. Several examples are given below; the GM and players are encouraged to develop additional abilities as well. See Flight (page 19), Hyperflight (page 22), Jumping (page 24), Speed (page 37), Teleport (page 39), Tunnelling (page 40), or Water Speed (page 40) for other methods of movement.

BALANCE

The character never loses his or her balance, even when running on a narrow rope or beam.

CAT-LIKE

The character will take half damage (round down) from most falls and always lands on his or her feet.

DIMENSION HOP

Upon a successful Stat check, the character can instantly travel between his or her home dimension to one other dimension, such as Asgard, Heaven, Hell, alternate Earth, the astral plane (the body is left behind), etc. Each time this method is assigned, the character can travel to another single dimension. Characters who can travel among many dimensions should probably have the Dynamic Powers (Dimensions) Attribute instead. The GM will determine if Dimension Hop is appropriate for his or her campaign.

LIGHT-FOOTED

The character can skim over sand, snow, or ice at full speed.

SLITHERING

The character can slither along the ground at normal walking/running speeds. This allows a character to move quickly while maintaining a very low profile.

SWINGING/BRACHIATING

The character can swing through forests and cities (areas with natural or artificial structures above swinging height) using vines/ropes/webbing or simply his or her arms.

UNTRACKABLE

The character never leaves footprints, tracks, or a scent when he or she walks or runs.

WALL-BOUNCING

The character can move at regular walking speed without touching the ground by bounding back and forth between nearby vertical surfaces (walls). For example, he or she can proceed down hallways or climb an alleyway between two buildings (bouncing from wall to wall).

WALL-CRAWLING

The character can cling to walls or ceilings as though they were on the ground or floor. This counts as two Special Movement abilities.

WATER-WALKING

The character can walk or run over water as if he or she was on land. This counts as two Special Movement abilities.

ZEN DIRECTION

When the character opens his or her mind to the natural world, he or she will always move in the "right" direction. The "right" direction is not always the desired direction, however.

SPEED

COST:	6 Points/Level
RELEVANT STAT:	Body
REQUIRED PMVs:	None
OPTIONAL PMVs:	None
PROGRESSION:	Medium Progression Chart, starting at 100 kph
REDUCTION:	Very specific utility
RESTRICTIONS:	Under certain conditions; time limit; Stat/Skill checks required to run safely

On average, a character can sprint up to 6 metres per round (4.3 kph) times his or her Body Stat. A character with Speed can move much faster than this, as well as perceive the world at an increased pace. At Speed Level 5+, the character moves quickly enough to run over any liquid surface as well.

In most genres, a fast-moving character can still interact with the world. This means that the character will not run into buildings along city streets because he or she can perceive them early enough and make sharp turns to avoid them. Speedsters can also read books quickly, write at incredible speeds, and perform normal chores and activities at enhanced rates. In addition to gaining +2 Initiative at each Level, the character is harder to hit due to the incredible speed at which the character is moving. For more information about Speed and its influence on combat, see page 66.

Speed is a modular Attribute that does not provide the character with many other benefits typically associated with speedsters, however. Many characters with Speed will also possess one or more Levels in the following Attributes: Combat Technique (Lightning Reflexes), Extra Attacks, Extra Defences, Heightened Awareness, Incorporeal, Massive Damage (Speed attacks), Regeneration, Special Movement, and Special Attack (Tied to Speed through the Dependent Defect).

SUPERSTRENGTH

COST:	4 Points/Level
RELEVANT STAT:	Body
REQUIRED PMVs:	None
OPTIONAL PMVs:	None
PROGRESSION:	Medium Progression Chart, starting at 1 tonne
REDUCTION:	Very specific utility
RESTRICTIONS:	Under certain conditions; no extra combat damage; Superstrength in single limb only

On average, a character can lift 30 kg times his or her Body Stat, but some characters are far stronger than their Body Stats indicate. This Attribute can represent the muscular strength of a large and powerful non-human, a supernatural ability, or the hydraulic systems of robotic muscles. Each Level of Superstrength determines the maximum mass the character can lift. Each Level also adds +10 close combat damage when using punches, kicks, body slams, melee weapons, Special Attacks with the Muscle-Powered Ability, or the Natural Weapon Attribute (page 27). Each Level also grants a +4 bonus for Body Stat checks where pure strength is involved.

A character's Superstrength is independent of his or her Body Stat. When someone or something has Superstrength, strength moves beyond the Stat scale; the Body Stat now represents fitness, durability, and agility rather than actual muscle. Thus, a player could create someone with a Body Stat of 2, but Levels of Superstrength (clumsy but powerful!).

SWARM

COST:	2 Points/Level
RELEVANT STAT:	Body
REQUIRED PMVS:	None
OPTIONAL PMVS:	None
PROGRESSION:	Linear; +1 critter for every current Health Point each Level
REDUCTION:	Attribute always used in same way
RESTRICTIONS:	Under certain conditions; fewer critters; suffer damage when transforming

A character with this Attribute can transform into a swarm of small creatures: rats, bats, wasps, crows or other creatures or things (such as tiny attack robots). Vampires and demons most often possess this dramatic ability.

The type of swarm must be determined during character creation. The character can create one critter from his or her body for every current Health Point, multiplied by the Level in this Attribute. Thus, a character with 130 current Health Points who has Swarm at Level 4 could transform into a mass of 520 creatures (130 x 4 = 520).

When transformed into a swarm, the character cannot use any of his or her existing Attributes or Skills. The actions of the swarm are basically limited to three options: move, observe, and attack. Additionally, all the critters of the swarm must remain within close proximity of each other (within a radius of five metres per Level).

A swarm's Attack Combat Value is equal to the Swarm Attribute Level + 4. Its attack damage is not based on Combat Value, though. Instead, it inflicts 1 damage for every 10 critters (round up; minimum one damage point) in the swarm. In many instances, the Armour and Force Field Attributes will protect the target character from all damage, since the Attributes stop sufficient damage from each critter attack. Against some critters, even regular clothing may be enough to stop some or all damage. Each situation will be different; the GM must determine how much damage, if any, will penetrate the target's defences.

A swarm can be attacked normally, and each creature in it dies if it is hit (no defence check is allowed). Unless an opponent is using an attack with the Area-Effect or Spreading Abilities (pages 32 and 34), however, only a single member of the swarm can be killed per attack (GM's discretion). Consequently, a swarm of 200 creatures requires 200 attacks to completely destroy. Attacks with the Spreading Ability can affect multiple critters at a time, while attacks with the Area Effect Ability can be devastating to the swarm.

A character who dissolved into a swarm may choose to revert into normal form during his or her Initiative in a combat round. To accomplish this, all available critters in the swarm (those not killed or trapped) must join together. Transforming back to normal form replaces a character's action for that round. The character will return to normal form with Health Points equal to the number of critters that recombined, divided by the Swarm Attribute Level (round down). For example, if a character with 130 current Health Points and Swarm at Level 4 divided into 520 creatures, and after a battle, recombined with only 100 available critters, the character would then have a current total of 25 Health Points (100÷4=25).

TELEKINESIS

COST:	2 or 4 Points/Level
RELEVANT STAT:	Mind
REQUIRED PMVS:	None
OPTIONAL PMVS:	Area, Range
PROGRESSION:	Fast Progression Chart, starting at 1 kg
REDUCTION:	Limited control
RESTRICTIONS:	Under certain conditions; time limit; more specific matter limitation

The character can concentrate on an object and move it without physically touching it. Telekinesis may represent psionic ability, magic, or some form of tractor beam. Characters with the ability to magically control the movement of a particular element (Earth, Water, etc.) may also use Telekinesis to represent their particular ability.

A character using Telekinesis can lift him or herself, a character, an object, or a group of adjacent objects and move it at a fast walking speed (10 metres/round) or manipulate it with the dexterity of a human hand. The higher the Attribute Level, the greater fine motor control the character has when manipulating objects as well. The character can also levitate an object and have it strike another person as if it were a short-ranged thrown weapon. The mass Telekinesis can lift is reduced by a factor of 10 when throwing an object hard enough to inflict damage. For example, a character with Level 4 could lift up to 1,000 kg but could only throw objects massing up to 100 kg. This is treated as a normal attack and thus can be negated by a successful defence. Damage depends on the mass of the object hurled: 5-15 points for an object massing up to 1 kg, 15-30 points for up to 10 kg, 45 points for one up to 100 kg, 60 points for one up to 1,000 kg (one tonne), etc. The same damage applies to the object being hurled. If Telekinesis is used to directly crush or constrict a target, damage delivered equals 5 points for each Attribute Level.

A character who uses Telekinesis to grab another person and throw him or her uses the same procedure, but this requires a successful Attack Combat check to "grab" the target. Accurately tossing an opponent so that he or she hits another target requires a second successful attack check. If attempting to disarm a character with Telekinesis, the subject should be allowed a Body Stat check to retain the weapon at a -1 Check Value penalty per Level of the disarming character's Telekinesis Attribute. If a character wishes to fly at speeds exceeding 10 metres/round, he or she needs the Flight Attribute (page 19) rather than Telekinesis.

Ordinary Telekinesis (capable of moving anything physical, but not forms of energy) costs 4 Points/Level. At a cost of only 2 Point/Level, the character may have a more focused Telekinesis. This restricts the character to telekinetically moving (or sculpting) a particular type of matter. Some examples are given below.

AIR

The character can only move air (or other gases). A cubic metre of air masses about 1.3 kg. Enough air to fill a 3 metre by 3 metre by 3 metre (roughly 1,000 cubic feet) room masses 35 kg.

EARTH

The character can only move dirt, rock, stone, sand, etc. He or she cannot affect treated metals. A cubic metre of packed dirt masses about 2 tonnes; the same mass of concrete masses about 2.5 tonnes, while a cubic metre of solid granite masses about 2.7 tonnes.

FIRE

The character can only affect flames of an existing fire, or can possibly start them with his or her mind as well (GM's discretion). Since fire does not have mass, the Level indicates the size of the flames that can be controlled and manipulated: small fires at Level 1 (like a candle or match flame), up to raging infernos that cover several city blocks at Level 10.

METAL

The character's Telekinesis only works on metal. This may be a mystical limitation, or it may be the character's Attribute is actually based in magnetics. A cubic metre of steel masses about 8 tonnes.

WATER

The character can lift and move water. A cubic metre of water (1,000 litres) masses about a tonne. A gallon of water (about 4 litres) masses about 4 kilograms.

WOOD

The character's Attribute only works on wood (living or dead). This ability is usually mystical in origin and common to nature priests and spirits. A cubic metre of wood masses just under a tonne.

TELEPATHY

COST:	1-3 Points/Level
RELEVANT STAT:	Mind
REQUIRED PMVs:	Targets
OPTIONAL PMVs:	Area, Range
PROGRESSION:	Descriptive
REDUCTION:	Attribute always used in same way
RESTRICTIONS:	Under certain conditions; time limit; usage weakens character

Telepathy is the classic psionic ability. Versions of telepathy may also represent other magical capabilities; demons that can tempt their victims often possess Telepathy, for example.

Telepathy costs 1 Point/Level if its utility is quite restricted (for example, "only works with canines" or "only with close friends"). It costs 2 Points/Level if its utility is somewhat restricted (for example, "only with humans" or "only with beasts"). It costs 3 Points/Level if it has universal utility.

This Attribute allows the character to read and transmit thoughts, and at higher Levels, to actually "invade" a person's mind and probe their memories or alter their thoughts. Telepathy works only if a subject is in very close proximity, unless the Range or Area PMV Rank is 2 or higher. Pinpointing a single target in a crowd can be difficult; the GM may require a Mind Stat check, modified by any Levels the character has in the Heightened Awareness (page 22) or Heightened Senses Attribute (page 22).

A subject cannot detect a telepath reading thoughts or sensory impressions unless he or she has the Telepathy or Mind Shield Attributes at an equal or higher Level. If so, he or she can choose to block the telepath, in which case the only way to get through is via mental invasion. A subject will always be aware of a mental invasion (although a non-telepath may not understand exactly what is going on). See the Mind Combat rules (page 71) in Chapter 8: Combat for details of mental invasions.

Once contact is made, a telepath at Level 6 or higher can temporarily gain a target's specific knowledge that is associated with a Skill. The actual Skill is not learned in full, however. For example, a telepath can scan the mind of a nearby surgeon to learn how to perform a specific operation on an ally, but he or she does not gain the Medical Skill. The telepath will soon forget this newly learned Skill-based knowledge.

Unlike most Attributes, Telepathy only has listed entries for Levels 2, 4, 6, 8, and 10. If necessary, the GM can extrapolate intermediate and higher Levels. When performing a Mind Stat check to determine if the Telepathy attempt was successful, the character receives a Check Value bonus equal to half the Attribute's Level (for example, a Level 8 Telepath makes his or her Mind Stat checks with a +4 Check Value bonus).

LEVEL 2 The character can, by concentrating, use mind reading to pick up the "loud" surface thoughts of a subject. A "loud" thought is something about which the subject is thinking intensely or that has a very strong emotional content. The character can also transmit a single feeling, such as "fear" or "love" to another person.

LEVEL 4 The character can, by concentrating, use mind reading to pick up the ordinary surface thoughts of a subject. The character can only read what a person is actually thinking at the time. Two telepaths can communicate with one another at conversational speeds by reading each other's thoughts. The character can also transmit a word, simple image, or simple concept (like "flower," or a person's face) to a non-telepath on which he or she concentrates. It requires an entire round of concentration to convey one concept, which makes telepath to non-telepath communication slow.

LEVEL 6 The character can easily read a subject's surface thoughts and sensory impressions (for example, seeing through a subject's eyes, feeling what the subject feels, etc.). The character can choose to ignore some senses if desired. The character can send and receive mental speech to a non-telepath at normal conversational speeds. If the Targets PMV is raised to Level 2 or higher, the character can broadcast the mental speech of one subject to others in the range/area as well.

LEVEL 8 The character has the same capabilities as at Level 6 Telepathy. In addition, he or she can invade another person's mind. This counts as an attack, and if the subject is unwilling or unaware, the character will enter Mind Combat with him or her (page 71). If the subject is willing or loses the mental combat, the telepath can probe his or her memory for information he or she needs. The character will also automatically read surface thoughts of anyone within the telepathy area.

LEVEL 10 The character has the same capabilities as Level 8 Telepathy. He or she automatically shares the sensory experiences of anyone within the telepathy area without need for concentration, unless he or she deliberately tries to block this ability. Additionally, a successful mental invasion can probe memories that the subject can no longer consciously remember, delete existing memories, and plant false ones.

TELEPORT

COST:	5 Points/Level
RELEVANT STAT:	Mind
REQUIRED PMVs:	None
OPTIONAL PMVs:	Area, Range, Targets
PROGRESSION:	Fast Progression Chart, starting at 10 m
REDUCTION:	Attribute always used in the same way
RESTRICTIONS:	Under certain conditions; teleport not accurate; naked form only

Teleport enables the character to transport him or herself instantly from place to place without crossing the intervening space. It is a common ability for psionic characters, sorcerers, and superhumans.

Teleporting is only possible if the character has visited the intended destination or can see or otherwise sense the destination (possibly through the Heightened Senses or Sixth Sense Attributes). The Game Master may allow characters to teleport to unknown destinations (such as "100 metres up," or "to the other side of the door"), perhaps for an additional 1 or 2 Character Points total. Accidentally teleporting into a solid object may be fatal or simply cause a failed teleport at the GM's option. A character can carry anything while teleporting that he or she could normally carry.

When Teleport is first assigned, the GM may ask the player to decide if velocity (speed and direction) is conserved during travel. Alternatively, the character might adapt velocity to each Teleport individually. In many campaigns, the effects of velocity will simply be ignored.

TOUGH

COST:	2 Points/Level
RELEVANT STAT:	None
REQUIRED PMVs:	None
OPTIONAL PMVs:	None
PROGRESSION:	Linear; +20 Health Points each Level
REDUCTION:	None
RESTRICTIONS:	None

Possessing this Attribute increases the Health Points of the character, allowing him or her to withstand more damage in combat. The Tough Attribute, along with the Body Stat, also reflects a character's resistance to sickness, disease, and other physical ailments. See page 57 for more information on Health Points. Note that characters with high Body or Soul Attributes may be very healthy even without this Attribute.

TRANSFER

COST:	5 or 10 Points/Level
RELEVANT STAT:	Soul
REQUIRED PMVs:	Duration
OPTIONAL PMVs:	Range
PROGRESSION:	Linear; transfer of +1 Attribute Level each Level
REDUCTION:	More than one but less than all
RESTRICTIONS:	Character loses Attribute while it is transferred; transfer to specific type of targets; transfer of specific Attributes

Upon a successful Stat Soul check, the character can temporarily grant the use of any one of his or her Attributes to any single willing target character within the Range PMV distance. Dynamic Powers and Power Flux cannot be transferred under normal circumstances. The Transfer Attribute Level determines the maximum Attribute Level that can be granted. The Level of a transferred Attribute replaces the target's corresponding Level (if applicable), which can be an increase or decrease. The target gains the benefits of a transferred Attribute as long as indicated by the Duration PMV. The GM may also decide that Stats, Skills, and/or Characteristic Attributes can be given to a target when Transfer reaches Level 5 or higher. To grant Attributes to multiple targets, the Transfer Attribute can be assigned multiple times.

For 5 Points/Level the character can only transfer one Attribute at any single time. When the character grants a new ability, the target ceases benefiting from any currently transferred Attribute. For 10 Points/Level, the character can transfer all desired Attributes simultaneously to a single target. When an Attribute is Transferred, the receiving character is in complete control of its abilities.

TRANSMUTATION

COST:	3-5 Points/Level
RELEVANT STAT:	Mind or Soul
REQUIRED PMVs:	Duration
OPTIONAL PMVs:	Range
PROGRESSION:	Medium Progression Chart, starting at 1 kg
REDUCTION:	Very specific utility
RESTRICTIONS:	Under certain conditions; creation is visually flawed; limited control over actual object created

This Attribute allows a character to transmute one non-living object (or set of connected objects) into another. Transmutation costs 5 Points/Level if the character can transmute any object into another (within the limits of his or her Level). It costs 4 Points/Level if the character can only transmute (to or from) a general class of objects such as "metal," "weapons," "clothing," or "food." It also costs 4 Points/Level if the character can only transmute one object to another of similar mass; the types of objects are unrestricted. Finally, the cost is 3 Points/Level if the character is limited to a transmutation within a specific category and of similar mass, such as "regular clothes to battle costume," "lead to gold," or "spoiled food to edible food." The GM may restrict any categories that seem overly broad or too powerful.

Few characters with the Transmutation Attribute will also possess the Creation Attribute (page 16). Since Transmutation allows a character to transform air, earth, and buildings into anything else, this Attribute effectively "trumps" Creation. Only in rare circumstances will a character find him or herself in a situation in which nothing in the immediate area can be transmuted.

The character cannot transmute material into new objects outside the character's experience. The character could transmute a weapon into a book, painting or videotape, but the content must be something with which he or she was already familiar. Likewise, a character who had no familiarity with computers could not transmute a television into one using Transmutation. The GM may choose to require a Mind Stat check (or relevant Skill check) if the character attempts a particularly complex transmutation. Failure may indicate the new object does not function properly; this is especially applicable when creating complex technological devices. Unless the GM decides otherwise, Transmutation is only able to make objects that could be classified as Gadgets; it cannot create Items of Power. When attempting to transmute an Item of Power, the character suffers a penalty to the Mind or Soul Stat check of -2 for each Level of the Item of Power.

The object will remain transmuted for a period of time indicated by the Duration PMV.

TUNNELLING

COST:	2 Points/Level
RELEVANT STAT:	Body
REQUIRED PMVs:	None
OPTIONAL PMVs:	None
PROGRESSION:	Medium Progression Chart, starting at 10 m/hour
REDUCTION:	Limited control
RESTRICTIONS:	Under certain conditions; in specific terrain; depth limitation

The Tunnelling Attribute allows a character to move earth and/or burrow underground. Tunnelling assumes that the character is going through sand or packed earth; boring through solid rock is one Level slower. The tunnel the character leaves behind will either be permanent or will collapse immediately (must be specified during creation of each tunnel).

UNIQUE ATTRIBUTE

COST:	1-10 Points/Level
RELEVANT STAT:	Variable
REQUIRED PMVs:	Variable
OPTIONAL PMVs:	Variable
PROGRESSION:	Variable
REDUCTION:	Any
RESTRICTIONS:	Any

This Attribute covers any and all powers and special abilities not detailed in the rules. Often one single Point in a Unique Attribute is sufficient to give the character "flavour," but more Points can be allocated to enhance the effects on game play and must be added if the Attribute would be of considerable benefit. Discuss the Attribute with the GM to determine what specific game effects the Unique Attribute possesses.

The GM should assign a Point cost per Level based on how the Attribute compares to other Attributes and how useful it is. An Attribute that is somewhat useful in the game should cost 1 Point/Level; one that is very useful should cost 2-3 Points/Level; one that is extremely useful should cost 4-6 Points/Level; and one that is exceptionally powerful and useful should cost 7-10 (or more) Points/Level.

UNKNOWN SUPERHUMAN POWER

COST:	Variable
RELEVANT STAT:	Variable
REQUIRED PMVs:	Variable
OPTIONAL PMVs:	Variable
PROGRESSION:	Special (see below)
REDUCTION:	Any
RESTRICTIONS:	Any

In some campaigns, the characters may be unaware of their superhuman Attributes until they manifest at crucial moments. To represent this, the player can allocate some Points to Unknown Superhuman Power when creating the character. The player does not purchase a Level in this Attribute — he or she simply spends a selected amount of Character Points. The GM takes those Points and adds a bonus of 50% (rounding up) and uses them to assign other Attributes to the character. The GM does not tell the player which Attributes have been assigned; they are revealed to the player (and character) as the game unfolds and the Attributes manifest. GMs are encouraged to reveal the character's Attributes slowly and when it is appropriate for the campaign's story. The GM should never feel pressured to tell the player what his or her character's unknown Attributes are before the time is right.

WATER SPEED

COST:	2 Points/Level
RELEVANT STAT:	Body
REQUIRED PMVs:	None
OPTIONAL PMVs:	None
PROGRESSION:	Medium Progression Chart, starting at 5 kph
REDUCTION:	Limited control
RESTRICTIONS:	Under certain conditions; only surface travel; time limitation

A character with Water Speed can float and travel on or under water. Aquatic creatures or amphibious non-humans such as mermaids usually possess this Attribute. The character can swim on the surface at high speeds and dive underwater for brief periods by holding his or her breath, or indefinitely if he or she has the Adaptation (Underwater) Attribute. To survive the pressure associated with deep diving, the Adaptation (Pressure) Attribute must also be assigned. Also, depending on the speed at which the character is moving, opponents may suffer a penalty to hit the character (see Attacking Moving Targets, page 66).

WEALTH

COST:	3 Points/Level
RELEVANT STAT:	None
REQUIRED PMVS:	None
OPTIONAL PMVS:	None
PROGRESSION:	Medium Progression Chart, starting at $500,000
REDUCTION:	Very specific utility
	Difficult to access funds; less non-liquid assets; spending limits on single items

The character is more financially stable ("liquid") than an average person. This will allow him or her to easily acquire commercially available goods, and bribe or hire people. Note that hirelings that are intensely loyal to the character should still be acquired through the Agents, Henchmen, or Servant Attributes. The character usually has non-liquid assets (like houses or real estate) commensurate with his or her wealth as well. In order to have access to things that are illegal or difficult to acquire without special licenses, the character should still acquire the Organisational Ties or Gadgets Attributes (pages 27 and 21).

STEP 5: SELECT SKILLS

Your character's Skills represent his or her extensive training and experience in a particular field. Skill Points, not Character Points, are used to acquire them.

A character's starting Skill Points is determined by the power level (see Table 4-1: Starting Skill Points). This value is increased by an additional 10 Skill Points for each Level of the Highly Skilled Attribute (page 22). A character with the Unskilled Defect (page 57) has 10-60 fewer Skill Points. Non-player characters created by the GM may have any number of Skill Points. Minor characters will usually have only 5-15 Skill Points, for example, while a major, recurring opponent may have 100 or more. The character's power level also indicates the maximum Skill Level he or she can achieve under normal circumstances (GM's discretion).

Table 4-1: Starting Skill Points

Power Level	Starting Skill Points	Normal Maximum Skill Level
Subhuman	10	2
Human	20	3
Posthuman	30	4
Superhuman	40	5
Inhuman	50	6
Godlike	60	10

The different Skills are divided into Levels 1 through 10. Increasing the value of a Skill by one Level requires 1-12 Skill Points, depending on the Skill. The higher the Skill Level, the better your character is and the broader his or her knowledge within the field. Characters with high Stats (or Combat Values) can be exceptionally proficient within a field even without high Skill Levels; they are considered "naturals."

Table 4-2: Skill Level Descriptions

SKILL LEVEL 1	Well-Trained. The character has some training and practice with the Skill.
SKILL LEVEL 2	Scholar. The character has moderate training and practice with the Skill.
SKILL LEVEL 3	Expert. The character has significant training and practice with the Skill.
SKILL LEVEL 4	Veteran. The character has comprehensive training and practice with the Skill.
SKILL LEVEL 5	World Leader. The character has rigorous training and practice with the Skill.
SKILL LEVEL 6	Master Apprentice. The character has extensive training and practice with the Skill.
SKILL LEVEL 7	Master. The character has complete training and practice with the Skill.
SKILL LEVEL 8	Grand Master. The character has exhaustive training and practice with the Skill.
SKILL LEVEL 9	Undisputed Master. The character has nearly unparalleled training and practice with the Skill.
SKILL LEVEL 10	Heavenly Master. The character has godlike training and practice with the Skill.

SKILLS AND SPECIALITIES

General and Combat Skills have a number of associated Specialisations, which describe the different ways that the Skill may be used. For example, Gun Combat is divided into Auto-fire, Pistol, and Rifle. When you assign a Skill to your character, choose one of the listed Specialisation or create a new Specialisation with GM approval. Your character will be significantly better in the chosen Specialisation than he or she will be in the other aspects of the Skill. A Specialisation is usually recorded in parentheses after the Skill, for example, "Gun Combat (Pistol) Level 3."

Instead of improving a Skill by one Level, it is possible to take an extra Specialisation. Each extra Specialisation costs only one Skill Point regardless of the Point cost of the Skill. If your character has Skill Points to spare, however, you may find it more advantageous to add an extra Skill Level rather than take many extra Specialisations.

USING SKILLS

Each Skill has its own description, which indicates game effects and the Stat which is usually most relevant to the Skill's use, should a Skill check be needed. Game mechanics for using Skills in play are described under Skill checks (page 60), but there is no need to worry about them while designing a character. Simply choose those Skills that most closely fit your concept.

A player should not assign a particular Skill to his or her character to justify some familiarity within the field. Even a Level 1 Skill assignment reflects a substantial amount of training, and will demonstrate that your character is quite knowledgeable or capable in the chosen area. If a character has only limited capabilities within a specific area, he or she should not possess the relevant Skill. For example, anyone can throw a punch or fire a gun without necessarily having any real talent. A character that knows how to drive a car safely on city streets does not automatically need the Driving (Car) Skill nor does someone with a first year university course in physics necessarily have Physical Sciences (Physics). Conversely, a character may have high Skill Levels without any formal training, because he or she has used the Skill in daily life for many years (such as a brawny farm worker having the Powerlifting Skill). Characters should rarely possess Skill Levels at their maximum allowed Level, since this achievement reflects an incredibly high degree of proficiency. A character with a Skill Level of one-half X is widely regarded as one of the best in his or her field.

Table 4-3a: Skill Point Costs

Skill	Multi-Genre All Campaigns	Modern Day Action Adventure	Modern Day Animal Adventures	Modern Day Conspiracy	Modern Day Law Enforcement
Acrobatics	5	5	6	2	2
Animal Training	1	1	2	2	2
Architecture	1	1	1	2	1
Area Knowledge	3	4	2	4	4
Artisan	1	1	1	2	1
Biological Sciences	3	3	2	4	4
Boating	2	4	1	1	2
Burglary	3	4	1	4	3
Climbing	2	3	3	2	2
Computers	4	3	1	5	4
Controlled Breathing	1	1	2	1	1
Cultural Arts	2	1	1	3	1
Demolitions	3	5	2	3	3
Disguise	3	3	3	4	3
Domestic Arts	2	1	1	1	1
Driving	3	5	1	3	4
Electronics	3	3	1	4	3
Etiquette	2	2	1	3	2
Foreign Culture	2	2	1	3	3
Forgery	2	3	1	4	3
Gaming	1	1	1	1	2
Interrogation	3	5	1	4	5
Intimidation	3	5	2	4	5
Languages	2	2	2	3	2
Law	2	3	1	3	4
Management/Admin	2	1	1	3	3
Mechanics	2	4	1	3	2
Medical	3	3	1	4	4
Military Sciences	3	2	1	3	3
Navigation	3	3	4	3	3
Occult	2	1	1	2	1
Performing Arts	1	1	1	2	1
Physical Sciences	3	2	1	5	4
Piloting	2	4	1	3	2
Poisons	2	5	2	4	5
Police Sciences	3	3	1	4	6
Power Usage	6	3	5	3	2
Powerlifting	5	3	2	2	2
Riding	2	2	1	2	2
Seduction	2	3	2	3	2
Sleight of Hand	3	4	2	3	3
Social Sciences	3	2	1	3	3
Sports	1	2	2	1	1
Stealth	3	4	3	4	4
Street Sense	2	4	1	4	4
Swimming	1	2	3	2	2
Urban Tracking	4	5	1	4	5
Visual Arts	2	2	1	2	2
Wilderness Survival	3	3	5	2	2
Wilderness Tracking	3	3	5	2	2
Writing	1	1	1	2	1
Combat Skills					
Archery	2	2	1	2	2
Gun Combat	6	8	1	5	6
Heavy Weapons	4	5	1	1	4
Melee Attack	5	8	1	4	6
Melee Defence	5	8	1	4	6
Ranged Defence	6	8	2	6	8
Special Ranged Attack	6	6	-	4	-
Thrown Weapons	4	6	1	3	6
Unarmed Attack	6	8	3	5	8
Unarmed Defence	6	8	3	5	8

Skill	Modern Day Loony Cartoons	Modern Day Occult / Horror	Modern Day Pulp	Modern Day Reality TV	Modern Day Romantic Comedy
Acrobatics	5	3	5	2	2
Animal Training	2	2	2	1	2
Architecture	1	2	1	1	1
Area Knowledge	3	4	3	3	3
Artisan	1	4	2	3	2
Biological Sciences	1	4	2	2	2
Boating	2	1	4	3	2
Burglary	3	4	4	2	1
Climbing	3	2	3	2	1
Computers	1	5	1	3	3
Controlled Breathing	1	2	2	2	1
Cultural Arts	1	3	3	2	3
Demolitions	4	3	5	2	1
Disguise	2	4	3	2	2
Domestic Arts	1	1	1	4	4
Driving	2	3	5	3	3
Electronics	1	3	1	3	3
Etiquette	2	3	2	5	3
Foreign Culture	2	3	3	3	3
Forgery	1	3	3	1	1
Gaming	2	1	2	5	2
Interrogation	1	4	4	3	3
Intimidation	3	4	4	3	2
Languages	1	3	2	2	3
Law	1	3	2	2	2
Management/Admin	1	2	1	2	3
Mechanics	1	3	3	3	2
Medical	1	4	2	2	2
Military Sciences	1	2	2	2	1
Navigation	3	3	4	3	3
Occult	1	6	3	1	1
Performing Arts	3	2	1	3	3
Physical Sciences	1	5	2	1	2
Piloting	1	2	3	1	1
Poisons	1	5	4	2	1
Police Sciences	1	3	2	2	1
Power Usage	6	6	4	-	1
Powerlifting	3	2	4	1	2
Riding	3	2	3	2	2
Seduction	3	2	3	4	6
Sleight of Hand	3	3	3	4	2
Social Sciences	1	3	1	3	4
Sports	3	1	2	3	2
Stealth	3	4	3	2	2
Street Sense	2	3	3	3	2
Swimming	2	2	2	2	2
Urban Tracking	1	4	4	3	3
Visual Arts	1	4	1	2	2
Wilderness Survival	1	2	3	3	2
Wilderness Tracking	1	2	3	3	2
Writing	1	3	1	2	3
Combat Skills					
Archery	4	2	2	1	1
Gun Combat	2	5	8	1	1
Heavy Weapons	1	1	4	1	1
Melee Attack	5	6	8	2	1
Melee Defence	5	6	8	2	1
Ranged Defence	8	6	8	1	1
Special Ranged Attack	4	2	-	-	-
Thrown Weapons	4	4	6	2	1
Unarmed Attack	3	5	8	2	2
Unarmed Defence	3	5	8	2	2

Table 4-3b: Skill Point Costs

Skill	Modern Day Soap Opera	Modern Day Superhero	Modern Day Urban Fantasy	Historical 20th Century War	Historical Age of Pirates	Skill	Historical Ancient China / Japan	Historical Ancient Egypt	Historical Ancient Rome / Greece	Historical Middle Ages	Historical Old West
Acrobatics	2	6	3	4	4	Acrobatics	4	1	1	1	3
Animal Training	2	1	3	1	1	Animal Training	3	3	2	3	4
Architecture	1	2	2	2	1	Architecture	2	3	3	2	2
Area Knowledge	3	3	5	3	3	Area Knowledge	1	1	2	2	3
Artisan	2	2	4	2	2	Artisan	3	4	3	2	2
Biological Sciences	3	4	3	4	1	Biological Sciences	1	1	1	1	2
Boating	2	1	2	2	6	Boating	2	1	2	2	1
Burglary	3	3	3	2	3	Burglary	1	1	1	2	3
Climbing	1	2	2	3	2	Climbing	1	1	1	2	3
Computers	2	4	3	5	-	Computers	-	-	-	-	-
Controlled Breathing	1	1	2	3	2	Controlled Breathing	2	1	1	1	2
Cultural Arts	3	2	3	1	2	Cultural Arts	3	3	4	2	1
Demolitions	2	5	3	4	3	Demolitions	1	1	1	1	2
Disguise	2	3	3	4	2	Disguise	2	2	2	2	3
Domestic Arts	4	1	1	1	2	Domestic Arts	2	2	2	2	1
Driving	3	2	2	4	-	Driving	-	-	-	-	-
Electronics	2	4	3	5	-	Electronics	-	-	-	-	-
Etiquette	3	1	2	2	3	Etiquette	3	2	2	3	2
Foreign Culture	3	2	3	3	2	Foreign Culture	2	2	3	2	1
Forgery	3	4	2	3	3	Forgery	2	2	2	1	3
Gaming	2	1	2	1	2	Gaming	2	2	3	1	5
Interrogation	4	4	4	5	3	Interrogation	2	2	2	2	4
Intimidation	4	3	4	5	3	Intimidation	2	2	2	2	4
Languages	2	1	3	2	3	Languages	2	2	2	2	1
Law	4	3	3	3	2	Law	2	2	2	1	2
Management/Admin	4	1	2	2	2	Management/Admin	1	1	1	2	1
Mechanics	2	4	2	4	4	Mechanics	2	2	2	1	1
Medical	3	3	4	4	3	Medical	2	2	2	2	3
Military Sciences	2	4	2	8	3	Military Sciences	2	2	2	2	1
Navigation	3	2	3	6	5	Navigation	4	3	2	3	4
Occult	1	2	6	1	1	Occult	2	2	2	2	1
Performing Arts	4	2	3	1	2	Performing Arts	2	2	2	2	2
Physical Sciences	1	5	4	4	1	Physical Sciences	1	1	2	1	1
Piloting	1	2	1	3	-	Piloting	-	-	-	-	-
Poisons	2	4	5	3	2	Poisons	2	2	2	2	3
Police Sciences	3	4	3	5	-	Police Sciences	-	-	-	-	1
Power Usage	1	8	6	1	1	Power Usage	2	2	2	1	2
Powerlifting	1	6	2	3	3	Powerlifting	2	1	1	1	2
Riding	2	1	2	2	2	Riding	1	3	3	4	4
Seduction	5	3	4	2	3	Seduction	2	2	2	2	2
Sleight of Hand	2	3	4	3	2	Sleight of Hand	1	1	1	2	3
Social Sciences	4	2	3	2	1	Social Sciences	2	2	3	2	1
Sports	2	1	1	2	1	Sports	2	2	4	1	1
Stealth	3	3	5	3	3	Stealth	2	2	4	2	3
Street Sense	3	2	4	3	2	Street Sense	1	2	2	2	2
Swimming	2	1	2	3	3	Swimming	1	1	2	2	2
Urban Tracking	3	3	4	5	2	Urban Tracking	1	1	1	1	2
Visual Arts	2	2	3	1	1	Visual Arts	3	3	3	2	1
Wilderness Survival	2	1	2	5	3	Wilderness Survival	2	2	3	3	4
Wilderness Tracking	2	2	2	5	3	Wilderness Tracking	2	2	2	3	4
Writing	3	1	2	2	1	Writing	2	3	3	2	1
Combat Skills						**Combat Skills**					
Archery	1	7	2	2	1	Archery	4	1	4	4	3
Gun Combat	2	8	5	10	3	Gun Combat	-	-	-	-	6
Heavy Weapons	1	9	1	6	2	Heavy Weapons	-	-	-	-	1
Melee Attack	2	7	6	8	6	Melee Attack	6	4	5	6	4
Melee Defence	2	7	6	8	6	Melee Defence	6	4	5	6	4
Ranged Defence	2	12	6	10	6	Ranged Defence	6	6	6	5	6
Special Ranged Attack	-	10	6	-	-	Special Ranged Attack	-	-	-	-	-
Thrown Weapons	2	8	5	8	2	Thrown Weapons	5	5	5	4	2
Unarmed Attack	2	8	6	8	4	Unarmed Attack	4	5	4	4	5
Unarmed Defence	2	8	6	8	4	Unarmed Defence	4	5	4	4	5

Table 4-3c: Skill Point Costs

Skill	Historical Stone Age	Historical Victorian	Fantasy High Fantasy	Fantasy Low Fantasy	Futuristic Cyberpunk / Biopunk	Skill	Futuristic Hard SF	Futuristic Mecha	Futuristic Post Apocalyptic	Futuristic Soft SF	Futuristic Space Opera
Acrobatics	2	3	4	3	4	Acrobatics	3	1	3	3	4
Animal Training	3	3	3	2	1	Animal Training	1	1	2	1	2
Architecture	1	2	1	1	2	Architecture	2	1	3	1	1
Area Knowledge	1	3	3	3	4	Area Knowledge	3	4	2	3	3
Artisan	1	3	2	3	2	Artisan	1	2	2	1	1
Biological Sciences	1	2	1	1	4	Biological Sciences	6	3	2	2	2
Boating	1	2	2	2	1	Boating	2	2	2	2	2
Burglary	1	2	3	3	3	Burglary	1	2	2	2	2
Climbing	2	2	2	2	2	Climbing	1	1	2	2	3
Computers	-	-	-	-	6	Computers	6	4	1	3	2
Controlled Breathing	1	4	2	2	1	Controlled Breathing	2	2	1	1	1
Cultural Arts	2	2	2	2	2	Cultural Arts	3	1	1	2	1
Demolitions	1	1	2	2	4	Demolitions	3	4	3	3	3
Disguise	1	2	3	2	2	Disguise	2	1	2	2	4
Domestic Arts	3	2	1	1	1	Domestic Arts	1	1	2	1	1
Driving	-	-	-	-	4	Driving	2	6	1	2	3
Electronics	-	-	-	-	6	Electronics	4	4	1	3	2
Etiquette	1	5	2	2	3	Etiquette	4	3	2	3	3
Foreign Culture	1	2	2	3	3	Foreign Culture	4	2	1	3	3
Forgery	1	2	1	2	3	Forgery	4	2	1	2	3
Gaming	2	2	1	2	2	Gaming	2	1	1	2	2
Interrogation	1	2	3	2	4	Interrogation	3	2	3	3	3
Intimidation	2	2	3	2	4	Intimidation	3	3	3	2	3
Languages	1	2	2	2	2	Languages	3	1	1	3	2
Law	1	3	1	2	2	Law	3	1	1	2	1
Management/Admin	1	2	1	1	2	Management/Admin	2	2	2	2	1
Mechanics	1	1	2	2	3	Mechanics	3	5	3	3	3
Medical	2	2	3	3	3	Medical	2	2	3	2	3
Military Sciences	1	2	1	3	3	Military Sciences	4	4	2	3	2
Navigation	2	2	3	3	2	Navigation	3	3	3	2	3
Occult	1	2	3	2	1	Occult	1	1	1	1	1
Performing Arts	1	3	2	2	1	Performing Arts	1	1	1	1	2
Physical Sciences	1	2	1	1	4	Physical Sciences	6	3	2	2	2
Piloting	-	-	1	-	2	Piloting	3	6	1	3	4
Poisons	1	2	4	3	2	Poisons	3	1	2	2	2
Police Sciences	-	2	-	2	3	Police Sciences	3	2	1	2	2
Power Usage	-	1	4	2	2	Power Usage	2	2	2	3	4
Powerlifting	3	2	3	2	3	Powerlifting	2	1	3	2	3
Riding	2	4	4	3	1	Riding	1	1	2	1	2
Seduction	2	3	3	2	2	Seduction	2	2	2	2	3
Sleight of Hand	1	1	2	2	2	Sleight of Hand	1	1	2	1	3
Social Sciences	1	3	1	1	2	Social Sciences	4	1	2	2	2
Sports	2	2	1	1	1	Sports	1	1	1	1	2
Stealth	2	3	3	3	3	Stealth	2	2	3	2	3
Street Sense	1	1	1	2	4	Street Sense	2	3	3	2	3
Swimming	2	2	3	3	1	Swimming	1	1	2	1	1
Urban Tracking	1	2	2	1	4	Urban Tracking	2	3	3	2	3
Visual Arts	1	2	1	1	2	Visual Arts	2	1	1	2	1
Wilderness Survival	4	1	3	3	2	Wilderness Survival	3	2	3	2	3
Wilderness Tracking	4	1	3	3	2	Wilderness Tracking	2	2	3	2	3
Writing	-	3	2	1	2	Writing	3	1	1	2	1

Combat Skills

Skill	Historical Stone Age	Historical Victorian	Fantasy High Fantasy	Fantasy Low Fantasy	Futuristic Cyberpunk / Biopunk	Skill	Futuristic Hard SF	Futuristic Mecha	Futuristic Post Apocalyptic	Futuristic Soft SF	Futuristic Space Opera
Archery	-	2	6	6	1	Archery	1	1	2	1	2
Gun Combat	-	2	-	-	8	Gun Combat	6	4	3	4	8
Heavy Weapons	-	-	-	-	6	Heavy Weapons	5	5	4	5	8
Melee Attack	2	5	6	5	6	Melee Attack	4	5	6	4	7
Melee Defence	2	5	6	5	6	Melee Defence	4	5	6	4	7
Ranged Defence	1	4	7	6	8	Ranged Defence	8	10	6	8	8
Special Ranged Attack	-	-	4	3	3	Special Ranged Attack	4	5	4	5	5
Thrown Weapons	2	2	3	3	3	Thrown Weapons	4	2	3	4	3
Unarmed Attack	2	5	5	4	5	Unarmed Attack	4	3	5	4	6
Unarmed Defence	2	5	5	4	5	Unarmed Defence	4	3	5	4	6

Skill Point Costs

In Tri-Stat dX, the Point cost of a Skill is based on its utility in the game and not on the difficulty of learning the Skill. Table 4-3: Skill Point Costs provides a list of Skill Point costs for 30 popular gaming genres, settings, and themes. For example, in a typical comic book setting, action, scientific, and combat-oriented Skills are fairly costly, while political, diplomatic, and business Skills are available for much less. The reverse is true in a soap opera setting. Skills are subdivided into General Skills and Combat Skills

Use Table 4-4: Skill Costs Descriptions as a guideline for determining how much a particular Skill should be worth in your particular campaign.

Reallocating Skill Points

In some campaigns, characters may end up travelling to another time or dimension. If this travel results in a high-cost Skill becoming useless, the Game Master may allow the player to reallocate Skill Points between adventures to reflect what the character has learned in the new land.

For example, if a 21st century investigator has travels back in time to ancient China, his Driving and Area Knowledge Skills are useless. After several adventures and some rough experiences the GM could allow the character to trade those Skills for Levels in Chinese Foreign Culture and Languages. If the character ever makes it back to his own time, he will be allowed to swap the Skills back after a period of readjustment.

Adjusting Skill Costs

While some genres bring to mind certain campaign styles instantly, such as the deniable assets of a cyberpunk setting, alternate campaigns may require some Skill cost adjustments. For example, if the GM runs a "Martial Law" cyberpunk campaign (using the Cyberpunk/Biopunk Skill costs) with player characters taking the roles of law enforcement, the Skill costs for Law and Police Sciences may be raised to 5 Points/Level each. Additionally, if the campaign will be exclusively urban, the Wilderness Survival and Wilderness Tracking Skills will each drop to 1 Point/Level.

The Game Master should also adjust Point costs when blending multiple campaign themes. It is recommended that the GM uses the highest Point value of amongst the themes for important Skills. This method will result in more Skills requiring a greater number of Points, and thus the GM should also reduce the costs of some less frequently used Skills. For example, when running an Occult/Action Adventure campaign, the Occult Skill is probably best set at the higher 6 Points/Level cost (the Occult campaign cost) to reflect its importance. Conversely, if the Artisan Skill will be used infrequently, they should be set at the lower 1 Point/Level cost (the Action/Adventure campaign cost).

Table 4-4: Skill Costs Descriptions

6+ Points/Level	This is appropriate for Skills that define a particular campaign setting and will be vital in nearly all aspects of a story.
5 Points/Level	This is appropriate for Skills that will be used multiple times in a particular game session, or give characters extreme advantages.
4 Points/Level	This is appropriate for general adventuring Skills that characters will find useful in most story lines, or give characters significant advantages.
3 Points/Level	This is appropriate for Skills that are specialised enough that a character might use them only once in a typical session, but which are either of moderate utility or are likely to be important to the campaign.
2 Points/Level	This is appropriate for Skills that may be beneficial, but for which opportunities for use will probably not come up frequently.
1 Point/Level	This is appropriate for Skills that are mainly used to flesh out character backgrounds, but which will not usually be important in play.

General Skills

Acrobatics
Relevant Stat: Body
Specialisations: Balance, Flexibility, Jumps, Tumbling

The ability to perform feats of agility with minimal chance for injury. Includes jumping, flipping, contorting, and reacting quickly.

Animal Training
Relevant Stat: Soul
Specialisations: Any single animal such as dogs, dolphins, horses, etc.

The ability to teach and train animals with an intellect above that of instinctive insects. An animal usually has a Mind Stat of 1-2.

Architecture
Relevant Stat: Mind
Specialisations: Aquatic, Bridges, Fortifications, Small Buildings, Skyscrapers

Knowledge of construction methods, architectural drafting, etc. A successful use of this Skill can also find weak points in constructions or help in locating old structural plans.

Area Knowledge
Relevant Stat: Mind
Specialisations: One specific locale (city, forest, sea, desert, mountain) within the area

Knowledge of the geography and people of a single area (choose one area) and a specific locale within it. The smaller the area, the more detailed and extensive the character's knowledge. This Skill may be assigned multiple times to indicate knowledge of several areas.

Artisan
Relevant Stat: Average of Body and Soul
Specialisations: Carpentry, Leatherworking, Metalworking, Plumbing, Tailoring, Woodworking

This Skill represents a character's ability to work with a variety of materials to repair or produce useful or aesthetically pleasing objects not electronic or mechanical in nature.

Biological Sciences
Relevant Stat: Mind
Specialisations: Bacteria/Viruses, Botany, Ecology, Genetics, Physiology, Zoology

This field covers scientific knowledge of how living things function.

Boating
Relevant Stat: Average of Body and Mind
Specialisations: Hovercraft, Large Ships, Small Boats, Submarines

The ability to safely operate a watercraft.

Burglary
Relevant Stat: Body or Mind
Specialisations: Breaking-and-Entering, Hot-Wiring, Safe Cracking.

The ability to open locks, quietly cut glass, hot-wire car ignitions, etc. The ability does not cover disarming electronic security systems, which is handled by Electronics (Security) Skill.

Climbing
Relevant Stat: Body
Specialisations: Natural Surfaces, Poles, Walls, Vegetation

The ability to scale vertical surfaces with or without the use of specialised climbing equipment.

Skill Groups (Optional Rule)

Some Game Masters and players prefer a less-rigid Skill system for their campaigns — one with which they can indicate general knowledge within an area of expertise without assigning specific Skills. To accommodate this preference, you can use the Skill Groups we provide below ... or create your own custom Groups.

A Skill Group represents a broad area of learning that provides dice roll bonuses the same way that normal Skills do (page 41). Skill Groups do not, however, provide combat bonuses. Rather than specific Skills, however, a Skill Group relates to all aspects within the field, as agreed upon by the GM and player. For example, the Scientific Skill Group usually indicates high levels of competency in: biological sciences, physical sciences, medical sciences, natural sciences, theoretical sciences, etc. A character may possess several Levels in multiple Groups when appropriate.

Skill Groups are acquired with Character Points rather than Skill Points. If Skill Groups are used in your game, Skill Points will probably not be used at all; we do not recommend mixing individual Skills and Skill Groups. Like normal Skills, Skill Group assignments can range from Levels 1 through 10, with a maximum Skill Group Level of one-half X. Skill Groups do not have any Specialisations, however.

Very brief descriptions of the Skill Groups are included to the right.

ADVENTURING Skills that apply to a broad spectrum of high-risk explorations of the unknown in urban or wilderness environments.

BUSINESS Skills that cover a wide variety of business applications, including management, sales, policy, and savvy.

DETECTIVE Skills relating to police sciences, investigations, urban immersion, and subterfuge.

DIPLOMATIC Skills common to world travellers and those with political interests.

EVERYMAN Skills that are often obtained without formal education, and that have applications in daily life.

MILITARY Skills connected to organised troop efforts, espionage, and combat support.

PHILOSOPHY Skills related to artistic endeavours and the social academic fields.

SCIENTIFIC Skills appropriate to trained academics in quantitative fields, such as biological, physical, medical, and natural sciences.

STREET Skills that reflect familiarity with underworld elements as well as urban culture and survival.

TECHNICAL Skills related to gadgets and their functioning, including aspects of mechanics, electronics, and computers.

Table 4-5: Skill Group Costs

Skill Groups	Adventuring	Business	Detective	Diplomatic	Everyman	Skill Groups	Military	Philosophy	Scientific	Street	Technical
Multi-Genre						**Multi-Genre**					
All Campaigns	6	3	5	4	2	All Campaigns	4	2	4	5	3
Modern Day						**Modern Day**					
Action Adventure	6	1	4	1	1	Action Adventure	4	1	2	4	3
Animal Adventures	4	1	3	1	2	Animal Adventures	2	1	1	3	1
Conspiracy	4	2	4	3	2	Conspiracy	2	2	3	3	3
Law Enforcement	4	2	5	2	2	Law Enforcement	3	1	3	3	2
Loony Cartoons	6	1	3	1	1	Loony Cartoons	1	1	1	2	1
Occult / Horror	4	2	4	3	2	Occult / Horror	2	3	3	4	3
Pulp	6	1	5	3	1	Pulp	2	1	2	3	2
Reality TV	3	3	2	2	6	Reality TV	1	2	2	2	4
Romantic Comedy	2	1	3	2	6	Romantic Comedy	1	1	2	3	2
Soap Opera	2	4	4	2	6	Soap Opera	1	3	2	3	2
Superhero	6	3	6	3	2	Superhero	5	2	5	4	4
Urban Fantasy	5	2	3	3	3	Urban Fantasy	2	3	2	5	2
Historical						**Historical**					
20th Century War	4	1	2	2	3	20th Century War	6	1	3	4	1
Age of Pirates	4	2	2	3	3	Age of Pirates	5	1	3	3	2
Ancient China/Japan	3	2	2	3	2	Ancient China/Japan	4	2	1	1	1
Ancient Egypt	3	2	2	2	2	Ancient Egypt	3	2	1	1	1
Ancient Rome/Greece	3	2	2	2	2	Ancient Rome/Greece	3	4	1	1	1
Middle Ages	3	2	2	3	4	Middle Ages	4	2	2	2	1
Old West	6	2	3	2	3	Old West	4	1	2	4	2
Stone Age	4	1	1	1	4	Stone Age	1	3	1	1	1
Victorian	3	2	3	3	4	Victorian	2	3	3	2	2
Fantasy						**Fantasy**					
High Fantasy	6	2	3	3	2	High Fantasy	3	2	2	3	2
Low Fantasy	5	3	3	4	2	Low Fantasy	4	3	3	3	2
Futuristic						**Futuristic**					
Cyberpunk/Biopunk	6	3	4	3	2	Cyberpunk/Biopunk	3	2	4	4	5
Hard SF	3	3	4	5	2	Hard SF	5	4	5	2	5
Mecha	5	1	3	2	2	Mecha	5	1	4	3	5
Post Apocalyptic	5	2	3	3	5	Post Apocalyptic	3	2	3	3	3
Soft SF	4	3	4	4	2	Soft SF	4	3	3	3	4
Space Opera	6	2	4	2	3	Space Opera	4	1	2	4	3

COMPUTERS

RELEVANT STAT: Mind

SPECIALISATIONS: Artificial Intelligence, Databases, Intrusion/Security, Networks, Programming

Practical knowledge of computer use. Computer engineering (hardware) is covered by Electronics.

CONTROLLED BREATHING

RELEVANT STAT: Body or Soul

SPECIALISATIONS: Cyclic Breathing, Holding Breath, Slow Heart Rate

The ability to control respiratory functions in order to maximise breathing efficiency or to perform tricks such as "playing dead."

CULTURAL ARTS

RELEVANT STAT: Mind

SPECIALISATIONS: Archaeology, Art Appraisal, History, Literature, Urban Legends

Knowledge of aspects of human culture (or another species' culture).

DEMOLITIONS

RELEVANT STAT: Body or Mind

SPECIALISATIONS: Artificial Structures, Bomb Disposal, Natural Structures, Safe Cracking, Underwater

The ability to set explosive charges without getting hurt in the process or inflicting undesired collateral damage. It is also used for deactivating explosives set by someone else.

DISGUISE

RELEVANT STAT: Body, Mind, or Soul

SPECIALISATIONS: Costume, Make-up, Prosthetics

The ability to change one's personal appearance in an attempt to deceive others.

DOMESTIC ARTS

RELEVANT STAT: Mind or Soul

SPECIALISATIONS: Cleaning, Cooking, Decorating, Home Budgeting

The ability to efficiently organise and run a domestic household.

DRIVING

RELEVANT STAT: Body or Mind

SPECIALISATIONS: Big Rig (large tractor/trailer trucks), Car, Motorcycle, Small Truck (vans, pick-ups, hi-cubes), Tank

The ability to operate a powered ground vehicle. Skill checks are only necessary in difficult situations such as performing vehicular stunts, avoiding hazards, etc.

ELECTRONICS

RELEVANT STAT: Mind

SPECIALISATIONS: Communications, Computers, Consumer Electronics, Robotics, Security, Sensors

The ability to maintain, repair, build, modify (and at high Levels, design) electronic equipment.

ETIQUETTE

RELEVANT STAT: Mind

SPECIALISATIONS: Lower Class, Middle Class, Upper Class

The knowledge of polite, proper, and inoffensive behaviour in social settings.

FOREIGN CULTURE

RELEVANT STAT: Mind

SPECIALISATIONS: One Specific Culture

Reflects knowledge of the history, religion, ethics, and lifestyle of one or more foreign countries or cultures: one foreign culture at Level 1, two at Level 2, three or four at Level 3, five to eight at Level 4, and more than nine at Level 5. Naturally, less than the maximum number of cultures can be assigned. Thus, multiple Specialisations may be listed for Foreign Culture.

FORGERY

RELEVANT STAT: Mind

SPECIALISATIONS: Electronic Documents, Handwriting, Paper Documents

The ability to counterfeit documents and papers. This Skill can be used in conjunction with the Computers Skill.

GAMING

RELEVANT STAT: Mind or Soul (Body for some video games)

SPECIALISATIONS: Board Games, Computer Games, Gambling/Card Games, Military Simulations, Role-Playing Games

The ability to play various games and simulations well.

INTERROGATION

RELEVANT STAT: Mind or Soul

SPECIALISATIONS: Drugs, Psychological, Physical

The ability to convince someone to provide information against their will. Can also be used to help withhold information when being Interrogated by an enemy.

INTIMIDATION

RELEVANT STAT: Body, Mind, or Soul

SPECIALISATIONS: Business, Political, Street

The ability to convincingly project a "tough guy" image. A successful check means someone witnessing your performance is convinced you mean any threats you make. How they react after that will depend on how tough they are themselves in relation to the kind of threat you present — they may respond with respect, fear, hatred, or amusement.

LANGUAGES

RELEVANT STAT: Mind

SPECIALISATIONS: Any one language, Braille, Code Language, Lip Reading, Sign Language

Reflects an aptitude for languages and their historical usage. Additionally, a character will be able to speak and write one foreign language at Level 1, two at Level 2, three or four at Level 3, five to eight at Level 4, and more than nine at Level 5. Thus, multiple Specialisations will be listed for Languages — the first is the character's native language (a free Specialisation), while the others are foreign languages.

LAW

RELEVANT STAT: Mind

SPECIALISATIONS: Civil, Criminal, Customs, Family, International, Political

Knowledge of legal procedure and practice. GMs may assume that anyone with Level 3 or more has a license to practice law. In addition to lawyers, many police officers, politicians, and superbeings have the Law Skill at Level 1 or 2. All Specialisations, except International, are specific to one country or region only (for example, "American Criminal Law").

MANAGEMENT AND ADMINISTRATION

RELEVANT STAT: Mind

SPECIALISATIONS: Accounting, Banking, Executive, Fraud, Government, Marketing, Small Business

The ability to organise, run, and understand part or all of an organisation (such as a business, government, or association). This Skill is also useful for locating new employees.

MECHANICS

RELEVANT STAT: Mind (sometimes Body)

SPECIALISATIONS: Aeronautical, Armourer, Automotive, Gunsmith, Locksmith, Micro, Traps

The ability to maintain, repair, or build mechanical and electro-mechanical devices. This also includes knowledge of tool use, welding, etc. Armourer applies to heavy vehicle-mounted weapons while Gunsmith covers personal weaponry. Use Artisan for archaic weapons.

MEDICAL

RELEVANT STAT: Mind (sometimes Body)

SPECIALISATIONS: Acupuncture, Dentistry, Diagnosis, Emergency Response, Homeopathy, Pathology, Pharmacy, Surgery, Veterinary

Knowledge of how to heal the body. GMs may assume that anyone with Level 3 or more has a license to practice medicine. A typical general practitioner would Specialise in Diagnosis, while most police officers or paramedics Specialise in Emergency Response.

MILITARY SCIENCES

RELEVANT STAT: Mind

SPECIALISATIONS: Hardware Recognition, Intelligence Analysis, Logistics, Strategy, Tactics, Teamwork

The character has military-style tactical, staff, or leadership training. In addition, SWAT (or other tactical police units) often include individuals who pick up similar Skills (and often recruit ex-military personnel).

NAVIGATION

RELEVANT STAT: Mind

SPECIALISATIONS: Air, Highway, Sea, Space, Urban, Wilderness

The ability to read maps or use specialised navigation equipment. The Navigation Skill will help a character find the fastest/safest route to a destination.

OCCULT

RELEVANT STAT: Mind

SPECIALISATIONS: Astrology, Channelling, Numerology, Rituals, Spirits, Tarot, Voodoo, Witchcraft

Knowledge of the arcane and mystical arts, and their applications in both historical and modern society.

PERFORMING ARTS

RELEVANT STAT: Average of Body, Mind, and Soul

SPECIALISATIONS: Comedy, Dance, Drama, Music, Public Speaking, Singing, Fast Talking

The ability to perform well before an audience, and to evoke an emotional response through the art form.

PHYSICAL SCIENCES

RELEVANT STAT: Mind

SPECIALISATIONS: Astronomy, Biochemistry, Chemistry, Engineering, Geology, Mathematics, Physics

Scientific training in the way the universe works, including the necessary background knowledge.

PILOTING

RELEVANT STAT: Average of Body and Mind

SPECIALISATIONS: Heavy Airplane (usually multi-engine), Helicopter, Jet Fighter, Light Airplane (usually single-engine), Lighter than Air Craft, Spacecraft

The ability to operate air or space vehicles. Skill checks are normally only necessary when performing an unusual manoeuvre, avoiding a hazard, piloting an unfamiliar aircraft, etc.

POISONS

RELEVANT STAT: Mind

SPECIALISATIONS: Alien, Natural, Synthetic

The ability to recognise, concoct, apply, and neutralise a variety of poisons and toxins.

POLICE SCIENCES

RELEVANT STAT: Mind

SPECIALISATIONS: Ballistics, Criminology, Forensics

This is the science behind detective work. Ballistics is the study of the wounds inflicted by projectiles; criminology focuses on studies of criminal behaviour and strategies; forensics covers evidence gathering (including hair-and-fibre, fingerprint and DNA-based identification techniques).

POWER USAGE

RELEVANT STAT: Body, Mind, or Soul

SPECIALISATIONS: One specific Attribute only

Unlike other Skills, Power Usage only offers a Check Value bonus to the Stat check (not Combat check) for one specific Attribute, which is also the Specialisation. To receive a bonus on multiple Attributes, this Skill must be assigned multiple times at 8 Points/Level. The Skill is useful to a character who may not have a high Stat (such as Mind) that is associated with one of his or her Attributes (such as Mind Control or Telepathy). When the character must make a Stat check for the specific Attribute, the Power Usage Skill adds a bonus to the Check Value as though the Stat check is actually a Skill check.

POWERLIFTING

RELEVANT STAT: Body

SPECIALISATIONS: Bulky Objects, Free Weights, Humans, Moving Objects, Small Objects (Hand-Held)

The ability to perform feats of strength with minimal chance for injury. Includes lifting or pushing heavy objects, stopping objects in motion, and supporting large masses.

RIDING

RELEVANT STAT: Body, Mind, or Soul

SPECIALISATIONS: By species (Camel, Horse, Tiger, etc.).

This is the knowledge of how to care for a riding beast, how to saddle, mount, and dismount the animal, how to get it to perform difficult or dangerous manoeuvres safely and without balking, and how to best pace it for long distance rides.

SEDUCTION

RELEVANT STAT: Body or Soul

SPECIALISATIONS: Alien, Female, Male

A character with this Skill is adept at exploiting their sex appeal. A successful Skill check will convince another person that the character is genuinely interested in them. Whether or not the subject actually responds will depend on his or her own romantic inclinations and sexual preferences.

SLEIGHT OF HAND

RELEVANT STAT: Body

SPECIALISATIONS: Card Sharking, Lock Picking, Pick Pocketing, Stage Magic

A character with this Skill (also known as prestidigitation) has superior manual dexterity, greater than that suggested by his or her Body Stat. This includes the ability to perform "magic" tricks, palm small objects, cheat at cards, plant an item on someone, etc.

SOCIAL SCIENCES

RELEVANT STAT: Mind

SPECIALISATIONS: Anthropology, Geography, Politics, Psychology, Social Work, Sociology, Theology

Understanding of the way people function in society as well as societal behavioural patterns.

SPORTS

RELEVANT STAT: Body (sometimes Mind or Soul)

SPECIALISATIONS: Baseball, Basketball, Cricket, Football, Hockey, Volleyball, etc.

The ability to play well with others in a team or individual sporting event with specialised rules.

STEALTH

RELEVANT STAT: Body (sometimes Mind)

SPECIALISATIONS: Camouflage, Concealment, Silent Movement

The ability to disguise objects or people so that they blend into their surroundings. This also includes the ability to conceal small objects on one's person and the ability to move silently.

Street Sense

RELEVANT STAT: Mind or Soul

SPECIALISATIONS: Gang Activity, Influential Individuals, Territorial Divisions (all by region)

The knowledge of street activity within a particular region or city. This is a vital survival Skill for a person on the streets.

Swimming

RELEVANT STAT: Body

SPECIALISATIONS: Competition, Deep-Sea Diving, Free Diving, Scuba, Snorkelling

The character is skilled at swimming or diving. The GM may assume that any character in a modern setting can swim even without this Skill. A swimmer can usually move at a speed equal to his or her Body in kilometres per hour for short distances.

Urban Tracking

RELEVANT STAT: Mind

SPECIALISATIONS: Academic, Corporate, Residential, Underworld

Urban Tracking is the ability to "shadow" someone (or follow a vehicle in another vehicle) through an industrialised, populated area or to find certain people in a particular sub-culture or environment by asking the right questions.

Visual Arts

RELEVANT STAT: Body, Mind, or Soul (often an average)

SPECIALISATIONS: Animation, Drawing, Flower Arranging, Painting, Photography, Sculpting, Video

The ability to produce a work of fine or commercial art in a particular visual field.

Wilderness Survival

RELEVANT STAT: Mind (sometimes Body)

SPECIALISATIONS: Aquatic, Arctic, Desert, Forest, Jungle, Mountain, Plains

The ability to find food and shelter in the outdoors, to avoid natural hazards, and to identify wild plants and animals.

Wilderness Tracking

RELEVANT STAT: Mind (sometimes Soul)

SPECIALISATIONS: Aquatic, Arctic, Desert, Forest, Jungle, Mountain, Plains

The ability to successfully trail or track someone or something while outdoors in a rural or wilderness setting.

Writing

RELEVANT STAT: Average of Mind and Soul

SPECIALISATIONS: Academic, Fiction, Journalistic, Poetic, Technical

The ability to communicate ideas or emotions in a written work.

Combat Skills

Archery

RELEVANT STAT: None (uses Attack Combat Value)

SPECIALISATIONS: Bow, Crossbow

The ability to accurately shoot with a bow or crossbow. This is an Attack Combat Skill.

Gun Combat

RELEVANT STAT: None (uses Attack Combat Value)

SPECIALISATIONS: Auto-fire, Pistol, Rifle

The ability to accurately shoot with a hand-held firearm and to keep it properly maintained. Auto-fire applies to firing bursts of fully automatic fire from any gun, whether it is a small submachine gun, a big assault rifle, or a heavy machine gun. Pistol applies to firing single shots from a handgun. Rifle covers firing single shots from guns with a shoulder stock including rifles and shotguns. This is an Attack Combat Skill.

Heavy Weapons

RELEVANT STAT: None (uses Attack Combat Value)

SPECIALISATIONS: Artillery (indirect fire weapons such as Howitzers), Gunnery (heavy machine guns, tank guns and other vehicle-mounted direct-fire weapons), Launchers (rocket and missile launchers)

The ability to accurately fire vehicle-, shoulder-, or tripod-mounted weapons such as a tank cannon or heavy machine gun, and to perform routine maintenance. This is an Attack Combat Skill.

Melee Attack

RELEVANT STAT: None (uses Attack Combat Value)

SPECIALISATIONS: Axe, Baton/Club, Knife, Improvised Weapons (chairs, lamps, ladders, etc.), Polearms (spears, naginata, etc.), Shield, Sword, Whips/Chains

The ability to attack effectively with a hand-to-hand melee weapon. This is an Attack Combat Skill.

Melee Defence

RELEVANT STAT: None (uses Defence Combat Value)

SPECIALISATIONS: Axe, Baton/Club, Knife, Improvised Weapons, Polearms (spears, naginata, etc.), Shield, Sword, Whips/Chains

The ability to defend well with a hand-to-hand melee weapon. This is a Defence Combat Skill.

Ranged Defence

RELEVANT STAT: None (uses Defence Combat Value)

SPECIALISATIONS: Personal, Air Vehicle, Ground Vehicle, Water Vehicle, Space Vehicle

The ability to avoid ranged attacks, but this does not enable a character to actually dodge bullets. Rather, it is a combination of situational awareness and tactical movement as well as knowing when to keep moving (to present a more difficult target) and when to drop for cover. This is a Defence Combat Skill.

Special Ranged Attack

RELEVANT STAT: None (uses Attack Combat Value)

SPECIALISATIONS: One specific Special Attack

This Skill is used for weapons created using the Special Attack Attribute (page 32) that emanate from the character's body, rather than a device or weapon. For example, eye beams, fireballs fired from the hand, or sonic blast shot from the mouth would qualify, but a laser gun or a deadly boomerang would not. This is an Attack Combat Skill.

Thrown Weapons

RELEVANT STAT: None (uses Attack Combat Value)

SPECIALISATIONS: Blades, Cards, Grenades, Rocks, Shields

The ability to accurately throw weapons or objects at a target. This is an Attack Combat Skill.

Unarmed Attack

RELEVANT STAT: None (uses Attack Combat Value)

SPECIALISATIONS: Strikes, Holds, Throws, Grappling

The ability to attack without weapons. This is an Attack Combat Skill.

Unarmed Defence

RELEVANT STAT: None (uses Defence Combat Value)

SPECIALISATIONS: Strikes, Holds, Throws, Grappling

The ability to block armed or unarmed melee attacks without using a weapon. This is a Defence Combat Skill.

STEP 6: SELECT DEFECTS

Defects are disadvantages through which your character must suffer in order to overcome the hardships of day-to-day life. Defects serve as an excellent and often comical role-playing opportunity. They only impede your character to a limited extent and are not intended to totally negate his or her many abilities. The Defects that have "Linked to Attribute" in their description are direct limitations on your character's Attributes, rather than more general disadvantages (BP returned by linked Defect cannot exceed Attribute cost).

My Overconfident, Lazy, Stubborn, Honourable Character

No, you don't get any Bonus Points for creating overconfident characters in Tri-Stat. Or truthful ones, or sadistic ones, or shy ones. Less desirable personality traits should appear in the game through role-playing, not Points on a character sheet. If your character is a coward, then portray him or her as cowardly. It's just that simple.

Defects represent disadvantages over which your character has little or no control (i.e. no free will). One example is Phobia — a person with an irrational fear has no choice but to be afraid of the specific trigger. A Phobia is not a personality trait.

By taking a Character Defect you can gain up to three (or occasionally more) Bonus Points (BP) to use when acquiring Stats or Attributes. The number of Points you receive is directly proportional to how much the Defect hinders your character; Defects that do not inflict a significant disadvantage (such as a weakness to bullets made from the earth of planet Neptune) are not worth any Bonus Points. After you have selected your character's Defects, return to the previous steps to use your Bonus Points.

It is recommended that you assign no more than eight Defects to your character (this limit does not apply to Defects linked to an Attribute). In most cases 2-5 Defects are appropriate.

DEFECTS AND DUAL IDENTITIES

If a character maintains a dual identity through the Skeleton in the Closet (Secret Identity) Defect, some other Defects may not affect him or her in one of the identities. For example, a masked vigilante may be wanted by the police on murder charges (the Wanted Defect), but his or her alternate identity may be a respected politician. In these instances, the character will receive Bonus Points at a reduced amount.

If either the character's normal or secret identity (but not both) suffers from a Defect, the Bonus Points granted are reduced by 1 BP. If both identities suffer from the identical Defect, at the same or different BP Levels, the character is granted Bonus Points equal to the higher BP Level. If a character only has one identity, the Defects return Bonus Points as normal.

Defects associated with an Alternate Form (page 12) usually provide Bonus Points directly to the Form's Point total. The GM may decide that some of these Defects function the same as they do for the Skeleton in the Closet Defect, though (at low BP ranks), rather than apply to the Alternate Form directly.

ACHILLES HEEL

The character loses twice as many Health Points as normal from a particular attack form, which must fit with the character concept. It might be something with appropriate mystic resonance, such as wooden stakes for vampires or silver for werewolves. It could also reflect the character's nature such as a fire-based villain taking extra damage from water, or an alien's weakness to weapons from his or her home planet. The GM must approve any Achilles Heel Defects. A character may have an Achilles Heel to either a common, uncommon, or rare attack form (in the context of the campaign).

1 BP The attack form is rare.

2 BP The attack form is uncommon.

3 BP The attack form is common.

Table 5-1: Defects

Defect Name	Progression	Page
Achilles Heel	1-3 BP	50
Activation Time	1-10 BP	50
Awkward Size	1-10 BP	51
Backlash	1-3 BP	51
Bane	1-3 BP	51
Blind Fury	1-3 BP	51
Burns Energy	1-10 BP	51
Concentration	1-3 BP	51
Conditional Ownership	1-3 BP	51
Confined Movement	1-3 BP	52
Cursed	1-3 BP	52
Dependent	2,4,6 BP	52
Detectable	1-3 BP	52
Diminutive	2,4,6 BP	52
Easily Distracted	1-3 BP	52
Famous	1-3 BP	52
Inept Attack	3,6,9 BP	53
Inept Defence	2,4,6 BP	53
Involuntary Change	1-3 BP	53
Ism	1-3 BP	53
Less Capable	1-10 BP	53
Limited Use, Instantaneous	1-3 BP	53
Limited Use, Ongoing	1-3 BP	53
Marked	1-3 BP	54
Maximum Force	1-3 BP	54
Nemesis	1-3 BP	54
Not So Tough	1-3 BP	54
One-Way Transformation	1-3 BP	54
Owned	1-3 BP	54
Part of Body	1-3 BP	54
Permanent	1-3 BP	54
Phobia	1-3 BP	54
Physical Impairment	1-3 BP	55
Recurring Nightmares	1-3 BP	55
Red Tape	1-3 BP	55
Reduction	Special	55
Restriction	1-3 BP	55
Sensory Impairment	1-3 BP	55
Significant Other	1-3 BP	56
Skeleton in the Closet	1-3 BP	56
Special Requirement	1-3 BP	56
Unappealing	1-3 BP	56
Unique Defect	1-3 BP	56
Unreliable Power	1-3 BP	56
Unskilled	1-3 BP	57
Vulnerability	1-3 BP	57
Wanted	1-3 BP	57
Weak Point	1-3 BP	57

ACTIVATION TIME

Linked to Attribute. A character with this Defect cannot use one of his or her Attributes whenever desired because the Attribute requires a short time to activate. Once activation has started, only the character can stop it from becoming active when the appropriate time is up. This could represent a physical change that is not instantaneous, the collection of spiritual energies to perform a task, a device that takes time to "power up," or an Attribute that only works when the character is mentally prepared (or angry, or overcome with another emotion).

Activation Time extends to 10 BP following the Time Progression Chart, starting at 10 Initiative (1 BP) and increasing to 1 month (10 BP). Additionally, the Defect may return an additional 1 or 2 Bonus Points to the character. 1 additional BP is granted if the activation can be interrupted temporarily, but restarted where it left off. One example of this is an Item of Power body suit that the character must put on. If the character stops activating the Attribute (i.e. stops dressing) to make a phone call, he or she can continue afterwards. 2 additional BP are granted if the activation must start again from the beginning if it is interrupted before the Activation Time has elapsed. An example of this is a spell that must be chanted completely before the Attribute activates; if it is interrupted, the spell must be started again from the beginning. The Concentration Defect (page 51) is often linked to these two applications of Activation Time.

AWKWARD SIZE

This Defect means the character is notably larger than an ordinary human. A character with Awkward Size may have trouble fitting through doors and moving through narrow hallways, and does not fit into many vehicles. A character with Awkward Size is also much easier to notice. The larger the character, the more BP this Defect will be worth. In most cases, Awkward Size above 1 BP is not appropriate for human characters, only for robots, aliens, giant monsters, or similar entities.

Awkward Size extends to Level 10 following the Slow Magnitude Chart, starting at 2.5 to 4 metres tall (x2 height; Level 1) increasing to 2000 metres tall (1000x height; Level 10). Mass increases proportionally as a cubed function of the height multiplier, starting at 0.8 tonnes (Level 1) increasing to 27,000 tonnes (Level 5), and finally to 1 billion tonnes (Level 10). An elephant, for example, would be Awkward Size Level 2.

BACKLASH

Linked to Attribute. The character suffers from an unfortunate side effect whenever an associated Attribute fails to work. If the character fails his or her Stat check when using the Attribute, the character is hit with the energy or essence that would have powered the Attribute's use. The Backlash could be physical damage, memory loss, Stat drain, disorientation, or many other effects that make the character's life more difficult. The player and GM should determine the game effect of the Backlash.

1 BP The backlash occurs if the character fails the check by 6 or more.

2 BP The backlash occurs if the character fails the check by 3 or more.

3 BP The backlash occurs if the character fails the check by 1 or more.

BANE

A character with the Bane Defect is vulnerable to an otherwise non-damaging substance such as water, sunlight, or a specific element, material, or object. The Bane should relate to the character's background or Attributes in some way.

The character suffers damage if his or her skin is physically touched by the Bane. If the Bane does not require direct physical contact (such as sunlight, seeing one's reflection, hearing the noise of a church or temple bell, or having the Bane in close proximity), the damage is halved. Alternatively, if the Bane only affects the character when ingested, the damage is doubled. Finally, the damage rating assumes that the Bane is common, such as water, sunlight, steel, or wood. If it is less common, such as a holy symbol, Buddhist scripture, or rare element, the damage is also doubled. If it is even more rare such as one particular artefact, the damage may be tripled or quadrupled.

1 BP The Bane causes minor damage (20 points/round of exposure).

2 BP The Bane causes moderate damage (40 points/round of exposure).

3 BP The Bane causes severe damage (60 points/round of exposure).

BLIND FURY

Under specific conditions selected by the player (and approved by the GM), the character will enter a state of unbridled anger. While enraged, the character will furiously attack the closest person, whether that individual is a friend or foe. Once that person is defeated or flees, the berserk character will attack the next closest "threat." Examples of conditions that might initiate Blind Fury include: receiving a certain amount of damage, sight of blood, a specific sound or smell, being outnumbered in combat, seeing a friend in mortal danger, confrontation with a specific opponent, etc.

The character can only return to a normal emotional state under another specific condition. This return could involve a Soul Stat check, or could be an automatic reversion. Examples of return conditions include: no opponents in the vicinity, a specific calming technique performed by an ally, solitude, injection of a particular drug, being knocked unconscious, etc.

1 BP Initiating the Blind Fury is difficult; reverting to normal emotional state is easy.

2 BP Initiating the Blind Fury and reverting to a normal emotional state are both moderately difficult.

3 BP Initiating the Blind Fury is easy; reverting to normal emotional state is difficult.

BURNS ENERGY

Linked to Attribute. This Defect is only available in campaigns where Energy Points are used. The character's Energy Points are used to power a particular Attribute. The Energy Points will either be reduced after the Attributes use (for Attributes for immediate effects, such as Teleportation or Special Attack), or while the Attribute is used (for Attributes that are used over a period of time, such as Flight or Invisibility).

Burns Energy extends to 10 BP. For immediate effects, reduce the Energy Points by: 1 (1 BP), 2 (2 BP), 5 (3 BP), 10 (4 BP), 15 (5 BP), 20 (6 BP), 30 (7 BP), 50 (8 BP), 80 (9 BP), or 100 (10 BP). For Attributes used over a period of time, reduce the Energy Points as follows: 10/day (1 BP), 1/hour (2 BP), 5/hour (3 BP), 10/hour (4 BP), 1/minute (5 BP), 5/minute (6 BP), 10/minute (7 BP), 5/round (8 BP), 10/round (9 BP), or 5/second (10 BP).

CONCENTRATION

Linked to Attribute (or the Activation Time Defect, page 50). The character must concentrate while using a specific Attribute that functions over a period of time; it does not apply to Attributes with an instantaneous effect. If the character's concentration is interrupted voluntarily or by an outside event, the Attribute ceases to function.

1 BP The Attribute requires slight concentration. The character can still perform other non-combat actions, but cannot engage in combat or use other Attributes that also require Concentration.

2 BP The Attribute requires intense concentration. The character can move at a slow speed and talk with others while using the Attribute, but cannot perform any complex actions or use any other Attribute.

3 BP The Attribute requires full concentration. The character cannot do anything else while using the Attribute; he or she must remain still and devote full attention to the Attribute.

CONDITIONAL OWNERSHIP

Linked to Characteristic Attribute. This Defect can only be acquired by a character who possesses either the Item of Power or Gadgets Attributes (pages 24 and 21). The character's possessions granted by those Attributes actually belong to another person or organisation. They are issued to the character, but the agency imposes "mild," "strict," or "severe" conditions on their use.

"Mild conditions" indicate that the character can use the objects for some personal business (such as travelling), but if he or she is released from the organisation or disobeys direct orders, the objects can be taken away. The character can also be assigned different objects at any time. For example, a police detective might have conditional use of an unmarked police car.

"Strict conditions" indicate that the character is only permitted to use the objects for activities as ordered by the organisation. This is the way most military and police equipment is issued. If the character is caught using the objects for personal activities, he or she will receive a severe reprimand.

"Severe conditions" indicate that the character can only use the objects under specific orders. A government-owned time travel device would probably fall under these conditions. Using the objects at any other time results in incarceration, physical punishment, or even death.

1 BP Mild conditions are imposed on the objects' ownership and usage.

2 BP Strict conditions are imposed on the objects' ownership and usage.

3 BP Severe conditions are imposed on the objects' ownership and usage.

CONFINED MOVEMENT

This Defect prevents the character from leaving a narrowly defined area. This may represent an undead creature that is cursed to haunt a particular place, an android that is programmed to follow a specific guard route, or a government-licensed superhero that is only registered for travel in a specific region.

1 BP Restricted to a large area (100 km radius), such as a single county or large city.

2 BP Restricted to a small area (1 km radius), such as a small town or large, multi-structure complex.

3 BP Restricted to a tiny area (100 m radius), such as a small village or single building.

CURSED

A Cursed character has likely offended a great being of power in his or her past, or is the direct descendent of someone who did (Curses often pass through bloodlines). The Curse can take a near limitless number of forms, but should not provide a character with an obvious advantage (remember, it's a Curse!). The exact nature, background, and limitations of the Curse should be discussed with the GM.

1 BP The character suffers from a slight disadvantage.

2 BP The character suffers from a moderate disadvantage.

3 BP The character suffers from a severe disadvantage.

DEPENDENT

Linked to Attribute. The character cannot use the chosen Attribute without first using a second (or more) Attribute. If the character fails a Stat check to activate the second Attribute, he or she cannot use the other one either. Examples of the Dependent Defect include: a character who can fly after activating his Force Field (Flight Dependent upon Force Field), a character who gains additional Armour when invisible (Armour Dependent upon Invisibility), a character that can run much more quickly after stretching his or her legs and growing (Speed Dependent upon Elasticity and Grow), etc. The player must justify the Dependent Defect to the GM to avoid silly combinations.

2 BP The Dependent Attribute cannot work until 1 other Attribute is activated.

4 BP The Dependent Attribute cannot work until 2 other Attributes are activated.

6 BP The Dependent Attribute cannot work until 3 other Attributes are activated.

DETECTABLE

Linked to Attribute. While using a specific Attribute, the character can be pinpointed and possibly identified by others who have specific detection techniques. For example, the Attribute's use may make a loud noise or a bright flash, send vibrations through the ground, or emanate mental shock waves. Detection techniques include: astral; ethereal; human sight, hearing, or sense of smell; infrared; mental; radar; radiation; sonar; spiritual; ultraviolet; vibration; and others. The Special Attack Attribute (page 32) is an exception to this Defect — characters must acquire an Attack Ability to make the attack undetectable.

1 BP The Attribute's use can be detected using 1-2 methods.

2 BP The Attribute's use can be detected using 3-5 methods.

3 BP The Attribute's use can be detected using 6-9 methods.

DIMINUTIVE

The character is permanently smaller than a human. Although a Diminutive character is physically weaker than an average human, he or she is able to get into spaces that a human cannot and may be small enough to hide in someone's pocket. The Level progression is similar to the Shrink Attribute (page 31), but Diminutive is a disadvantage — the character does not have the option of shrinking to different Levels whenever desired, since the Defect is permanent.

Diminutive provides 2, 4, or 6 Bonus Points.

2 BP The character is the size of a cat or small dog. His or her running speed and weapon range is reduced to 20%, and he or she can only lift up to one hundredth (1%) normal capacity (for an average human, this is approximately 1 kilogram). Any damage the character inflicts using physical melee attacks is reduced by 10, while attacks from human-sized enemies inflict an additional 10 damage. Enemies making ranged attacks, however, suffer a -4 Attack penalty. Finally, he or she suffers a -6 penalty on any Body Stats checks that require lifting, carrying, or grappling with objects larger than cat size.

4 BP The character is the size of a rodent. His or her running speed and weapon range is reduced to 5%, and he or she can only lift up to one ten thousandth (0.01%) normal capacity (for an average human, this is approximately 10 grams). Any damage the character inflicts using physical melee attacks is reduced by 15, while attacks from human-sized enemies inflict an additional 15 damage. Enemies making ranged attacks, however, suffer a -6 Attack penalty. Finally, he or she suffers a -12 penalty on any Body Stats checks that require lifting, carrying, or grappling with objects larger than cat size (-6 penalty for larger than rodent size).

6 BP The character is the size of a bug. His or her running speed and weapon range is reduced one two hundredth (0.5%), and he or she can only lift up to one ten millionth normal capacity (for an average human, this is approximately 10 milligrams). Any damage the character inflicts using physical melee attacks is reduced by 20, while attacks from human-sized enemies inflict an additional 20 damage. Enemies making ranged attacks, however, suffer a -8 Attack penalty. Finally, he or she suffers a -18 penalty on any Body Stats checks that require lifting, carrying, or grappling with objects larger than cat size (-12 penalty for larger than rodent size; -6 penalty for larger than bug size).

EASILY DISTRACTED

Some characters are Easily Distracted by events, objects, people, or ideas, which are collectively known as triggers. Notable examples of triggers include attractive members of the opposite (or same) sex, wealth, food, movie stars, hobbies, gossip, hot cars, music, one's own looks, books or scrolls of ancient lore, and magical items. A character with this Defect will become enthralled with the trigger until it can no longer influence him or her. Many characters have interests in a variety of triggers but do not possess this Defect because their interest is moderated by their sense of judgement.

1 BP The character is distracted by a trigger that is encountered infrequently.

2 BP The character is distracted by a few infrequent triggers, or by one trigger that is encountered frequently.

3 BP The character is distracted by several infrequent triggers, or by one trigger that is encountered constantly.

FAMOUS

The character is recognizable by many people, and thus it is difficult for him or her to keep secrets or maintain a private life. Journalists and photographers may hound the character regularly, and report his or her actions on television, in newspapers, and on websites. While being Famous may have some privileges (preferred seating at restaurants, daily special treatment, etc.), it can be a significant disadvantage for someone who maintains a secret identity.

1 BP	The character has regional fame.
2 BP	The character has national fame.
3 BP	The character has international fame.

INEPT ATTACK

This Defect reflects a character's poor judgement in offensive combat situations, which makes it much more difficult to strike an opponent successfully. A character with the Inept Attack Defect suffers a penalty to the Attack Combat Value. The penalty cannot lower the Value below 1. See page 57 more information on the Attack Combat Value. Inept Attack provides 3, 6, or 9 Bonus Points.

3 BP	The character's Attack Combat Value is decreased by 1 Point.
6 BP	The character's Attack Combat Value is decreased by 2 Points.
9 BP	The character's Attack Combat Value is decreased by 3 Points.

INEPT DEFENCE

This Defect reflects a character's poor judgement in defensive combat situations, which can often place him or her in precarious positions. A character with the Inept Defence Defect suffers a Defence Combat Value penalty. The penalty cannot lower the Value below 1. See page 57 for more information on the Defence Combat Value. Inept Defence provides 2, 4, or 6 Bonus Points.

2 BP	The character's Defence Combat Value is decreased by 1 Point.
4 BP	The character's Defence Combat Value is decreased by 2 Points.
6 BP	The character's Defence Combat Value is decreased by 3 Points.

INVOLUNTARY CHANGE

This Defect is only available to characters who have the Alternate Form Attribute. The character may accidentally change from human form to the Alternate Form (or vice versa), or an external trigger (opponent, ally, natural force, etc.) may induce the change. This Defect may represent a character who: transforms between identities upon hearing or uttering a specific sound or word, reverts to normal form when a particular chemical in the body is in low quantities (such as sugar or salt), transforms when a button on a gadget or Item of Power is pushed, transforms in times of stress, etc.

This Defect is assigned once to indicate the character can accidentally change from human to the alternate identity, or vice versa. The Defect is assigned twice if the character can transform both ways unintentionally.

1 BP	It is difficult to trigger the Involuntary Change.
2 BP	It is moderately easy to trigger the Involuntary Change.
3 BP	It is very easy to trigger the Involuntary Change.

ISM

Ism is discrimination based solely on one particular aspect of a character. Examples of Ism include: ageism, elitism, racism, sexism, or discrimination based on education, species, genetics, sexual preference, occupation, religion, physical features, etc. The players and GM are strongly encouraged to discuss these contentious discrimination issues, and their role in the game, before play begins.

1 BP	The character experiences a small degree of discrimination.
2 BP	The character experiences a large degree of discrimination.
3 BP	The character experiences a severe degree of discrimination.

LESS CAPABLE

Currently, the three game Stats indicate the same level of ability in all aspects of each Stat: the Body Stat represents all physical aspects, the Mind Stat represents all mental aspects, and the Soul Stat represents all spiritual and willpower aspects. Some characters may have one or more aspects of a Stat at a less proficient level than the rest of the Stat aspects, however, and this is where the Less Capable Defect comes in.

For example, a bulky brawler might have a high strength, excellence endurance, fast running speed, good manual dexterity, and healthy immune system ... but be rather clumsy. This would fit a character with a Body Stat of 8 or 10, with the Less Capable (Agility) Defect at 2 BP. Similarly, a witty, perceptive, and insightful academic genius that happens to have a surprisingly bad memory might have a Mind Stat of 9, with the Less Capable (Memory) Defect at 1 BP.

Every Stat has a multitude of aspects associated with it, that are considered either Major Aspects (aspects that arise frequently in a game) or Minor Aspects (aspects that arise infrequently). For each BP Level of the Less Capable Defect, Stat or Skill checks for which the specific Major Aspects is important suffer a -3 penalty, while Stat or Skill checks for which the specific Minor Aspects is important suffer a -6 penalty. Less Capable can typically extend to 6 BP for Major Aspects or 3 BP for Minor Aspects. Derived Values are not recalculated.

Each Stat has three Major and three Minor Aspects listed below. Players may create additional Aspects with the Game Master's input.

BODY

Strength, Agility, Endurance (Major); Manual Dexterity, Running Speed, Immune System (Minor)

MIND

Intelligence, Wits, Perception (Major); Memory, Intuition, Savvy (Minor)

SOUL

Luck, Willpower, Charisma (Major); Presence, Empathy, Composure (Minor)

ALL STAT ASPECTS

There are rare occasions in which a character may need the Less Capable Defect to apply to all aspects of a specific Stat. This usually applies to characters that undergo a radical change from one form to another, such as that induced by the Alternate Form Attribute (page 12). For example, a scientist character with a Mind Stat of 11 who transforms into a hulking beast may need to reduce his or her Mind Stat to 3 with a Less Capable Mind Defect. For this application, a -1 is applied to the character's specific Stat checks for every 2 BP Levels of the Less Capable Defect assigned. All Derived Values must be recalculated for this application of Less Capable.

LIMITED USE, INSTANTANEOUS

Linked to Attribute with an instantaneous effect. The character can only use a specific Attribute occasionally. This may result from a need to recharge the Attribute (or a device), an incredible drain on the character's internal reserves, or a different form of limitation. Only under exceptional circumstances (and at a great sacrifice) can the character use the Attribute more often than indicated by this Defect. This Defect is usually incompatible with the Burns Energy Defect.

1 BP	The character can only use the Attribute three times a day.
2 BP	The character can only use the Attribute twice a day.
3 BP	The character can only use the Attribute once a day.

LIMITED USE, ONGOING

Linked to an Attribute that can be used on an ongoing basis. After the character uses a specific Attribute, he or she cannot use it again for a specific period of time; the longer the Attribute is used, the longer the rest period must be. For example, the muscles of a character with Superstrength may need time to recuperate after use, or an Item of Power that grants Flight may need to be recharged between uses. Only under exceptional circumstances (and at a great sacrifice) can the character use the Attribute again before the waiting period has elapsed. This Defect is usually incompatible with the Burns Energy Defect.

1 BP	For every minute the character uses the Attribute, he or she must wait 1 minute before the Attribute functions once again.
2 BP	For every minute the character uses the Attribute, he or she must wait 5 minutes before the Attribute functions once again.
3 BP	For every minute the character uses the Attribute, he or she must wait 10 minutes before the Attribute functions once again.

MARKED

A character is considered Marked if his or her body hosts a permanent and distinguishing design that may be difficult to conceal. The design may be a family symbol, an identifying birthmark, a permanent scar, or a unique tattoo. If the mark is not considered out of the ordinary (such as freckles or a common tattoo), this Defect does not apply. Characters who are obviously non-human (robotic, demonic, alien, etc.) in a setting where most people are human (or vice versa) would also have the Marked Defect.

1 BP The mark is easily concealable because it is small or in an inconspicuous location.

2 BP The mark can be concealed, but this is difficult because it is large or in an obvious location.

3 BP Under most circumstances, the mark cannot be concealed because it affects the character's entire body.

MAXIMUM FORCE

Linked to Attribute. The character cannot use a specific Attribute at the lowest end of its power range. This could represent a character who is too talented for his or her own good, an item that only functions within certain parameters, a powerful character who pushes the Attribute's limits so often that he or she has forgotten how to use it at a low Level, or something different.

This Defect is only appropriate for the following Attributes: Animal Summon/Control, Creation, Dynamic Powers, Elasticity, Flight, Grow, Hyperflight, Illusion, Insubstantial, Jumping, Mass Increase, Plant Control, Projection, Shrink, Special Attack (applies to damage only), Speed, Teleport, Transmutation, and Water Speed.

Maximum Force extends to Level 10, providing 1 BP each Level. The restriction on an Attribute's use is given below, where Z is the number of Bonus Points granted and (Z+1) is one Level higher than the BP Level.

Z BP The character cannot use up to Level Z of the Attribute. The Attribute must be at Level (Z+1) or higher.

NEMESIS

The character has someone in his or her life that actively interferes with goal achievement on a regular basis. This Nemesis can take several forms. He or she could be a professional rival such as someone competing for the favour of the character's boss. The Nemesis could also be personal; for example, a criminal may be pursued by a specific law enforcement officer who devotes his or her existence to putting the character behind bars. The Nemesis may even be a romantic rival such as someone chasing the same person the character is pursuing.

The Nemesis should be someone who makes the character's life difficult frequently (and cannot easily be removed), but the Nemesis does not need to be a mortal enemy. It might be someone the character loves very much, but one whom they cannot avoid. An overbearing parent who lives at home is an example of this. If for any reason the Nemesis is defeated or goes away, the GM should create another Nemesis, unless the player also wishes to use Advancement Points (page 73) to eliminate the Defect permanently.

1 BP The Nemesis is merely annoying and/or interferes infrequently.

2 BP The Nemesis may actively try to harm the character and/or interferes frequently.

3 BP The Nemesis will always harm the character given the opportunity, and/or interferes constantly.

NOT SO TOUGH

The character is less durable than his or her Body and Soul Stats would otherwise suggest. This Defect is appropriate for characters with a "glass jaw," or those who succumb to physical trauma easily.

1 BP The character's Health Points are decreased by 10 Points.

2 BP The character's Health Points are decreased by 20 Points.

3 BP The character's Health Points are decreased by 30 Points.

ONE-WAY TRANSFORMATION

Linked to Attribute. This Defect can only be taken in conjunction with the Alternate Form, Elasticity, Grow, Insubstantial, Invisibility, Mass Increase, or Shrink Attributes. Once the character has transformed from a normal state, he or she cannot transform back to a prior form without meeting certain conditions. This might include a magical ritual, work by mechanics or lab technicians, consuming a specific substance, or simply the passage of time.

1 BP It takes several hours of work or special circumstances to enable the character to transform back to an earlier form.

2 BP As 1 BP, but the process requires expensive (or hard to find) replacement components, ingredients, or other prerequisites.

3 BP As 2 BP, but the process takes several days.

OWNED

Free will has little meaning for a character who is Owned by a corporation, government, crime ring, or other organisation or individual. Control over the character can be exerted through a variety of methods including blackmail, brainwashing, legal contract, technology, or just highly effective propaganda. Dire consequences await a character whose actions conflict with the mandate of the owning body.

1 BP The organisation has partial ownership of the character; the character is subject to slight punishment for opposing the owners.

2 BP The organisation has significant ownership of the character; the character is subject to moderate punishment for opposing the owners.

3 BP The organisation has total ownership of the character; the character is subject to severe punishment for opposing the owners.

PART OF BODY

Linked to Attribute. Only part of the character's body is affected by a specific Attribute, most commonly used for: Adaptation, Alternate Form, Armour, Damage Absorption, Damage Conversion, Insubstantial, Invisibility, and Superstrength. For example, a character might only receive Armour benefits against abdominal attacks, possess the ability to turn his or her left arm invisible, or have bionic legs with Superstrength.

1 BP The Attribute affects a large part of the body (torso, both legs, both arms, etc.).

2 BP The Attribute affects a small part of the body (one leg, one arm, abdomen, chest, head, etc.)

3 BP The Attribute affects a tiny part of the body (one hand, face, one foot, groin, knee, etc.).

PERMANENT

Linked to Attribute. A specific Attribute is always functioning, and the character cannot turn it off. This Defect only applies to Attributes that would inconvenience the character if the Attribute was always active, such as: Force Field, Insubstantial, Invisibility, or Nullify. The player and GM should discuss the problems and limitations associated with an eternally active Attribute.

1 BP The Attribute is a slight inconvenience to the character.

2 BP The Attribute is a moderate inconvenience to the character.

3 BP The Attribute is a severe inconvenience to the character.

PHOBIA

A Phobia is a fear (often irrational) of an event, object, or person that can limit a character's choice of actions. Avoiding situations that could trigger the phobia may take a high priority in the character's life. Note that a Phobia that effectively cripples the character with fear does not add constructively to the role-playing experience.

1 BP The character has a slight phobia or one that is encountered infrequently.

2 BP The character has a moderate phobia or one that is encountered frequently.

3 BP The character has a severe phobia or one that is encountered constantly.

PHYSICAL IMPAIRMENT

The character has a physical impairment that makes aspects of daily life more challenging. Possible impairments include: one or more missing (or unusable) limbs, loss of speech, constant sickness, nagging injury, severe headaches, an android that requires frequent repairs, etc. The player and GM should discuss the problems and limitations associated with the impairment.

1 BP   The impairment is a slight inconvenience to the character.

2 BP   The impairment is a moderate inconvenience to the character.

3 BP   The impairment is a severe inconvenience to the character.

RECURRING NIGHTMARES

When the Recurring Nightmare Defect haunts a character, he or she has trouble sleeping at nights and functions at less-than-optimum performance during the day. The nightmare can be a memory of a tragic event or traumatic experience, or it might be something else such as a prophetic vision or warning. The nightmare may not occur every night but it will haunt the character on a regular basis. Additionally, the nightmares do not need to portray the exact same events repeatedly, but the visions should be related in some way. The details concerning the subject matter of the nightmares and why they occur is the responsibility of the GM and the player to create.

1 BP   The nightmares occur infrequently and have a slight effect on the character's lifestyle.

2 BP   The nightmares occur frequently and have a moderate effect on the character's lifestyle.

3 BP   The nightmares occur constantly and have a severe effect on the character's lifestyle.

RED TAPE

The character must negotiate his or her way through a complicated bureaucracy in order to accomplish tasks. This Defect is often associated with characters who are members of law-enforcement organisations or similar government agencies that require paperwork. A large criminal organisation, however, may also require a character to receive permission from several levels of bosses before undertaking certain high-profile jobs.

Red Tape also includes whatever measures the character must take "after the fact" to appease the organisation to which he or she belongs. For example, a cop may need to fill out a report every time his or her weapon is fired or may have to follow a complicated series of steps to obtain a search warrant. A thug may be required to pay a percentage of his or her take to the regional crime organisation or face some very strict penalties.

The Red Tape Defect is inappropriate for characters created via the Agents, Henchmen, or Servant Attributes.

1 BP   The Red Tape only impedes the character before or after a major action (but not both) and/or the Red Tape is easy to manage most of the time.

2 BP   The Red Tape impedes a character both before and after a major action, and/or is difficult to manage most of the time.

3 BP   The Red Tape impedes a character before, after, and during a major action, and/or is extremely difficult to manage most of the time.

REDUCTION

Linked to Characteristic or Attribute. One of the character's Attributes is limited greatly, resulting in a Reduction of its Point cost per Level. This Defect offers a near-endless number of limitations, and consequently the player and GM should discuss the game ramifications and the Attribute's new Level costs.

Each Attribute description provides one sample Reduction. This entry is only a suggestion, and does not represent the only Reductions available. A list of suggested Reductions are shown in Table 5-2: Sample Reductions.

Unlike other Defects, Reduction does not return Bonus Points to the character; the Attribute cost changes instead. The Point cost change is directly related to the original cost of the Attribute. For example, a Reduction that limits a 4 Points/Level

Attribute to half of its power might be a 2 Points/Level Reduction; the same limitation on a 10 Points/Level Attribute could be a 5 Points/Level Reduction. This Defect is not usually appropriate for 1 Point/Level Attributes.

Table 5-2: Sample Reductions

Fewer sub-Points awarded
Less frequent usage
Limited control
More than one but less than all
One aspect
Partial effectiveness
Attribute always used in same way
Very specific utility

RESTRICTION

Linked to Characteristic or Attribute. One of the character's Attributes is associated with one or more disadvantages that limits its use. This Defect offers a near-endless number of limitations, and consequently the player and GM should discuss the ramifications of the selected Restriction. A list of suggested Restrictions are shown in Table 5-3: Sample Restrictions.

Each Attribute description provides a short list of three of the more commonly associated Restrictions. These entries are only suggestions, and do not represent the only Restrictions available. The GM may increase the Bonus Points returned to the character to an alternate progression (such as 2 BP, 4 BP, 6 BP; or 3 BP, 6 BP, 9 BP) if the Attribute this Defect is restricting has a high Character Point cost at each Level (see Dynamic Powers, Extra Attacks, or Power Flux for examples). Severe limitations on an Attribute, which will affect the Point cost per Level, is covered by the Reduction Defect (see above).

1 BP   The Attribute has a minor Restriction.

2 BP   The Attribute has a moderate Restriction.

3 BP   The Attribute has a major Restriction.

Table 5-3: Sample Restrictions

Cannot use on oneself
Check needed to maintain control
During specific times of the day
Easy to counteract
Flawed results
In particular locations
Initiative penalty to use
Limited functioning
Loss of specific effect
Naked form only
Requires consumable focus
Requires maintenance
Requires special equipment
Requires Stat checks
Restricts movement
Specific targets
Time limit
Under certain conditions
Usage inflicts pain
Use weakens character

SENSORY IMPAIRMENT

One or more of the character's senses (sight, hearing, taste, touch, smell) are either diminished or lost. An example of a diminished sense is being near-sighted or hard of hearing; the GM should take the impairment into consideration when deciding what the character is able to perceive, and may apply a -4 penalty on checks to notice things with that sense. An example of a lost sense is blindness or deafness. Any diminishment or loss is based on the character's status after benefiting from any technological aids such as eyeglasses or hearing aids in the setting. For example, if a character has a hearing aid but is still hard of hearing, he or she has Sensory Impairment (diminished hearing, 1 BP). In a setting where a hearing aid was unavailable or could not correct his or her particular impairment, he or she would have Sensory Impairment (deaf, 2 BP) instead.

1 BP The character has a diminished primary sense (such as short-sightedness or being hard of hearing), or has lost a secondary sense (such as taste or smell).

2 BP The character has completely lost a primary sense (sight or hearing), has two diminished primary senses, or has completely lost multiple secondary senses.

3 BP The character has completely lost a primary sense (sight or hearing) and multiple secondary senses.

SIGNIFICANT OTHER (S.O.)

A character with this Defect has someone for whom he or she will go to any lengths to keep safe from harm, even at the risk of his or her own life. The S.O. should be a regular fixture in the campaign. A one-night stand, or a cousin visiting for two weeks is a plot complication and not an appropriate S.O. The character's sense of obligation towards the S.O. is enough that the character will take great pains to ensure his or her safety and well-being. Examples include spouses and steady boy or girl friends, teammates, immediate relatives (parents and grandparents, brothers and sisters, perhaps very close cousins), and close co-workers (such as a cop's partner). It is acceptable for a character to take another character as an S.O., provided the players role-play this relationship appropriately. In this case, the S.O. relationship is always worth just 1 BP but is treated as a 3 BP Defect by the GM in terms of the frequency with which it affects the game.

The S.O. Defect is inappropriate for most Agents, Henchmen, and Servant characters.

1 BP The S.O. is rarely placed in grave danger and appears infrequently.

2 BP The S.O. is often placed in grave danger and appears frequently.

3 BP The S.O. is always placed in grave danger and appears constantly.

SKELETON IN THE CLOSET

The character has a dark secret. Exposure of this secret could cause the character harm in the form of public humiliation, loss of a job, arrest, injury, or even death. The number of BP gained from this Defect is based on the severity the consequences if the secret is revealed. The secret must be important enough that the character will actively take steps to keep others from learning of it. If the Skeleton is ever revealed, the character will suffer the associated consequences, and the GM should replace it with an appropriate Defect or Defects worth at least as many BP as Skeleton in the Closet.

For example, most criminals have a 1 BP Skeleton in the Closet: they have committed crimes that could send them to jail or worse, but usually there is no easily available evidence. If their secret is discovered, they will usually have Skeleton in the Closet replaced by an equal or higher value Wanted Defect. A 3 BP Skeleton is usually reserved for characters who face destruction or death if their secret is discovered such as a flesh-eating alien living among humans or an undercover agent that has infiltrated a terrorist organisation.

If a character has a secret identity, the Skeleton in the Closet Defect applies. The number of Bonus Points associated with the identity depends on the consequences if the secret is revealed, and thus is heavily Dependent on the nature and actions of the character. For instance, if an undercover agent's identity is revealed, enemies can target the character and his or her family more easily. Whether this is a 1, 2, or 3 BP Defect depends on the position of the character, popularity of the character, how many enemies he or she has, how easily the character can maintain a normal lifestyle, etc. When in doubt, assume that most characters who have secret identities gain the 2 BP Defect.

The Skeleton in the Closet Defect is inappropriate for most Servant characters.

1 BP The Skeleton is difficult to discover, and/or the consequences of discovery are slight, and/or the character's reputation will be impacted slightly.

2 BP The Skeleton is relatively easy to discover, and/or the consequences of discovery are moderate, and/or the character's reputation will be seriously impacted.

3 BP The Skeleton is very easy to discover, and/or the consequences of discovery are severe, and/or the character's reputation will be devastated.

SPECIAL REQUIREMENT

This Defect forces the character to meet a Special Requirement before an action or task can be completed. The Special Requirement may involve a physical object, an event, an action, an environmental condition, or even a state of mind. Everyday activities, such as eating and sleeping, are not considered to be Special Requirements unless they must be carried out under unusual conditions or more frequently for some reason. This Defect covers a wide range of possibilities, and thus the details should be discussed with the GM.

1 BP The Special Requirement is easy to obtain and/or needed infrequently.

2 BP The Special Requirement is difficult to obtain and/or needed frequently.

3 BP The Special Requirement is extremely difficult to obtain and/or needed constantly.

UNAPPEALING

An Unappealing character may find it difficult to blend into a crowd because their appearance is distinctive. The term "unappealing" does not necessarily mean ugly but can also refer to a bad smell, manner of speech, or even an unpleasant habit that provokes a consistently negative reaction.

This Defect is often taken in conjunction with the Marked Defect (page 54). A monstrous, ugly creature is usually both Unappealing and Marked. On the other hand, a beautiful, winged angel would be Marked (the presence of wings) but not Unappealing.

1 BP The character is slightly unappealing. He or she receives a -2 penalty on any Seduction Skill use.

2 BP The character is moderately unappealing. He or she receives a -4 penalty on any Seduction Skill use.

3 BP The character is severely unappealing. He or she receives a -6 penalty on any Seduction Skill use.

UNIQUE DEFECT

This section covers any and all possible Defects that a character might possess but are not detailed in the rules. The boundaries and limitations of the Defect should be discussed with the GM.

1 BP The Defect occurs infrequently and/or has a slight effect on the character.

2 BP The Defect occurs frequently and/or has a moderate effect on the character.

3 BP The Defect occurs constantly and/or has a severe effect on the character.

UNIQUE DEFECT EXAMPLE: HARD CODING

A character with the Attack Restriction Defect has limitations on whom he or she can attack due to a reduction of free will (such as "hard coded" commands). The attack restriction can only be overcome during exceptional circumstances and may result in harsh consequences, including unbearable guilt or punishment by superiors. This Defect obviously does not apply to heroic characters who will not "attack innocent people."

1 BP The character's restriction applies to very few people, or the character has slight reservations.

2 BP The character's restriction applies to many people, or the character has strong reservations.

3 BP The character's restriction applies to a large group of people, or the character has extremely strong reservations.

UNRELIABLE POWER

Linked to Attribute. One of the character's Attributes frequently does not function when desired. Before the character can use the Attribute, he or she must make a successful Stat check with a penalty. If the Attribute does not have a "Relevant Stat" entry, the character's Soul Stat should be used as a default. If the Stat check fails, the character can try to use the Attribute again during the next round (when the character is in combat), or in a short period of time (when the character is not in combat).

At the GM's and player's discretion, Unreliable Power can also represent an Attribute that does not always function in the manner desired. For example, a character with Grow might not always grow to the desired size, or a Force Field might not always appear in the correct place. For this alternative, the Stat check determines if the Attribute operates properly; a failed check indicates that it activates in an unexpected manner.

1 BP The character suffers a -2 Stat check penalty. In non-combat situations, the character cannot attempt to use the Attribute again for 1-10 minutes.

2 BP The character suffers a -4 Stat check penalty. In non-combat situations, the character cannot attempt to use the Attribute again for 10-30 minutes.

3 BP The character suffers a -6 Stat check penalty. In non-combat situations, the character cannot attempt to use the Attribute again for 30 minutes to 2 hours.

UNSKILLED

An Unskilled character starts with less than the usual number of Skill Points: -10 Skill Points (up to the character's starting Skill Point total) for each BP returned. This Defect cannot be combined with the Highly Skilled Attribute.

VULNERABILITY

The character has a critical weakness to a specific object, environment, thought, activity, or condition. When in close proximity to the Vulnerability, it can temporarily strip the character of his or her Attributes. The Vulnerability should only affect the character rarely, however, since it impacts him or her so severely.

1 BP The character's accessible Attribute Levels all drop by one-quarter (round up) when affected by the Vulnerability.

2 BP The character's accessible Attribute Levels all drop by one-half (round up) when affected by the Vulnerability.

3 BP The character cannot use any Attributes when affected by the Vulnerability.

WANTED

The character is wanted by the law, a powerful criminal, or private organisation that has placed a price on his or her head. Being Wanted is different from having a Nemesis; there is no single person devoting his or her life to annoying or hunting down the character. The character will need to conceal his or her identity or move around regularly to avoid having complete strangers calling the police or pursuing the character (depending on the circumstances).

1 BP The incentive to hunt the character is minor. For example, he or she may be wanted on outstanding warrants, but there may be no actual reward posted, or the reward is fairly small.

2 BP The reward, contract, or other incentive offered to hunt the character is significant.

3 BP The reward, contract, or other incentive offered to hunt the character is extreme.

WEAK POINT

The character's body possesses an abnormal weak point (in addition to the normal human weak points, like the heart and head). If the weak point is ever hit during combat with a Called Shot (page 63), the result is an automatic critical hit (page 69). If the attacker rolls a natural critical hit (a natural 2), the target is immediately reduced to 0 Health Points and falls unconscious. The opponent, or even the character, may not be aware the weak point exists, however, until its presence is discovered by accident or through careful study.

1 BP The weak point is tiny (-6 Called Shot attack check penalty).

2 BP The weak point is small (-4 Called Shot attack check penalty).

3 BP The weak point is large (-2 Called Shot attack check penalty).

STEP 7: CALCULATE DERIVED VALUES

Calculate the character's Derived Values. These numbers are based directly on the Body, Mind, and Soul Stats and thus do not afford any choices of Point distribution.

COMBAT VALUE

This value governs all facets of physical conflict including your character's abilities in attacking, defending, and delivering damage. A higher Combat Value reflects fighting spirit and an increased knowledge of all physical combat forms: armed, unarmed, martial arts and ranged weapons. There are two separate components of the Combat Value — Attack and Defence. Character Attributes and Defects may modify either component separately, but unless otherwise noted, the term Combat Value refers to both Attack and Defence.

Increased skill in combat can only be achieved through harmony of the Complete Self. Lack of self-unity through weakness of any facet of the character will restrict his or her ability in combat. Consequently, the Body, Mind, and Soul are all of equal importance to the combat master: Body Stat for a forceful attack and defence, Mind Stat for quick wit, knowledge of combat techniques and anticipation of an opponent's actions, and Soul Stat for the winning spirit and good fortune. For example, a petite female standing five feet tall with martial arts training can take down an opponent nearly twice her size; knowledge and determination is just as important as brute force.

To calculate the base Attack Combat Value, add together all the Stat Values and divide by three, rounding down ([Body + Mind + Soul] ÷ 3).

The base Defence Combat Value is two less than the Attack Combat Value ([Body + Mind + Soul] ÷ 3 - 2).

HEALTH POINTS

This Derived Value dictates the amount of physical damage your character's body can sustain before it ceases to function (for example, your character is knocked unconscious or even dies). Damage delivered in combat are subtracted from your character's current Health Point total. If the total ever falls below zero, the character is rendered unconscious and may die if he or she does not receive medical attention. Attributes or Defects may further modify Health Points.

The base number of Health Points is equal to the sum of the Body Stat and Soul Stat multiplied by 5 ([Body + Soul] x 5).

HENCHMEN RULE

To reflect the ease with which unimportant NPCs are dispatched in combat, the GM is encouraged to assign such "extras" as the Not So Tough Defect at 2 or 3 BP, therefore reducing their Health Points by 20 or 30. The GM will decide which characters constitute minor NPCs.

ENERGY POINTS (OPTIONAL RULE)

This Derived Value can be used for games where the GM feels that characters possess a personal reserve of energy that is depleted when carrying out difficult tasks. Energy Points are needed to fuel Attributes that are associated with the Burns Energy Defect and Special Attacks that have the Uses Energy Disability. If your character's Energy Point total is ever reduced to 0, he or she will fall unconscious from exhaustion.

Caution! The use of Energy Points can slow the pace of a game and greatly increase the amount of bookkeeping. Additionally, your character may tire quickly if you assign the Burns Energy Defect to several Attributes, preventing him or her from using them over sustained periods. Whether this is appropriate for your character or not depends on how you envision your hero. Energy Points may be further modified by the Energy Bonus Attribute (page 18).

To calculate your character's initial Energy Point total, add together the Mind Stat and Soul Stat and multiply by 5 ([Mind + Soul] x 5).

SHOCK VALUE (OPTIONAL RULE)

For games in which damage should have more realistic effects, characters should also calculate their Shock Value. This value is not recommended for cinematic/heroic games. If a character suffers an amount of damage equal to his or her Shock Value, there is a danger that the character will be stunned. If the attack penetrates the skin (such as from a bullet or knife), the Shock Value also represents the damage necessary to inflict a major wound, which, if untreated, can result in the character bleeding to death. For more information on Shock Value and its applications, see page 70.

The Shock Value is equal to the character's maximum Health Points divided by 5. ([Health Points] ÷ 5).

STEP 8: EARN BACKGROUND POINTS

Now that the numerical component of your character is complete (Stats, Attributes, Defects, Skills, and Derived Values), you should concentrate on fine-tuning his or her personality, while still leaving room for the character to grow in the future. One of the most effective ways to better visualise your creation is to provide detail through a background history, a character story, or a character drawing. Spending time to develop your character without a rule structure will enhance your role-playing greatly, and can give the GM a window into your character's motivations. Additionally, your Game Master might hand out a character quiz for you to answer. As an incentive, the GM will award you from 1 to one-half X Background Points for each contribution that you complete, which are then distributed among the Attributes. If any of your character's Stats are changed after using the Background Points, you must recalculate the three Derived Values.

This final step in character creation also serves as your last chance to answer important character questions before game-play begins. What formed his or her outlook on life? Where does he or she live? Work? Earn money? What are your character's likes? Dislikes? What about family? Friends? Romantic interests? Enemies? Details add depth to your character, but you should not become obsessed with them. Leaving room for growth can provide numerous character development opportunities during the course of the adventures.

GAME MECHANICS

INTRODUCTION

In a role-playing game, most character or NPC actions do not require any particular rules. A player simply says his or her character walks across a room, picks up an object, drives a vehicle, or talks to someone, etc., and if the GM agrees that it is possible, this simply happens. Personal interaction between characters or NPCs normally consists of the players and GM talking "in character" and describing what their characters are doing. In the GM's case, he or she describes what the characters are seeing, hearing, smelling, touching, and tasting.

In the course of a game, circumstances may arise where specific rules can help determine what happens. This is usually the case when the outcome of an action or event is uncertain and the result is important to the story. If a character needs to fix a broken reactor pump to prevent a nuclear meltdown, can he or she do it in time? If a character's car drives off a cliff, can he or she jump clear in time, and if not, how badly will the crash injure the character? If two people fight, who wins?

A character's Stats, Attributes, Skills, and Derived Values help resolve these dramatic questions. In many cases, dice rolls can add additional hazard and drama to the action. The dice rolls represent elements beyond the direct control of the character or the uncertainty that results when opposing characters interact. In some situations, the GM may elect to determine the results by simple fiat, without rolling dice (see Should I Make My Players Roll Dice?, page 59). The GM may do so if he or she thinks a particular outcome is certain or is dramatically necessary to the game.

One situation the rules cover in greater detail is combat. The rules for combat are extensive, giving players a greater sense that they are in control of their characters' every step. If they lose, they will know the GM has not arbitrarily killed or injured their characters. The GM can also follow a similar procedure with any other actions that affect a character's fate: treat routine activities in passing and delve into more detail whenever an action influences the player character physically or emotionally.

IMPORTANT! Do not hesitate to go beyond the rules if you are the Game Master. If you dislike a rule presented in Tri-Stat dX, you are encouraged to modify it to suit your needs and those of the players. Do not let your own vision of a role-playing game be superseded by anything you read in this book. These pages are filled with guidelines and suggestions, but certainly do not reflect the "One True Way" to role-playing success. Use what you like, discard what you do not, and fill in the blanks with your own ideas.

THE PASSAGE OF TIME

"In game" passage of time in a role-playing game is fluid. In some situations, like a conversation between two characters, the movement of game time normally matches real world time. More often, the amount of time that passes depends on the characters' activities as set by the players' actions — things happen as soon as dramatically appropriate. Climbing a high mountain takes a few short minutes. It does not take the several hours that climbing a mountain would really take. The GM should telescope time until something interesting happens: "Two weeks pass while you investigate the crime. Then the terrorist broadcasts a message to the world, announcing his plans to destroy the UN if his demands are not met...." Finally, in very dramatic situations such as combat, the GM may keep very precise track of time, using individual "combat rounds" (see Combat, page 61). GMs may go back in time as well to employ flashback scenes. A flashback is a useful tool to establish the background for a story without simply recounting the information in dry lecture fashion, allowing the player to work through the event.

SCENE, ROUND, AND INITIATIVE

Three common measures of game time in Tri-Stat dX are a scene, round, and Initiative. A scene is any situation where the events remain linked, moment-to-moment. Think of it in movie terms — a scene lasts until the camera cuts to an entirely new setting, potentially with new characters. If, for example, a character is speaking with an informant in a diner, the conversation constitutes a scene. Once the GM switches scenes to the character entering a back alley, following up on the informant's lead, the diner scene ends and a new scene begins in the back alley. If the conversation was interrupted by a villain attacking the informant, intent on shutting him up before he could reveal any important information, the scene would not yet end when the character chased after the villain down a back alleyway. Since the events are still linked moment-to-moment, it is still a part of a scene although the setting has changed.

A round is a measure of time of approximately 1-10 seconds in length (usually averaged to 5 seconds), while an Initiative is one specific moment in time. When combat occurs, characters roll Initiative (page 61) and each is allowed to act on his or her Initiative. The round is broken into a number of Initiatives equal to the highest Initiative rolled for the round. For example, in a combat between three characters who roll an 11, 19, and 24, the combat round has 24 Initiatives. The round remains 5 seconds in length, but for the purposes of action within the conflict, there are 24 potential individual moments — 24 instances where a character could decide to act. On the following combat round, when the characters roll 16, 23, and 39, there are now 39 Initiatives within the round.

TAKING ACTION

Every character is capable of performing or attempting a nearly endless list of actions. These can be mundane activities (talking, breathing, thinking), skilled activities (building a suit of power armour, hacking into a computer, moving silently, climbing the side of a building), or combat activities (fighting, dodging, shooting). The Combat section covers combat action in detail and thus is not discussed here. Additionally, players can assume that characters carry out routine skilled activities successfully on a regular basis unless specified otherwise by the GM. For example, the GM can assume that characters with the Gun Combat Skill routinely keep their weapons clean, safely stored, and properly maintained.

Every GM has a preferred method for having players describe their characters' actions. Usually this involves the GM moving from player to player asking, "What is your character doing?" Experienced GMs try to give each person equal role-playing time so that everyone is an important facet of the story (switching between characters as necessary). Conversely, players are responsible for relating their characters' intended actions to the GM. In return, the GM will describe the results of those actions or will request a Stat or Skill check to determine the outcome.

Consider the three action descriptions below:

Action 1:"My character, Maxwell, is going to search for the artefact."

Action 2:"My character, Maxwell, is going to search for the artefact in the basement of the building."

Action 3:"My character, Maxwell, is going to quickly search for the artefact in the basement of the building. He will knock down doors if he has to, in order to find it as fast as possible."

All three accounts involve Maxwell looking for the artefact, but the level of detail is quite different. You should not be overly concerned with detail if it is irrelevant to your character's actions (such as exactly how Maxwell is forcing open the doors in Action 3), but sometimes a little detail can greatly alter the GM's interpretation of the event.

ATTRIBUTES AND ACTIONS

In some situations, it is important to know how many Attributes a character can activate at one time and how quickly he or she can activate the Attribute. Innate Attributes, such as Armour or Superstrength, are considered always active, unless the character selects a Restriction Defect (page 55) whereby the Attribute is not always active. Attributes which must be activated but do not usually require a dice roll, such as Force Field, can be activated at a rate of one per Initiative starting on the character's Initiative roll; these activations do not require the character to use an action. Attributes that must be activated and do require a dice roll demand focus, and thus the character must spend one or more actions to activate the Attribute. A character can have any number of Attributes active at any moment, though GMs may wish to impose penalties if the character is focusing on too many things. It is usually obvious which Attributes fall into which category, but the final classification is at the Game Master's discretion.

Using Attributes at Reduced Levels

Unless a character assigns the Maximum Force Defect (page 54) to an Attribute, he or she can voluntarily use the Attribute at reduced Levels and PMV Ranks. For example, a character with Level 6 Teleport (maximum distance of 1,000 km) could choose to teleport any distance up to 1,000 km. Similarly, if the character also assigned a Targets PMV of Rank 4 (50 people/1 tonne) to Teleport, he or she could use the Attribute on any number of people or objects up to 50 people/1 tonne.

Fractional Attribute Use

The GM might also allow the character to use a fraction of an Attribute's effect. A character with Level 10 Insubstantial, for instance, may only want to turn a single body part, such as a hand or head, incorporeal. The GM could decide that fractional Attribute use is more or less difficult than using an Attribute's full effect, assigning appropriate Check Value modifiers (see Table 7-1: Check Value Difficulty Modifiers).

DICE AND DICE ROLLS

Tri-Stat dX uses polyhedral (multi-sided) dice during game play, though usually only a single die type in each adventure or campaign. This game dice, represented by

Should I Make My Players Roll Dice?

It is important for the GM to realise that not all actions require a dice roll. Obviously mundane character activities, such as hammering a nail, riding a horse down a road, or eating lunch, should never need dice rolls unless there are exceptional circumstances surrounding the character's actions. In other situations, the necessity to roll dice is less obvious. If a character is virtually guaranteed to succeed at a task, then the GM should consider whether the check is really necessary. While it is true that the character might fail, having the player roll the dice will slow the game down. Thus, GMs should recognise when a character is almost certainly going to succeed at a task and, in those situations, not request the check and allow game play to continue, uninterrupted.

Conversely, one might think that if a character only succeeds if the player rolls a really high number, then the GM should similarly not request a check and, instead, state that the action fails. This, however, is not the case — player characters should always be given that one slim chance of success, even at difficult tasks that seem doomed to failure (with the exception of tasks that the GM deems impossible). While the dice roll may slow game-play down a bit, that slim chance of success allows characters to accomplish heroic feats that will be remembered for years. GMs may wish to allow only player characters to make this roll, even in the face of near-certain failure — since NPCs are not the stars of the game, they should not be allowed the same chance of pulling off superhuman feats.

The following is a list of suggestions when the dice should and should not be rolled. If a check is unnecessary, the character should gain an automatic success for the action.

Roll dice when...
- the unpredictability of dice adds to the excitement of the game
- the action is foreign to the character
- the action has been a weakness for the character in the past
- the character is distracted or cannot concentrate
- another character or NPC is working directly against the character
- the action is not of trivial difficulty
- outside forces influence the actions
- the player wants to roll the dice

Do not roll dice when...
- a roll would reduce the enjoyment of the game
- the action is routine for the character
- the action requires a trivial amount of talent compared to the character's Skill Level

X, usually has one of the following number of sides: 4, 6, 8, 10, 12, or (rarely) 20. When a random number needs to be generated, two dice are rolled. By adding the two numbers shown on each die, values between 2 and 2X can be generated. The distribution of values almost follows a bell curve, with the middle value of X + 1 generated most frequently. For example, when X = 6, the value of 7 is generated most often; when X = 12, 13 shows up most frequently. There are three major types of dice rolls, or checks, a GM or player may use during game play: a Stat check dice roll, a Skill check dice roll and an Attack/Defence Combat check. When a player announces the intended actions of his or her character, the GM must decide if a dice roll is necessary. Should a roll be required, the GM chooses which type of check is most appropriate.

In most cases, a player rolls dice to determine the success of an action his or her character performs, while the GM rolls the dice to determine the results of NPC actions when they impact the characters. In situations where NPCs are only involved with other NPCs, the GM should simply decide what happens rather than rolling dice.

In some circumstances, the GM may roll the dice to determine the results of a character's action instead of having a player roll, keeping the actual dice roll — and the reason for rolling — secret. This is normally done when the player rolling would give away an event that should remain unknown to the character. If, for example, there is something hidden that the character may or may not notice, the GM can secretly roll dice to see if the character spots it. If the GM allowed the player to roll the dice, the player would know that a clue existed even if the character did not succeed in noticing it.

STAT CHECKS

A Stat check is used when the GM believes that innate ability is more important than any learned expertise or combat capability. During a Stat check, the GM decides which Stat (Body, Mind, or Soul) would be most relevant to the action in question. If two or three Stats are closely related to the action, an average Stat Value should be calculated instead, rounding up to the closest whole number. For actions that fall under the domain of an Attribute, the relevant Stat is usually given in the Attribute description.

A successful Stat check involves the player rolling less than or equal to the Check Value on two dice. The base Check Value is equal to the appropriate Stat or Stat average, as determined by the GM. The Stat check is unsuccessful if the dice roll generates a value greater than the Check Value. The greater the difference between the Check Value and the dice roll, the greater the degree of success or failure.

CHECK VALUE DIFFICULTY MODIFIERS

The GM has the option of modifying the Check Value should the action the character is undertaking be particularly easy or difficult (see Table 7-1: Check Value Difficulty Modifiers). Difficult actions gain a negative modifier to the attempt, while easier actions receive a positive modifier.

Table 7-1: Check Value Difficult Modifiers

Check Value Modifier						Difficulty of the Action
d4	d6	d8	d10	d12	d20	
+4	+6	+8	+10	+12	+20	Practically Guaranteed (why roll dice?)
+3	+4	+6	+7	+9	+15	Extremely Easy
+2	+2	+4	+4	+6	+10	Easy
+1	+1	+2	+2	+3	+5	Below Average Difficulty
0	0	0	0	0	0	Average Difficulty
-1	-1	-2	-2	-3	-5	Above Average Difficulty
-2	-2	-4	-4	-6	-10	Difficult
-3	-4	-6	-7	-9	-15	Extremely Difficult
-4	-6	-8	-10	-12	-20	Practically Impossible

CRITICAL SUCCESS OR FAILURE

Regardless of the actual Check Value, an unmodified or "natural" roll of 2 always succeeds (it is considered at least a "marginal success"), and an unmodified roll of 2X always fails (it is considered at least a "marginal failure"). This rule is important in

<table>
</table>

The difficulty term "average difficulty action" more correctly means "action that is considered of average importance in the campaign, for which the GM would actually want the player to make a dice roll." Parallel parking a car is not an average action — even though many drivers cannot do it — since it is unimportant in almost any campaign using d6 through d20. It might be of some relevance in a d4 subhuman game, though.

When you are thinking about a specific task, if you cannot say "that's a fairly average action for a player character to accomplish in my campaign," then it's not an average action.

an RPG, because it reflects the extreme possibilities that even the most talented characters sometimes fail in their tasks, while even the most awkward characters can succeed. Due to the limited dice range available, the GM may modify this suggestion for games that use d4 (subhuman).

CONTESTED ACTIONS

If two or more characters are working directly or indirectly against each other (such as two people pulling on a contested object), each character must make a Stat check. The character with the greatest degree of success (or least degree of failure if both characters fail) is considered to have the advantage over the contested action.

SKILL CHECKS

A Skill check is similar to a Stat check, except it is used when the task is one that the GM decides would be governed by both a particular Stat and a particular Skill. For example, if a task required general intellectual ability (such as remembering the name of a person the character had met), a Mind Stat check would be made. Determining the origin of a rare alien species would also require a Mind Stat check, but this task is governed by the Biological Sciences Skill (more specifically, the Zoology Specialisation). In game terminology, this task would require a "Mind-Based Biological Sciences (Zoology) Skill check."

The base Check Value of a Skill check is equal to the appropriate Stat. Thus, for a Mind-based Skill check, the base Check Value is the character's Mind. If the character possesses the appropriate Skill (even without the exact Specialisation), he or she receives a bonus to the Check Value. This bonus is equivalent to the character's Skill Level (if the task does not fall under his or her Specialisation) or one more than the character's Skill Level (if his or her Specialisation does apply). A successful Skill check involves the player rolling less than or equal to the modified Check Value on two dice. The degree of the action's success or failure is determined by the difference between the Check Value and the dice roll.

The GM is responsible for deciding which Stat, Skill, and Specialisation are relevant to a particular task, using the Stat and Skill descriptions given in Chapters 2 and 4. Since these questions can often be tricky, the GM should listen to the player's reasoning why a particular Skill or Specialisation might apply. The final decision belongs to the GM, however.

COMBINING SKILL CHECKS

When more than one character tries the same Skill at the same time towards the same goal, their efforts may overlap — they can work together and help each other out. In this case, one character is considered the leader of the effort and makes master Skill check. Each helper also makes a Skill check, and for every success, the leader gets a +2 circumstance bonus to his or her master Skill check. The GM limits co-operation as he or she sees fit for the given conditions.

SKILL SYNERGY

It is possible for a character to have two Skills that work well together, such as Street Sense and Urban Tracking, or Computers and Electronics for a computerised lock. The GM should apply reasonable Skill check bonuses (up to a maximum of one-half X) when an appropriate situation arises.

UNSKILLED ATTEMPTS

Often, a character will attempt an action for which he or she does not possess the relative Skill. The Check Value in these situations is dependent on the nature of the action.

Familiar Action

If the character is undertaking a familiar action, the Check Value is simply equal to the relevant Stat. The familiarity should have been established previously, such as in the character's background story, or be consistent with the character's role within the setting. The player should explain to the GM why his or her character is familiar with the current task. The GM, of course, has final say whether the character is sufficiently familiar to avoid an unfamiliar action Check Value penalty (see below).

For example, a student who attends university to study astronomy undoubtedly has at least a cursory familiarity with many academic fields. Similarly, almost all characters living in a big city will be familiar with the process of driving a car, even if they do not possess the Driving Skill; in North America, attempting car-related actions is familiar to nearly everyone. A hermit living in the depths of the Amazon, however, is likely not familiar with motor vehicles and therefore driving would be an unfamiliar action.

Unfamiliar Action

If the character is undertaking an action with which he or she is unfamiliar, the task should be treated as a normal Stat check with an unskilled penalty applied to the Check Value. This reflects how difficult it is for an unskilled character to accomplish the task. The unskilled penalty should range from -1 to -X, depending on how much the GM feels training is required and how background aspects of the character could affect the attempt. This unskilled penalty is in addition to any penalty (or bonus) that is applied as a reflection of how easy or difficult the task itself is to accomplish.

For example, keeping a plane in the air in a human-level campaign (X = 6) after the cabin crew suddenly falls unconscious is a daunting task for anyone who is not trained as a pilot. An average character might therefore suffer a -6 penalty to the Check Value. A character who is an aficionado of combat jets and aircraft documentaries might only suffer a -2 Check Value penalty ... even if he or she has never actually piloted a plane before.

Required Skill

The GM may decide certain tasks automatically fail when performed by characters lacking the required Skill. Examples of required Skill activities include: performing brain surgery, deciphering ancient hieroglyphics, concocting an antidote for a poison, estimating the value of a rare piece of art, etc.

POWER USAGE SKILLS

Some characters may select the Power Usage Skill for one or more of their Attributes. This Skill provides a bonus when the character makes any check involving the specific Attributes. Unlike other Skills, Power Usage does not provide an additional +1 bonus for Specialisations. For example, a teleporter with a Mind Stat of 9 and the Power Usage (Teleportation) Skill at Level 3 makes Teleportation checks against a Check Value of 12 (a Mind Stat of 9 plus 3 for his Level in the Power Usage Skill).

ADDITIONAL MODIFIERS

GMs should remember to also apply normal Check Value difficulty modifiers based on how easy or difficult the task is (see Table 7-1: Check Value Difficulty Modifiers). For instance, landing a crippled airliner on an icy runway at midnight during a blizzard might be a quite difficult task. Landing the same crippled jet during daylight in fair weather might not incur a difficulty penalty. Any difficulty modifiers that are assigned to a character's task are cumulative with his or her Skill Level bonus.

COMBAT DICE ROLLS

The combat check resolves any type of physical combat including armed, unarmed, martial arts, and ranged weapons attacks. The combat check is very similar to a Skill check except the Check Value is now the character's Attack Combat Value (for attack combat checks) or Defence Combat Value (for defence combat checks) rather than a Stat. A successful combat action involves the player or GM rolling less than or equal to the Check Value on two dice. The attack or defence is unsuccessful if the dice roll (after any modifiers) is greater than the Check Value.

A character can attack or defend with a weapon (or unarmed) even if he or she does not possess the relevant attack combat Skill (combat is a Familiar Action). Consequently, attacking or defending characters lacking the appropriate Skill do not suffer a Check Value penalty; a character without the appropriate combat Skill simply does not receive a Check Value bonus.

Skills adjust the Check Value, but other Attributes may also provide modifiers as well. The GM also has the option of modifying the Check Value should the attack or defence be particularly easy or difficult (see Table 7-1: Check Value Difficulty Modifiers, page 60). A natural dice roll of 2 ("snake eyes") is a critical success and cannot be negated by an opponent's defence (the defender does not even have the opportunity to make a defence check). The critical success rule may not apply in games that use d4 (GM's discretion).

USING ATTRIBUTES

If an Attribute does not specifically require a Stat or Skill check or a combat check, GMs can assume they function automatically in most situations, though the Game Master may decide that a Stat or Skill check is necessary in unusual circumstances. For example, a character with the Features (Appearance) Attribute always looks good, but the GM might require a Soul Stat check were he or she attempting to attract someone's attention.

Certain Attributes occasionally require Stat checks (or sometimes Skill checks) to properly use the Attribute. Other Attributes provide favourable modifiers to Stat checks or Skill checks. If an Attribute interacts with Stat or Skill checks, this is noted in the Attribute's description in Character Creation.

COMBAT INTRODUCTION

Conflict is an essential component of any role-playing game. Physical conflict, or combat, is an important element of the Tri-Stat dX RPG, but important is not the same as frequent. Combat should be a vital element of a scene, and not just a distraction that the GM uses to pass the time.

The combat rules for Tri-Stat dX were designed to mimic dynamic, fast-paced combat. Whenever a character enters physical conflict with another character or NPC, the physical Combat Phase begins. Each round of combat covers from 1 to 10 seconds of time from the characters' perspectives, depending on the characters' actions and the circumstances (the exact time scale is not relevant; a five-second round is usually appropriate). Characters are permitted to take one offensive and one defensive action each round. They may also choose to take more than one defensive action, but suffer a Check Value penalty to each subsequent attempt (see the Defence section). Alternatively, a character may forfeit his or her attack in favour of one non-combat action. Should the conflict not be resolved at the end of the first combat round, subsequent rounds of combat will follow.

The Physical Combat Phase is subdivided into four parts: Initiative, Character Action, Defence, and Damage.

INITIATIVE

Initiative determines the order in which characters act and is checked at the beginning of each round. Each player involved in the fracas rolls two dice and adds the result to his or her character's Attack Combat Value. A bonus is applied if the character possesses the Combat Technique (Lightning Reflexes; page 14) or Speed (page 37) Attributes. The GM does the same for any NPCs engaged in the conflict. The GM may also grant bonuses or penalties if he or she believes the situations calls for it. Alternatively, the players and Game Master can roll once at the beginning of combat to determine their characters' Initiatives for the entire battle (i.e. their Initiatives will remain the same every round).

The character with the highest total has "gained Initiative" and acts first, followed by others in descending order. Should two or more characters or NPCs have the same Initiative, their actions are simultaneous. This means both characters attack and deliver damage at the same time; if one character drops below zero Health Points as a result, he or she still acts before falling unconscious.

A character may delay his or her action until any time later in the round to see what the other characters intend to do. If all his or her opponents also delay their

COMBAT FLOWCHART

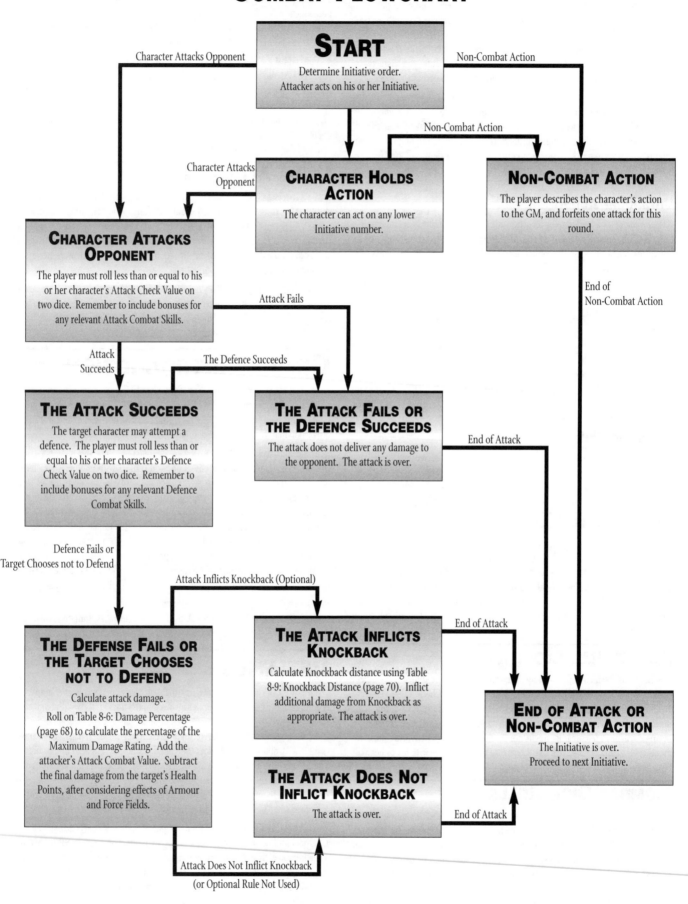

START
Determine Initiative order.
Attacker acts on his or her Initiative.

Character Attacks Opponent

Non-Combat Action

Non-Combat Action

CHARACTER HOLDS ACTION
The character can act on any lower Initiative number.

Character Attacks Opponent

NON-COMBAT ACTION
The player describes the character's action to the GM, and forfeits one attack for this round.

CHARACTER ATTACKS OPPONENT
The player must roll less than or equal to his or her character's Attack Check Value on two dice. Remember to include bonuses for any relevant Attack Combat Skills.

Attack Fails

Attack Succeeds

The Defence Succeeds

THE ATTACK SUCCEEDS
The target character may attempt a defence. The player must roll less than or equal to his or her character's Defence Check Value on two dice. Remember to include bonuses for any relevant Defence Combat Skills.

THE ATTACK FAILS OR THE DEFENCE SUCCEEDS
The attack does not deliver any damage to the opponent. The attack is over.

End of Attack

End of Non-Combat Action

Defence Fails or Target Chooses not to Defend

Attack Inflicts Knockback (Optional)

THE DEFENSE FAILS OR THE TARGET CHOOSES NOT TO DEFEND
Calculate attack damage.
Roll on Table 8-6: Damage Percentage (page 68) to calculate the percentage of the Maximum Damage Rating. Add the attacker's Attack Combat Value. Subtract the final damage from the target's Health Points, after considering effects of Armour and Force Fields.

THE ATTACK INFLICTS KNOCKBACK
Calculate Knockback distance using Table 8-9: Knockback Distance (page 70). Inflict additional damage from Knockback as appropriate. The attack is over.

End of Attack

END OF ATTACK OR NON-COMBAT ACTION
The Initiative is over.
Proceed to next Initiative.

THE ATTACK DOES NOT INFLICT KNOCKBACK
The attack is over.

End of Attack

Attack Does Not Inflict Knockback
(or Optional Rule Not Used)

actions waiting for something to happen, the round ends in a dramatic stand-off and a new one begins.

If a character holds one or more actions until the end of a round and does not act, he or she acts on the first Initiative in the next round. The character does not gain an additional action — he or she simply acts first regardless of Initiative rolls. All held actions occur during the first Initiative. If two (or more) characters hold their actions until the following round, then both characters act simultaneously (assuming neither continues to hold their action) and then everyone else involved in the combat acts based on Initiative rolls.

CHARACTER ACTION

Characters act in the sequence determined by the Initiative roll. When it is time for a character to act, he or she may make one offensive action (i.e. attack) or one non-combat action, unless the character has the Extra Attacks Attribute (page 19). Attacks are normally against a single target, though some weapons or attack Abilities may allow the character to engage multiple targets simultaneously.

Before rolling the dice, the player should clearly describe the method of attack, the weapon his or her character uses (if any), and the target. If the character is trying something unusual (such as a Called Shot or attacking with two weapons), he or she should specify this beforehand.

To successfully attack an opponent, the player (or GM for an NPC) must roll less than or equal to his or her character's Attack Combat Value on two dice as described under Combat Dice Rolls on page 61. Remember to include all relevant Attribute, Skill, Defect, Weapon Ability/Disability, and difficulty modifiers (refer to Table 7-1: Attack Check Modifiers, page 60).

If the attack check succeeds, the character is on target and will hit unless the opponent can defend against the attack. Refer to defence checks, page 67, for more information. If the target fails the defence check or does not defend at all, he or she suffers the effects of the attack. This is normally damage and/or any other special effects associated with the attack. To reflect some of the brutally successful attacks demonstrated in game adventures, a natural dice roll of 2 is a critical success and cannot be negated by an opponent's defence (an optional rule for d4 games).

If an attack check fails, the character has missed. The attacker's action is over, and the attack has no effect, though a miss with a ranged weapon may cause collateral damage if the shot strikes somewhere else instead (this is up to the GM). A natural roll of 2X (for example, 12 for a d6 game or 20 for a d10 game) will always miss and may result in an exceptional failure, such as hitting an innocent bystander or a weapon malfunctioning (an optional rule for d4 games).

MELEE VS. RANGED ATTACKS

Some attacks are useful at a distance, while others are limited to close, hand-to-hand fighting. For simplicity, ranges are grouped into the four categories listed below. It is up to the GM to decide whether he or she wishes to track ranges and distances, or abstract them.

The distance given for each attack range is the effective reach of that attack. Many may be fired out to twice that range at -4 penalty or five times the distance at -8, though the GM may decide that some attacks or weapons cannot exceed their listed ranges.

MELEE

The attack is only usable against adjacent opponents within touching distance (usually one to five metres). This is the range for swords, melee combat, etc.

SHORT

The attack has an effective range out to about 50 metres. Most pistols, shotguns, grenades, submachine guns, and hurled weapons such as a thrown rock or throwing knife, are short-ranged.

MEDIUM

The attack has an effective range out to about 500 metres. Most energy blasts as well as bows, crossbows, rifles, and machine guns are medium-ranged. This is the default range for weapons if none other is listed.

LONG

The attack is effective out to considerable ranges: about 5 km (or more if specifically noted). A surface-to-air missile, an anti-tank rocket, or a tank's main gun are examples of this.

SPECIAL COMBAT SITUATIONS

The following are special situations that can occur during combat.

ATTACKING MULTIPLE TARGETS WITH ONE ATTACK

When a character absolutely must take down a number of targets but he or she does not have enough Extra Attacks to do so, the character may attempt to use one attack to strike multiple targets. For each additional target beyond the first, the character suffers a -4 attack combat penalty. Only one attack combat check is made, not one check per target. Each target, however, is allowed to make a defence combat check as normal. Additionally, any damage inflicted is reduced by 2 ranks, to a minimum of 0% (see Amount of Damage Inflicted, page 68). Thus, if a character attempted to swing his sword and strike three people in one blow, he would make one attack check with a -8 penalty (-4 for each of the two extra targets). If he successfully hits any of the targets, his damage is reduced by 2 ranks.

Attacking Multiple Weaker Opponents

Sometimes a character wants to attack multiple significantly weaker opponents with one offensive action. This action is very cinematic (representative of a powerful warrior battling hoards of lowly minions), and consequently the attack penalties are not as severe. For each additional target who is at least 50 Character Points lower than the attacker, the penalty is only -2 instead of -4. The attacker does not suffer any penalties for each additional target who is at least 100 Character Points lower than the attacker.

For example, a 200 Point superhero uses her optic blast Special Attack to combat a hoard of eight villains with the following Character Points: 50, 50, 50, 50, 50, 125, 175 and 175. The heroine suffers no penalty for the five villains at 50 Character (since they are at least 100 Character Points lower than she), a -2 penalty for the single villain at 125 Character Points (since he is at least 50 Points lower), and a full -4 for the two villains at 175 Points (since they are only 25 Points lower). The final attack check penalty the heroine suffers for her one attack is -10 (-2 -4 -4 = -10).

Attacks With Two Weapons

A character with a one-handed weapon in each hand may use both at once against the same target or attack two different targets (even if he or she does not have Extra Attacks) but at a severe penalty to both checks. A two-weapon attack incurs a -8 Check Value penalty if the attacks are aimed at the same target or a -12 penalty if aimed at different targets. If a character has Extra Attacks, he or she can only use this option with one attack and not every attack.

CALLED SHOTS

An attacking character may opt to suffer an unfavourable difficulty modifier to hit in exchange for a Called Shot that provides some special advantage. For example, a Called Shot may ignore Armour (by attacking a small, unarmoured spot) or strike a vital point, inflicting greater-than-normal damage results. Players must specify a Called Shot before rolling the dice.

Called Shot — Disarming

A character may attempt to shoot or knock a weapon out of another person's hand. If using a ranged attack, this requires an attack at a -8 penalty. If the attack hits and the opponent fails his or her defence check, the character knocks away the weapon (probably damaging it). If using a melee weapon or unarmed attack to disarm, the character only suffers a -4, but the target may make a Body Stat check to retain control of the weapon. If the Body Stat check succeeds, the weapon's user still suffers a -4 Check Value penalty on his or her next action with that weapon (since it is off balance), but he or she retains control of it.

Called Shot to Partial Armour

Some armour may provide partial protection, like a flak vest only protecting a person's torso. An attack aimed at a thin or unarmoured area suffers a -4 attack check penalty and ignores the effects of the Armour if successful.

Called Shot to Vital Spot

A character attacking a living being can specify he or she is aiming for a vital spot (heart, brain, spine, etc.) rather than simply shooting at the centre of mass as usual. He or she suffers a -8 attack check penalty, but, if successful, the attack inflicts full, 100% damage. If the character rolls a natural 2 on this attack check, subtract 6 from his or her dice roll for determining the effects of the critical hit (page 69; optional for games using d4).

Called Shot to Weak Point

If the character knows his or her enemy has a Weak Point Defect (page 57), a Called Shot can be made to hit it in combat. The attack check penalty depends on the size of the Weak Point: a tiny spot gives a -6 penalty; a small spot gives a -4 penalty; and a large spot gives a -2 penalty.

COMBINED ATTACKS

Sometimes, characters will find themselves facing an extremely tough opponent whose Armour or Force Field is tough enough to prevent the characters from inflicting harm. In these situations, characters will often co-ordinate their attacks, attempting to strike the same point at the same time in the hopes of overwhelming the target's defences. For each character attempting a combined attack after the first, the attackers each suffer a -2 penalty to their attack check. Each character must hold his or her attack until the slowest character's Initiative (or later) before launching the attack. Each character makes an attack combat check to see if he or she hits the target. If the character hits, he or she determines how much damage is inflicted by the attack normally (page 68). All successful attackers combine their damage values into one total and this amount is inflicted upon the target as if from one attack.

If one attack fails to hit with the combined attack penalty but otherwise would normally hit, the character still hits the target but does not successfully co-ordinate with the other characters. Naturally, if only one character co-ordinates, a combined attack does not occur. The character determines how much damage is inflicted but

Combined Attacks Make No Sense

Some people might point out that a character's failure to combine an attack with allies, which results in a reduction of damage inflicted, makes no sense. The decision for implementing this rule is twofold.

First, it was done for a game balance purpose. While Tri-Stat makes every attempt to reflect the cinematic reality common in action games, it is first and foremost a game. It therefore attempts to maintain both game balance and a fun atmosphere. Combined attacks, when successful, are very effective and provide attackers with a tremendous advantage. They can quickly overwhelm Force Fields and Armour to bring down a foe. To offset this advantage, there needs to be a counter-balance — a detriment to prevent characters from constantly using it as a mode of attack. There has to be a reason that characters do not always combine their efforts into one massive attack upon their opponents. Thus, a mechanic was built into the Combined Attack rule that penalised characters when they failed their attack roll. While a successful Combined Attack remains incredibly effective, a failed attempt is enough of a detriment to force characters to consider if the attempt is worth it. If they can bring the foe down individually, the combined attack is not necessary and the risk of inflicting reduced damage is incentive to not try. If they cannot affect the character normally, then the risk of reducing the damage they inflict is not a consideration — reducing the damage of an ineffective attack still results in an ineffective attack.

Secondly, GMs can easily explain the reduction of damage by pointing out that failure to combine one's attack with allies results in a glancing blow. The character hits the target but his or her effort to hit a precise spot results in a less-than-solid strike.

reduces the damage delivered by two ranks (minimum of 0% damage). If the character misses, no damage is delivered.

The target of a successful combined attack may avoid all damage from the attackers' combined effort with a single defence combat check. If he or she is successful, all damage from the combined attack is avoided. A penalty of -1 is applied to the roll for each opponent who successfully participates in the combined attack. Any failed combined attacks, however, must be defended against separately.

Characters who possess the Combination Attack Attribute (page 15) have special rules for performing this manoeuvre, and are not subject to the same limitations.

EXTRA AIM

A character making a ranged attack may deliberately take extra time to aim. If a character aims a ranged weapon for an entire round and does not move or defend during that period, he or she receives a +2 attack check bonus, or +3 if he or she is using a scope. If an aiming character chooses to make a defence check or suffers any damage before he or she can fire, the character loses the benefit of Extra Aim.

STRIKING TO INCAPACITATE

A character attacking in hand-to-hand combat or with a blunt melee weapon may attempt to knock a surprised opponent unconscious. The target of the attack must be unaware of the attack to be vulnerable. The attacker makes his or her Attack Combat check with a -6 penalty. If the target suffers any damage (after all defensive Attributes are applied), he or she must make a Body Stat check. If the target succeeds on this Body check, he or she maintains consciousness. If the target fails this check, however, he or she falls unconscious. Damage inflicted by an Incapacitating Strike is then divided by ten, rounding down.

For example, a special ops cyborg wants to capture the terrorists alive so he strikes to Incapacitate. He rolls to hit with a -6 penalty and successfully hits his opponent, forcing the target to make a Body Stat check. His punch, after rolling, inflicts 40 damage. Regardless of whether or not the target remains conscious, he takes 4 (40÷10 = 4) damage from the blow.

STRIKING TO WOUND

A character in combat can elect to reduce his or her delivered damage below the normal damage value to a minimum of 1 point (known as striking to wound). He or she may not attempt this with attacks possessing the Area Effect, Auto-Fire, or Spreading Ability, however.

THROWING HEAVY THINGS

A character with the Superstrength Attribute (or a high Body Stat) can lift heavy things — up to 10% of his or her maximum capacity — and throw them to deliver damage. It takes one action to grab and lift a large, awkward object, and another to throw it. Consequently, throwing objects is slower than firing most weapons. The advantage of throwing an object is that big things are harder to dodge than smaller ones. The GM should assign objects a number of BP of Awkward Size based on their size and mass; see Awkward Size on page 51. Defence checks suffer a penalty of -1 for each BP of Awkward Size of the object thrown (or equivalent). Damage delivered to both the target and the thrown object is equal to the attacker's Combat Value, plus bonuses for Superstrength and Massive Damage, plus 10 for each BP of Awkward Size Defect of the thrown object.

TOTAL ATTACK

A character can take this option in conjunction with an attack. It means he or she focuses completely on an offensive action with no thought given to defence. The character may opt to forfeit one defence action to perform a Total Attack, gaining a +2 bonus to his or her attack check. Only one defence may be forfeited per attack, though a character with both the Extra Attacks and Extra Defences Attributes can initiate more than one Total Attack each round.

TOUCHING A TARGET

Some Attributes require a character simply touch his or her target. It is much easier to just touch a person than it is to physically strike him or her with enough force to cause damage. Thus, any character who is simply attempting to touch an opponent gains a +6 bonus to his or her attack check. Touching a specific part of a target's body may require a Called Shot (page 63). This assumes the character is simply attempting to make physical contact with the target. If prolonged contact is required, the target must either be willing or the character must grapple the target (below).

TRICK SHOTS

Some characters are known to make trick shots (such as ricocheting weapons or energy blasts off several walls before striking the target). Trick shots make the attack much harder to defend against, but likewise it is harder for the attacker to successfully hit. If the attacker takes a voluntary penalty to his or her Attack Combat Check Value, reflecting the difficult nature of the trick shot, the defender will suffer the same penalty to his or her Defence Combat Check Value.

Table 8-1: Trick Shot Modifiers

Trick Shot Degree of Difficulty	Attack's Penalty To Hit	Defender's Penalty To Evade
Fancy Trick Shot	-2	-2
Challenging Trick Shot	-4	-4
Complex Trick Shot	-6	-6
Difficult Trick Shot	-8	-8
Fantastic Trick Shot	-10	-10

GRAPPLING

Instead of striking to inflict damage in melee combat, a character can attempt to grab someone and pin him or her. This is a grappling attack, and a character must have at least one empty hand free. Grabbing a small, inanimate object not in an individual's Sphere of Control (page 71) does not require a full action.

Game Masters resolve a grappling attempt like a normal attack with the applicable Unarmed Attack (Grappling) Skill. If the attack hits and the target's defence (if any) fails, then the attacker successfully grabbed his or her opponent. The target of a grappling attack defends by making a defence check. The Unarmed Defence (Grappling) Skill is applicable. The attacker gains a grappling advantage if he or she has more free hands than the defender. "Free" means not holding weapons or other objects, or not otherwise incapacitated. In this case, the defender suffers a cumulative -2 attack or defence check penalty for each free hand the attacker uses to grapple in excess of the number of free hands the defender is using. The maximum penalty assigned for this disadvantage is -8.

For example, if a knight (two hands) tries to escape from the grasp of a lizard man (four hands), he suffers a -4 defence check penalty (4-2 = 2; 2 x -2 = -4). If the lizard man is holding an object in one of its four hands, however, the knight only suffers a -2 defence check penalty (3-2 = 1; 1 x -2 = -2). Characters with the Elasticity Attribute (page 18) gain a bonus to attempts to grapple.

The attacker can hold a grabbed character relatively stationary. The target suffers a -4 penalty on all attack and defence checks when performing other melee attacks or defences (including grabbing, biting, kneeing, etc.) or -8 when attempting to perform other tasks requiring freedom of movement like using hand-held equipment. Exception: if the grabbed character is much stronger (or more agile, at the GM's discretion) than the opponent, his or her penalty is halved, and the character can still move freely. The GM may consider a character much stronger if his or her Body Stat is at least four Levels higher or if the character has Superstrength at a higher Level. For this purpose, each Level of Less Capable (Strength) counts as a -3 to Body. Thus, a small child (Body 2) could not stop a strong man (Body 6) from pinning him or her while the strong man would be able to move freely if grabbed by the small child. It is, of course, possible for one character to grab an opponent who then grabs the character in return (this is what often happens when grappling).

Grappling Manoeuvres

Once a character grabs an opponent, he or she can attempt a grappling special manoeuvre (Lock, Throw, or Pin) as his or her next attack (see below).

Lock

Instead of attacking normally, a character who (on a previous attack) successfully grabbed his or her opponent can choke, crush, or strangle that foe. This attack automatically hits and inflicts damage equal to the character's Combat Value plus bonuses from Superstrength and Massive Damage.

Throw

Instead of attacking normally, a character who has already grabbed an opponent and is standing can hurl the foe to the ground. A character must make an attack check at a +4 bonus, modified by the Unarmed Attack (Throws) Skill. If successful, the opponent receives a defence check using the Unarmed Defence (Throws) Skill. A throw delivers damage equal to the Attack Combat Value plus 5 additional points of damage (as well as bonuses from Superstrength). Additionally, if the defender fails his or her defence check, the attacker may throw the character out a window or off a ledge, and the GM can assign extra damage based on the situation. If the attacker throws the opponent at another enemy, the target must make a defence check or suffer equal damage as well. A throw normally breaks the grip on the target unless the attacker attempts to maintain a hold and succeeds in an Unarmed Attack (Grappling) check with a -4 penalty (which must be made whether the throw is successful or not).

Pin

A character who has grabbed someone may attempt to improve his or her hold during the next attack by completely immobilizing the opponent in a pin. Game Masters may treat this manoeuvre the same as the first grab attack. If the attack succeeds and the opponent fails to defend, then the foe is pinned, usually under the weight of the attacker's body. Attackers may not attempt a pin if the opponent is much stronger (see earlier for definition of much stronger). Once a character pins an opponent, the target suffers a -6 penalty on checks when attempting to escape. A pinned character cannot attack or defend.

Biting

Since biting does not require the use of hands, it is an effective tactic when a character has either grabbed or been grabbed by an opponent. Game Masters should treat this as a normal attack that inflicts only one half of the Attack Combat Value in damage (round down), unless the aggressor is using a Natural Weapons Attribute (Fangs, Beak, or Mandibles).

Escaping

A grabbed character may attempt to struggle free. On the character's Initiative to act, he or she can attempt to escape instead of attack. Both characters roll a Body Stat check with modifiers for the Unarmed Attack (Grappling) Skill. The character with the highest degree of success (or least degree of failure) wins. If the grabbed character wins, he or she escapes, and may also attack or take another action. If the characters tie, the grabbed character escapes, but forfeits his or her current action. If the grabbed character loses, he or she is immobilised and forfeits one attack action and one defence action that round. If a grabbed character chooses to attack the person who grabbed him or her (with appropriate penalties) and inflicts damage equal to or greater than his or her foe's Body Stat, he or she escapes the grab.

Fighting from the Ground

Fighters thrown to the ground or who are otherwise forced to fight from a prone position defend and make all attacks at a -4 penalty.

Disarming via Grappling

A character can try grabbing an opponent's weapon instead of the opponent's body. He or she makes the attack at a -2 attack check penalty. The opponent earns a +2 bonus to the defence check if holding onto the weapon with two or more hands. A successful attack might dislodge the weapon, but the defender is allowed a Body Stat check to maintain his or her grip. If the defender fails, he or she drops the item; if successful, the defender is at a -4 penalty to use the weapon until the end of his or her next action (after which time, the defender can use the weapon without penalty, unless the attacker attempts another disarm manoeuvre).

MOVEMENT IN COMBAT

The GM decides whether he or she wishes to keep detailed track of movement, ranges, and distances. In most close-in combat situations, GMs should not worry about exact speeds and distances — a general idea of the overall situation is sufficient. Alternatively, GMs can measure ranges in a more abstract fashion: "you're behind him and in melee range" or "you can reach her in three rounds, if you hurry." The GM should judge how quickly range shifts from relative speeds to dramatic necessity. For example, in a race between two opponents with equal speeds, the GM can allow the character who keeps winning Initiative to increase the gap gradually between him or her and the other runner. A good way to resolve long distance chases is for the GM to establish a certain number of combat rounds between the starting point and the goal. It then becomes a simple matter of reaching the target first.

If the GM wishes to keep precise track of movement and distances, assume an average human adult can sprint approximately 6 metres per round times his or her Body Stat over short distances (one metre times Body Stat if swimming or crawling). The speed is reduced when a character is running a long distance. This guideline assumes five-seconds per round, but the GM can modify exact speeds when necessary.

JUMPING

GMs can allow characters to jump as far as seems dramatically appropriate for the game. If distance is important, a person can jump about two metres forward, or one up or back, with range doubled on a short running start. A successful Body Stat check allows a fast moving character (or vehicle) with a running start to jump, in metres, one-quarter of his or her current speed in kilometres per hour — an average character can reach 5 kph times his or her Body. A failed Stat check means the character falls short. A wheeled or tracked vehicle or a boat can only jump if it has a ramp.

MOVEMENT ATTACK PENALTIES

When a character is moving in combat, he or she may incur penalties to attack and Block Defence checks (see Table 8-2). The penalty incurred depends on how quickly the character is moving relative to his or her maximum movement ability. The following chart indicates the movement rates and penalties incurred. For a normal character who does not have or is not using an Attribute to move (Speed, Flight, Water Speed, etc.), the character's movement rate is dictated by his or her Body Stat, as outlined in the Normal Character column. Characters who are using a movement Attribute refer to the Movement Attribute column to determine their rate of movement.

If a character is sprinting, he or she incurs a -4 penalty to attack and Block Defence checks. If the character is running, he or she incurs a -2 penalty on attack and Block Defence checks. Characters who are jogging do not incur penalties. Additionally, characters do not incur penalties when attempting Parry/Dodge Defence checks regardless of their speed. GMs do not need to keep exact track of movement rates unless they wish; they may simply keep movement abstract.

Table 8-2: Movement Attack Penalties

	Normal Character	Movement Attribute	Penalty
Jogging	up to Body x 4 metres per round	Up to Maximum Attribute Level -2	no penalty
Running	Body x 5 metres per round	Maximum Attribute Level -1	-2
Sprinting	Body x 6 metres per round	Maximum Attribute Level	-4

FIRING WEAPONS FROM MOVING VEHICLES

Characters who are inside a fast-moving vehicle fire their weapons at a penalty. Firing weapons when moving at moderate speeds incurs a -2 penalty, while moving very quickly earns a -4 attack check penalty. Game Masters should impose an additional -4 penalty for characters also piloting the vehicle while firing.

ATTACKING MOVING TARGETS

Attempting to hit a target that is moving at exceptional speeds is very challenging. When attempting to hit a target that is moving quickly, the character suffers an attack combat check penalty. See Table 8-3: Attack Situation Modifiers for the appropriate penalty based on the target's speed.

ATTACK CHECK MODIFIERS

The GM may impose appropriate modifiers when the players make an attack check. An attack action normally assumes characters are engaged in active combat — dodging enemy attacks, making quick strikes when the opportunity arises, moving about, etc. The GM should not apply any penalties for this sort of normal combat-related activity. If circumstances are such that a character's aim or

Table 8-3: Attack Situation Modifiers

Attack Situation	Modifier
Attacker is:	
Taking an action to aim	+2, or +3 with scope
Attacking Multiple Targets with one action	0, -2, or -4 per additional target
Attacking with two weapons (same target)	-8
Attacking with two weapons (different targets)	-12
Attempting a Combined Attack	-2 per attacker after the first
Attempting to Touch the Target	+6
Making a Total Attack	+2
Firing personal weapons from a moving vehicle	-2 or -4
Firing personal weapons while piloting a vehicle	-8
Firing personal weapons while swimming or performing acrobatics	-4
In an awkward position (on the ground, etc.)	-4
Attacker is Attempting a Trick Shot:	
Fancy Trick Shot	-2
Challenging Trick Shot	-4
Complex Trick Shot	-6
Difficult Trick Shot	-8
Fantastic Trick Shot	-10
Attacker is:	
Jogging: At Body Stat x 4 metres per round or lower	no modifier
Running: At Body Stat x 4 to Body Stat x 5 metres per round	-2
Sprinting: At Body Stat x 5 to Body Stat x 6 metres per round	-4
Jogging: At two Levels below maximum Attribute rate	no modifier
Running: At one Level below maximum Attribute rate	-2
Sprinting: At maximum Attribute rate	-4
Attacker is Attempting a Called Shot:	
Disarming (with melee attack)	-4
Disarming (with a ranged attack)	-8
Targeting a partially armoured point	-4
Targeting a vital spot	-8
Targeting a Weak Point	-2, -4, or -6
Target is Moving at:	
up to 99 kph (Flight 1 or 2)	no modifier
100 to 499 kph (Flight 3; Speed 1)	-2
500 to 999 kph (Flight 4; Speed 2)	-4
1,000 to 4,999 kph (Flight 5; Speed 3)	-6
5,000 to 9,999 kph (Flight 6; Speed 4)	-8
10,000 to 49,999 kph (Flight 7; Speed 5)	-10
50,000 kph or more (Flight 8+; Speed 6+)	-12
Target within melee range, and:	
Concealed by trees or brush	-2 to -6
Concealed by darkness, fog, or smoke	-2 to -4
Taking cover	-2 to -8
Target beyond melee range, and:	
Concealed by trees or brush	-4 to -8
Concealed by darkness, fog, or smoke	-4 to -6
Taking cover	-4 to -10
Range Modifiers:	
Attacking at up to twice range	-4
Attacking at up to five times range	-8

concentration seems likely impeded (such as shooting someone whom the character cannot clearly see or attacking a foe while hanging upside down), the GM may assign penalties to the attack check. Likewise, in stress-free situations (such as whacking an immobile victim, or target range shooting with nothing riding on the outcome), the GM can apply favourable bonuses or assume automatic success.

A number of possible penalties or bonuses are described on Table 8-3: Attack Situation Modifiers. The GM may adjust or ignore these modifiers if he or she prefers.

NON-COMBAT ACTIONS

Rather than taking an offensive action during any combat round, a character may use a non-combat action on his or her Initiative. Such actions include untying a rescued captive, running, changing weapons, climbing into or out of a vehicle, writing a note, changing clothes, etc. Players may also use non-combat actions to safely withdraw from armed or melee combat, provided the opposition does not attack at a later Initiative number in the same round. Note that speaking a few words during combat, running about while attacking, or making a short dramatic speech does not constitute an action.

A non-combat action may succeed automatically, or the GM can require a Stat check, or Skill check to determine whether it succeeds. Some non-combat actions may require several rounds to perform at the GM's option.

OTHER ACTIONS

Some activities do not count as attack or non-combat actions. A character can perform all of the following activities in addition to an attack or non-combat action:

• Move a short distance or manoeuvre his or her vehicle.

• Say anything that fits within the span of 1-10 seconds.

• Perform defensive actions in response to any attacks against him or her. Note that if the character performs more than one defensive action in a round, subsequent defensive actions after the first (or later, if he or she has the Extra Defences Attribute, page 19) in the same round suffer penalties.

DEFENCE

If a character is the target of a successful attack, he or she may attempt to defend against it with a Dodge/Parry Defence (avoiding the attack by moving out of the way, or using a weapon to push the attack to the side or "off-line"), an Attribute Defence (page 72), or a Block Defence (interposing an object between the attack and the target). Defensive actions are not dependent on Initiative order but resolved immediately after the attack before the attack damage is calculated or revealed.

To successfully defend, the player must roll less than or equal to the character's Defence Combat Value. Each character can attempt a defence only once against a particular attack (including grapples). A character may defend against more than one attack in a round, but with an appropriate penalty to each defence after the first (unless the character has the Extra Defences Attribute; the penalty then applies to each defence after the final bonus defence). Should the opponent not defend (perhaps in anticipation of a more powerful attack still to come), he or she cannot change that decision later in the round.

If a vehicle is the target of an attack, its driver or pilot makes the defence checks. If a vehicle is unable to manoeuvre (trapped in a confined space, for example) the GM may rule that it cannot defend at all. Likewise, a vehicle cannot normally defend against attacks made by a character who is riding in or on it.

DEFENDING AGAINST MULTIPLE ATTACKS

When defending against multiple attacks in a single round, each defence after the first incurs a cumulative Check Value penalty of -4: -4 for the second defence, -8 for the third, -12 for the fourth, etc. This means that even the greatest fighter may be overwhelmed if badly outnumbered. Remember to include all relevant Attribute, Skill, Defect, and difficulty modifiers. If successful, the defender blocks, dodges, or otherwise negates the attack, and suffers no damage.

RELEVANT DEFENCE SKILLS

When a character defends against a ranged attack, the relevant Skill is Ranged Defence. For a hand-to-hand or other melee-ranged attack, the relevant Skill is either Unarmed Defence (if the character is dodging, or blocking the attack with his or her body), or Melee Defence (if the character is using a weapon to parry or block).

BLOCK DEFENCE

Rather than attempting to avoid an attack with a Dodge/Parry Defence, the character may instead choose to block the attack with a shield or other suitably large and resistant object (a Block Defence). When a character attempts to block, he or she gains a +2 bonus to his or her defence combat check. If successful, the character has interposed the object in front of the attack. The object's Armour Rating provides protection to the character. Thus, a plank of wood can be used to block a powerful energy blast but, if the attack does more damage than the wood's Armour Rating, it will still strike the character, inflicting reduced damage. See Breaking Objects (page 82) for suggested Armour Ratings of common items or Table 9-5 Armour and Protective Devices (page 81) for shields. If the attack delivers five times the object's Armour Rating, the object is destroyed. Characters may only attempt to block melee or unarmed attacks unless they have the Block Ranged Attack Combat Technique (page 14).

Why is Block Defence Easier?

Of the two defence options — Block Defence or Dodge/Parry Defence — we have decided to make the Block Defence easier for two reasons. First, we believe that interposing an object, like a sword or shield, between your own body and an attack is indeed easier than completely avoiding any contact (a dodge). We also think it's easier than using your own weapon to parry, which requires some skill.

Secondly, we assigned the +2 bonus for Block Defences for game balance reasons. With a successful Parry/Dodge Defence, the defender avoids all damage completely. Powerful attacks can potentially break the object the defender uses in a Block Defence, however, still inflicting partial damage. In exchange for a higher-risk defence manoeuvre, we are awarding your character a +2 bonus.

INDEFENSIBLE ATTACKS

A character may not attempt a defence check if he or she is unaware of the attack, unable to move, or is struck with a Critical Hit (page 69).

TOTAL DEFENCE

A character can make fewer offensive or non-combat actions in a round to improve his or her chances of avoiding an attack. Instead of attacking or engaging in another activity, he or she concentrates completely on defence. A character performing a Total Defence may still move normally, but may not attack or take non-combat actions; the character is dodging and weaving, parrying frantically, ducking, and hiding. The character receives a +2 bonus to all defence checks for each attack sacrificed. This lasts until the character acts again next round. Additionally, a character who is employing Total Defence reduces any Knockback suffered (page 70) by half, representing the character bracing for the attack. Total Defence is a good tactic for anyone retreating, or someone buying time until his or her allies arrive.

Table 8-4: Defence Situation Modifiers

Defence Situation	Modifier
Dodge/Parry Defence	No Modifier
Block Defence	+2
Total Defence	+2 per attack sacrificed
Defending Against Additional Attacks	-4 per additional attack (cumulative)
Defending Against Undetectable Assailant	-8
Defending When Surprised	Defence Check Not Possible
Defending Against Critical Hit	Defence Check Not Possible

DEFENDING OTHERS

A character can defend the target of an attack in three ways: by pushing/pulling him or her out of the way, by interposing an object (such as a shield, or the character's body) between the target and the attacker, or using an Attribute. The first two methods are described below, while the final method is detailed under Defending With an Attack (page 72).

The first option, pushing or pulling (or grabbing a target as the character swing by), is similar to a Dodge/Parry Defence. The character uses a defence action, and rolls a defence check. It is difficult to defend someone else, however, and the attempt usually suffers a significant penalty (see Table 8-5). Obviously the action has to make sense — if the character has no way to reach a target, he or she cannot defend the individual.

To shield another person is akin to a Block Defence. Like any other Block Defence, the character gains a +2 bonus to his or her defence combat check, and must have the Block Ranged Attacks Feat in order to defend against missile weapons. A character can Block for another person with a Shield, weapon, extendable Force Field, or simply by standing in the way and absorbing the brunt of the attack.

If the character is out of defence actions, however, he or she normally cannot attempt to defend another (although in dire situations a GM might allow the character to make a roll with the normal cumulative penalty for additional defences, plus any other modifiers).

Table 8-5: Defending Others

Defence Situation	Modifier
Target is within reach	-2
Target is at medium range	-4
Target is at long range	-6
Target is in an awkward position	-2
Defender is in an awkward position	-2
Target concealed by trees or bush	-2
Target concealed by darkness, smoke	-4
Defending against additional attacks	-4 (cumulative)
Defender is surprised	Defence Not Possible
Defending against undetectable assailant	Defence Not Possible

DAMAGE

Characters suffer damage through combat, accidents, or other hazards. Damage ratings indicate the maximum amount of damage that an attack can inflict. The target character subtracts any damage inflicted from his or her Health Point total if the attack successfully penetrates Armour.

AMOUNT OF DAMAGE INFLICTED

Each attack has a Maximum Damage Rating, which is equal to the base damage of the attack (which includes a weapon's damage value) plus any bonuses from Massive Damage, and Superstrength, as is appropriate for the attack. When the character successfully strikes an opponent, he or she rolls on Table 8-6: Damage Percentage to determine the amount of damage the attack inflicts (always round fractions up). The character's Attack Combat Value, a reflection of the balance between Body Stat (force of the blow and manual dexterity), Mind Stat (knowledge of a body's vulnerable areas), and Soul Stat (determination and luck), is added to that value to determine how much damage is inflicted upon the target. The Maximum Damage Rating for normal, unarmed attacks by characters lacking Superstrength and Massive Damage is zero — the only damage delivered is equal to the character's Attack Combat value (do not roll on Table 8-6). In some circumstances it may be still important to determine the damage percentage for a Special Attack with the No Damage Disability (page 36), since the result determines the effectiveness of the attack's other Attack Abilities.

Characters may choose to inflict less damage than the dice roll indicates, if they desire. Thus, a heroic character who scores a crushing blow against an opponent on his last legs can reduce the damage inflicted to ensure that he does not kill the villain by mistake, rendering him unconscious instead.

Some effects reduce the percentage of damage delivered by one or more ranks. Each rank of reduction reduces the damage delivered by 25% to a minimum of 0% damage, though the attacker's Attack Combat Value is still added to this result.

If an attack delivers a percentage of damage, such as a Special Attack with the Burning Ability (page 33), the percentage of damage is based on the Base Damage of the attack, not on the amount of damage that the successful attack inflicts upon the target. If an attack inflicts multiple hits, such as Special Attacks with the Auto-Fire Ability (page 33), each additional hit inflicts the same percentage of damage as the first hit.

Players should record, on their character sheets, the Maximum Damage as well as the 25%, 50%, and 75% damage values of each of their attacks to avoid slowing down game play.

Table 8-6: Damage Percentage

Dice Roll						Damage percentage
d4	d6	d8	d10	d12	d20	
2	2-3	2-4	2-5	2-6	2-10	100% Maximum Damage
3-4	4-6	5-8	6-10	7-12	11-20	75% Maximum Damage
5-7	7-10	9-13	11-16	13-19	21-32	50% Maximum Damage
8	11-12	14-16	17-20	20-24	33-40	25% Maximum Damage

UNARMED COMBAT

The attack's Maximum Damage is equal to the character's bonuses for Superstrength, and Massive Damage. The character's Attack Combat Value is added to the damage inflicted.

MELEE WEAPONS

The attack's Maximum Damage is equal to the weapon's damage value, plus bonuses for Superstrength and Massive Damage. If the weapon has Abilities or Disabilities, refer to the relevant section (pages 32-36) for their effects. See Table 9-2: Weapons (page 75) for damages delivered by various melee weapons. The character's Attack Combat Value is added to the damage inflicted.

RANGED WEAPONS

The attack's Maximum Damage is equal to the weapon's damage value, plus bonuses for Massive Damage. A Superstrength bonus may also be added when appropriate (such as for thrown weapons). If the weapon has Abilities or Disabilities, refer to the relevant section (pages 32-36) for their effects. See Table 9-2: Weapons (page 75) for damages delivered by various ranged weapons. The character's Attack Combat Value is added to the damage inflicted.

SPECIAL ATTACKS

The attack's Maximum Damage is equal to the Special Attack's damage value, plus bonuses for Superstrength (as appropriate), and Massive Damage. The character's Attack Combat Value is added to the damage inflicted.

IMPACT DAMAGE

Damage may also result from a non-combat action such as crashing a speedboat into land or falling from a tree. Characters always suffer the maximum damage indicated from falls and crashes — do not roll on Table 8-6: Damage Percentage. Naturally, some non-combat actions may result in an NPC's death, but these events should only kill a player character in exceptional circumstances.

Crashing

During the course of an adventure, a character's vehicle may accidentally (or deliberately) crash into objects along the road, in the sky, in or on water, or in space. GMs should assess whatever damage they deem appropriate upon both the vehicle and occupants in a crash. The Armour and Force Field Attributes may protect against this damage. Similar damage can be applied to a character who jumps or is pushed from a speeding vehicle, or is struck by one.

ALTERNATE DAMAGE OPTIONS

Players interested in exploring additional options for damage should take a look at some of GUARDIANS OF ORDER's other RPGs.

Big Eyes, Small Mouth (BESM)

BESM, and our licensed Tri-Stat anime RPGs, use a fixed damage system. In *BESM*, having all attacks inflict their maximum damage upon a successful hit reflected the anime genre it was attempting to emulate — a genre where mecha are often destroyed after one or two hits and combat is fast and furious. If players wish to utilize a simpler system, they can return to the fixed damage ratings — damage inflicted equals the maximum damage of the attack. This will speed up combat greatly but, in the grand scheme, should not change the outcome of most fights — a character who would win with Tri-Stat dX's variable damage will probably also win using *Big Eyes, Small Mouth*'s fixed damage. Simply be aware that using a fixed damage value will greatly speed up combat and change the style and feel of the game. The choice of game style, however, is for the players and GMs to discuss.

Hong Kong Action Theatre! (HKAT!)

Some players will prefer a grittier combat system, where a successful Defense Combat check is not absolute, and where the Margin of Success is important. *HKAT!* illustrates an alternate damage system.

In this variant, the degree by which someone avoids an attack depends on how well a character defends against it. To completely defend against an attack, the player must score a Margin of Success equal to or greater than the attacker's Margin of Success on the attack check. If successful, the defender blocks, dodges, or otherwise negates the attack, and suffers no damage.

If the defender makes a successful defense combat check but scores a Margin of Success less than the attacker's Margin of Success, then the defender partially avoids the attack and only suffers half damage (rounding down). This reflects the character successfully blocking a punch but still taking some damage (perhaps after the attacker's fist hits his or her arm) or someone who dives through a window to avoid being shot, etc. If the defender fails his or her defense combat check completely, then he or she does not avoid the attack and suffers full damage.

Table 8-7: Crashing and Falling Damage assists the GM in determining the damage for hitting the ground, water, a building, or some other immovable object based on how fast the vehicle was moving during that round. If a speed falls between two damage values, use the greater of the two.

Falling

A character who falls a great distance will suffer damage depending on the height he or she plummeted. He or she may also make an Acrobatics Skill check with success halving the sustained damage to indicate a proper break fall. The Armour and Force Field Attributes may protect against this damage (GM's discretion).

Table 8-7: Crashing and Falling Damage

Speed	Falling Distance	Damage Delivered
20 kph	3 to 4 meters	10
30 kph	5 metres to 9 metres	20
50 kph	10 metres to 29 metres	30
100 kph	30 metres to 59 metres	50
150 kph	60 metres to 149 metres	70
200 kph	150 metres to 499 metres	90
500 kph	500 metres (or greater)	120
1,000 kph		150
2,500 kph		180
each additional 2,500 kph		an additional 30

ARMOUR OR FORCE FIELDS AND DAMAGE

If a character has Armour (page 13) or a Force Field (page 19), this reduces the delivered damage from each successful attack by an amount equal to its rating. The character suffers any damage not negated by the Armour or Force Field, subtracting it from his or her current Health Point total. See Effects of Damage (below) for the result.

CRITICAL HITS

In the event of a natural attack dice roll of 2, the attacker automatically hits, preventing the target from making a defence check at all (this rule is optional for games that use d4). The target also receives double Maximum Damage from the attack, plus the character's Attack Combat Value — do not roll on Table 8-6 when an attacker rolls a critical hit.

EFFECTS OF DAMAGE TO A CHARACTER

Total loss of Health Points can cause a character to pass out or die. Should a character or NPC's Health Points ever drop below zero, he or she suffered a severe wound and is rendered unconscious. If a character is reduced to the negative value of his or her Health Points, he or she has suffered a mortal wound and will die (or fall into a coma, depending on the tone of the game) unless medical attention arrives immediately. The GM may allow the character to linger long enough to say a few last words or perform some other final, heroic action.

WOUND DIFFICULTY PENALTIES

The Game Master may wish to assign difficulty penalties to characters who have been injured in combat. When the character's Health Points are reduced to 75% of their original value or less, all tasks suffer a -2 penalty. This penalty applies to all Stat, Skill, and combat checks. At 50% Health Points, tasks suffer a -4 penalty; at 25%, tasks suffer a -6 penalty.

Second Wind

If an event occurs during the course of combat that induces a powerful emotional response within a damaged character, the character is given an opportunity to refocus on the combat and eliminate all damage difficulty penalties — getting a "second wind." The GM decides which events are significant enough to evoke such a reaction. In these situations, the penalties are removed if the character makes a successful Stat check, without any modifiers, against his or her highest Stat Value.

If a character drops below one of the remaining damage tiers (50% or 25% of original Health Points) after getting a second wind, he or she will immediately suffer from the corresponding damage difficulty penalties once again: -4 at 50% or -6 at 25%. A character can only get a second wind once during any combat scene.

Table 8-8: Damage Difficulty Penalties

Percentage of Original Health Points	Modifier
100-76%	0
75%-51%	-2
50%-26%	-4
25%-0%	-6

CHARACTER DEATH

Death in a game can occur rarely, often, or never, depending on the tone and theme of the story in question. The default rule in Tri-Stat dX is that death is a real consequence of extreme actions; it happens rarely, but is the end result of deadly force or careless negligence. Characters are responsible for keeping their powers in check, and not laying waste to their targets haphazardly.

Not all stories should have the possibility for death, or the chance of accidental death, however. In these games, characters may hit an enemy full force and be comfortable that the GM won't announce they've unwittingly decapitated their opponent. Wounds may require medical attention, and knockouts, concussions, and comas are all possible, but death only occurs when a player announces that his or her character has had enough, and finally steps over that line. Playing with this rule gives players the freedom to let loose a little, but still maintains the option for intense role-playing, if a character is ever driven so far as to make that choice.

SHOCK AND CRITICAL INJURY
(Optional Rule)

The rules for Shock and Critical Injuries are appropriate for gritty or realistic games but are not recommended for cinematic or heroic games.

SHOCK

If a character suffers more damage from a single attack than his or her Shock Value (page 58), he or she must make a Soul Stat check. If the check fails, the character is stunned and will collapse. The character will also let go of anything he or she is holding. The character's incapacitation will last for a number of rounds equal to the amount by which the Soul Stat check was failed. An incapacitated character is effectively out of action, either knocked out or awake but immobilised by pain or shock. He or she may not take any offensive, defensive, or non-combat actions. The duration of incapacitation from multiple failed Soul Stat checks from several injuries occurring in a short period of time is cumulative.

CRITICAL INJURY

A character that suffers more damage than his or her Shock Value from an attack that breaks the skin (such as from a bullet, knife, arrow, grenade fragment, etc.) has taken a critical injury. A character who suffers a critical injury loses one additional Health Point every round (every minute, if out of combat) until given successful first aid. Just stopping the bleeding through first aid is not enough, however — it only slows the loss of Health Points. A critically injured character that has undergone successful first aid will lose one Health Point every 10 minutes until he or she undergoes successful surgery (best performed in a hospital). Thus, a character who is badly hurt might die because of shock and internal injuries before he or she can be stabilised. A character can suffer multiple critical injuries. If so, each must be treated separately, and Health Point losses are cumulative.

MEDICAL TREATMENT FOR CRITICAL INJURIES

If a character suffered a critical injury, he or she will lose one Health Point every round (or every minute if out of combat) until treated via first aid. This requires a successful Mind/Body-average based Medical (Emergency Response) Skill check. Each attempt takes 10 rounds (or one minute); several tries can be made until successful. If the character is trying to perform first aid on him or herself, apply a -2 penalty. If the character does not have an actual first aid kit handy but is forced to improvise dressings, etc., apply an additional -2 penalty.

As mentioned before, a critical injury that is treated will still result in the loss of one additional Health Point every 10 minutes until the character undergoes surgery. This requires a Mind/Body-average based Medical (Surgery) Skill check. There is no penalty if performed with a full staff in a modern hospital, but a -4 penalty applies if it is performed with less adequate medical facilities (for example, in a doctor's office or a poor third-world hospital) or -8 if performed with completely improvised equipment. Each attempt will take at least 10 minutes. Success stabilises the patient while failure causes him or her to lose additional Health Points equal to twice the margin of failure. Another try is possible, however.

Optionally, a character who has been badly injured (negative Health Points) because of cumulative Health Point loss may also require treatment, even if he or she did not suffer a critical injury. This may be dependent on the nature of the injuries — someone who was badly burned may be in worse condition than someone who was beaten up. The GM can rule that keeping the character alive until adequate medical attention is available requires a successful Medical (Emergency Response) Skill check and that full recovery (at doubled healing rate) will require a Medical (Surgery) Skill check. In both cases, use the average of the caregiver's Body and Mind Stats.

KNOCKBACK
(Optional Rule)

Blunt attacks (such as punches, kicks, or blunt melee weapons) and Special Attacks with the Knockback Ability (page 34) can inflict Knockback upon a successful hit with this optional rule. Attacks such as a slash from a sword or a piercing spear do not normally inflict Knockback. The target is knocked back one metre for each point of damage delivered after rolling on Table 8-6: Damage Percentage (before adding the attacker's Attack Combat Value, unless the character has the ACV Knockback Combat Technique; page 14). This distance is reduced by the target's Body Stat, in metres. Additionally, the Immovable Attribute (page 23) and Force Fields without the Full Impact Disability (page 19) reduce Knockback.

Table 8-9: Knockback Distance (in Metres)
Add:
+ Percentage of Maximum Damage delivered (see Table 8-6: Damage Percentage)
+ Attacker's Attack Combat Value (only if the character possesses the ACV Knockback Combat Technique)
Multiply by:
x Critical Hit damage multiplier, if the attack delivered a critical hit (page 69) or Called Shot to Vital (page 64)
Subtract:
- Target's Body Stat
- Target's Immovable Attribute Level x 20
- Target's Force Field Attribute Level x 20 (only for Force Fields without the Full Impact Disability)

KNOCKBACK IMPACT DAMAGE

Characters who are knocked back usually tumble along the ground or sail through the air, but do not suffer any additional damage. When a character is knocked back into an object, however, he or she suffers 1 point of impact damage for each metre of Knockback, up to a maximum of five times the Armour rating of the object into which he or she is knocked (see Breaking Objects, page 82).

OTHER KNOCKBACK EFFECTS

If a character is knocked high into the air, off a building, or some other similar situation, additional damage may be suffered when the character falls to the ground. The Special Movement (Cat-Like) Attribute and Acrobatics Skill can mitigate damage (GM's discretion). If a character is knocked up into the air, reduce his or her Knockback distance by half; the character falls back to the ground and suffers full damage from the fall. A character that falls to the ground as a result of Knockback only suffers damage from the fall (see Table 8-7: Crashing and Falling Damage, page 69), not the Knockback impact damage outlined above.

Additionally, if the character can fly and is knocked back a great distance, the GM can determine if he or she is able to recover his or her senses soon enough to begin flying before colliding with an obstacle. The GM may require a successful Body or Mind Stat check for a character to accomplish this (possibly with penalties on the check).

GMs may, however, alter any of this to reflect specific situations or game styles, as is appropriate. For example, a GM may decide that a character who is knocked back 80 metres and comes to a skidding stop on the pavement will still suffer some damage (perhaps equal to one tenth the Knockback distance), even if he or she does not collide with a building or object.

MIND COMBAT

Mind combat is a special type of conflict, that uses the Telepathy Attribute (page 39) to forcibly invade another's mind. Most telepaths make mental attacks using the Special Attack Attribute with the Mind Attack Ability. This mental conflict, however, is a clashing of two psyches, each struggling to subdue the other — it is akin to two people getting into a mental fist fight. Mental combat can become lethal if either person begins tearing down neural pathways, erasing memories, or destroying brain cells. Physical strength does not play a role in this battle, only the power of the Mind. Each round of mind combat covers from 1 to 10 seconds of time from the characters' perspectives. The exact time scale is not relevant, since one round of physical combat should cover the same amount of time as one round of mind combat.

Mind combat can only be carried out once mental contact has been established, usually using the Telepathy Attribute. Once two minds have touched, the initiator of the contact may withdraw at any time. Alternatively, physical damage to the initiator or perhaps use of an appropriate Item of Power can break the contact. For the target to break unwanted mind contact, the player cannot initiate any other actions for one round and must make a successful Mind Stat check with a -4 penalty. If the check is successful, the aggressor is forced from the character's mind and the mind combat ends immediately.

If any character in mental contact forfeits all physical actions for the round (including attack, defence, and non-combat action), he or she can attack through mind combat. A successful attack requires the player to make a successful Stat check using the average of his or her Mind and Soul Stats. The GM has the option of modifying the Check Value should the attack be particularly easy or difficult. The target can attempt to defend with a Stat check using the average of his or her Mind and Soul Stats with a -2 penalty.

The psychic damage of a successful attack is equal to the average of the attacker's Mind and Soul Stats. If using the optional rules for Energy Points, this damage is subtracted from the target's current Energy Points. Otherwise, it is removed from the character's Health Points. If a character is ever reduced to or below zero Health (or Energy) Points while in mind combat, his or her mind has been broken and is now at the mercy of the opponent. The victor can end the character's life, search through memories, plant powerful suggestions, erase thoughts, or simply render the character unconscious. Any changes to a character's mind (other than death) will remain until reversed by another character skilled in the Telepathy Attribute. The GM should decide exactly how this must be accomplished. Role-playing a character whose mind has been altered is challenging but can also be very rewarding when played with consistency.

A telepath who wishes to alter a target's mind after winning a mind combat battle must spend a great deal of time to alter it. Minor changes such as removing unimportant memories or implanting unessential false memories can take a couple of hours. Massive changes, such as instilling (or removing) a prejudice or phobia, rebuilding a large portion of the target's memories, or similar large scale remodelling should take days to complete. Characters may rush the procedure, if pressed, but there is a risk of the alteration failing over time. The target may notice a gap in his or her memory and question what happened, or a personality adjustment (new phobia, for example) may weaken over time. If the character wishes to perform a change quickly, the character may perform minor changes in a matter of rounds while the character can accomplish massive changes in about an hour.

When a character attempts to alter a target's mind, he or she must make a Mind-based Social Sciences (Psychology) Skill check. The GM may impose a penalty if the alteration is particularly severe or drastic. The character's Margin of Success determines how long the modification lasts, measured in years if the character took his or her time with the procedure or measured in days if the character rushed things. GMs should make this Skill check secretly and not inform the player of the result unless it is a failure — he or she will not know how long the change will hold, only that it has occurred or not.

The Mind Shield Attribute (page 26) provides a bonus to the character's attempt to resist mind combat and mental alterations, as well as Armour against mind combat damage.

RECOVERY

A character who suffers lost Health Points due to damage may heal naturally (or be repaired, for mechanical characters).

RECOVERING HEALTH POINTS

Health Points regenerate at a rate equal to the character's Body Stat for each day (or hour for less "realistic" campaigns) of rest. For example, a character with a Body Stat of 5 rejuvenates 5 Health Points every day while resting. The healing rate doubles if the character is in the care of someone with Medical Skill but halved if he or she does not spend time resting.

RECOVERING ENERGY POINTS

This rule is only used in campaigns where Energy Points are used. The average of the Mind and Soul Stat (rounded up) equals the number of Energy Points the character recovers every hour whether the character rests or not. A character with a 7 Mind Stat and a 3 Soul Stat, for example, regains 5 Energy Points ever hour (7+3=10; 10÷2=5).

REPAIRING EQUIPMENT

Equipment, such as weapons, vehicles, or other gadgets can become damaged in the course of fighting crime. Characters can repair damage to equipment by making a Mind-based Mechanics Skill check. If the object has Health Points, each Skill check repairs 10 Health Points. Each Skill check should take approximately one day of work (approximately six to ten hours), depending on the extent of the repairs required. Most mechanical, or non-organic, characters do not recover Health Points, and must also be repaired.

USING ATTRIBUTES IN COMBAT

In some situations, players will want to use various Attributes in inventive ways in the middle of a fight. The following rules outline the use of Attributes in combat. In many instances, the appropriate Power Usage Skill (page 48) can influence the chances of success.

USING ATTRIBUTES AGAINST OPPONENTS

Creative characters can use a number of seemingly inoffensive Attributes in very effective ways in the middle of combat. Special Attacks are obviously designed for offensive use against an opponent, but what about Teleportation? Could a character not teleport an opponent in front of a moving truck or simply out of a fight entirely? When a character wishes to use a normally inoffensive Attribute against an unwilling opponent, the character must give up a non-combat action and make a Stat check using the relevant Stat for the Attribute. If the check is successful, the target is allowed a Soul Stat check to resist the effect (Body or Mind can be substituted if the GM deems it appropriate). If the target fails the Soul Stat check, he or she is affected by the Attribute. Otherwise, the target resists the effect entirely.

Characters must have PMVs at a Level sufficient to be able to accomplish their desired effect. If a teleporter does not have the Targets PMV, for example, he or she cannot use the Attribute against an opponent.

SPHERE OF CONTROL

If a character attempts to use an Attribute on an object within the sphere of control of a character, the character is allowed to make a Soul Stat check to resist the effect as though he or she was the target of the attack. For example, a teleporter who wished to teleport the bullets out of an opponent's gun would still be required to make a Mind Stat check and the person holding the gun would be allowed a Soul Stat check to resist the effect. Other common objects usually in a target's sphere of control include: the ground beneath the target, air around the target, objects the target holds or carries, etc. The GM determines what objects are under the defender's sphere of control.

ALL-OR-NOTHING OR PARTIAL EFFECTS

When an Attribute is used against a group of targets, GMs may use one of two options for resolving the resistance check. When a large group of people attempt to resist the effect of an Attribute, the GM makes one check, using the average Soul Stat value of the targets. Important characters (player characters or key NPCs) should be allowed to make individual rolls for themselves to prevent villains from teleporting a group of 50 people, including the players characters, thereby using the more vulnerable citizens to avoid the player characters' higher Stats. In this way, either all of the targets are affected by the Attribute (on a failed Soul Stat check) or none are affected (on a successful check).

Alternatively, the GM may wish to use one dice roll which is used as the same roll for each character's check — characters with high Soul Stats within the group may successfully resist the effects of the Attribute while characters with low Soul Stats are affected.

ATTRIBUTE VS. ATTRIBUTE

When two characters pit their Attribute against each other, who wins? In most situations, the character with the highest Level wins. For example, a villain is attempting to make his get-away by Flight. The hero grabs the villain and tries to hold the character back, preventing him from flying away. The hero has Superstrength at Level 5 while the villain has Flight at Level 3. The hero, therefore, is strong enough to prevent the villain from escaping.

If the two Attribute are close in Level (usually the same or differing by one Level), the GM may request an opposed Stat check to see who wins the contested action. Using the above example, if the villain's Flight Level was 4, instead of 3, the GM could request an opposed Stat check. The villain makes a Body Stat check (since Body is the relevant Stat for Flight) and scores a Margin of Success of 4. The hero must now make a Body Stat check (again, since Body is the relevant Stat for Superstrength) and score a Margin of Success greater than 4 to prevent the villain from escaping.

What if a character has two or more Attribute that can be used in the opposed check? What if the villain, in the first example, also has Superstrength at Level 4? In a situation like this, the GM should simply add the two Attribute Levels together to determine who wins the opposed action. Thus, the villain has Flight at Level 3 and Superstrength at Level 4 for a total of 7 which is much higher than the hero's Superstrength Level of 5. The villain is therefore able to make his escape (possibly lifting the hero into the air or simply breaking free of his hold, depending on the GM's discretion).

Note: Superstrength provides a +4 bonus to Body Stat Checks. Do not apply this bonus in Attribute vs. Attribute contests — it is only applied when the character is attempting something like breaking open a door or bending steel bars.

USING ATTRIBUTES AS ATTACKS

In many adventure stories, character regularly use seemingly passive, non-hostile Attribute to attack opponents, causing harm. A character who can teleport may disorient foes by teleporting them repeatedly within one combat round or selectively teleporting portions of mechanical sentries away, causing massive trauma, for example. The list of possible attack applications of an Attribute is endless. Most Attribute, however, do not account for these offensive tricks and stunts — they are accomplished using Special Attacks. A Special Attack is not limited simply to powerful energy blasts — it can be any "attack" that causes harm or detriment to an opponent. The teleporter who repeatedly teleports a target in a combat round may have a Special Attack with the Drain Body Ability and the No Damage Disability, reflecting the disorientation the target feels after the attack and the fact that no real physical harm is inflicted on the opponent. Alternatively, if the teleporter is capable of teleporting just a select portion of a target away causing harm to the target, the Special Attack may be designed to do an incredible amount of damage. By using the Attack Abilities and Disabilities, players can create any sort of attack, which will account for the numerous and creative ways that heroes and villains use their abilities. Some Special Attacks designed this way will have the Dependent Defect (page 52) — the character must first activate his or her Teleportation before being able to use his or her Special Attack: Teleportation Disorientation, for example.

USING ATTRIBUTES DEFENSIVELY

Just as characters can find imaginative ways to use their Attributes against opponents, they are just as likely to think of ways to use their Attributes to defend themselves from harm. Automatic Attributes are those that work without a necessary Stat check. A teleporter, for example, is capable of teleporting him or herself without the necessity of a Stat check. Thus, in combat, if an attack is directed against him or her, the character can teleport out of harm's way. The character must attempt a defence check and, if successful, activates his or her teleportation and vanishes before the attack hits home. The defence check is used to determine whether or not the character activates the Attribute in time to avoid the attack, not whether or not the Attribute activates at all. If the character fails the defence, the Attribute may still activate after damage is delivered. The character defends him or herself from attacks exactly the same way all characters do — with a defence check.

DEFENDING WITH AN ATTACK

By holding an action until attacked by an opponent, a character can defend him or herself with the offensive use of an Attribute. This simultaneous attack and defence option combines the advice under Using Attributes Against Opponents and Using Attributes Defensively into a single action. To succeed, the character must activate the Attribute with an appropriate Stat check (the target can make a Soul Stat check to resist as normal) and also make a successful defence check to time the effect properly. For instance, when a hero attacks a villain who has a held action remaining, the villain might attempt to use Teleportation to place a bystander between him and the hero's power blast. The villain must first make a successful Mind Stat check to see if the Teleportation works. If the attempt is successful, and the bystander fails to resist with a Soul Stat check, a defence check determines if the villain activates the Teleportation in time.

PUSHING YOUR ATTRIBUTES
(Optional Rule)

To encourage players to develop their characters through role-playing, characters may push themselves beyond their normal abilities, sometimes exerting their Attributes beyond their normal limits and other times pushing them in ways they have never done before.

Any time the character wishes to push him or herself, the player spends one unused Advancement Point and attempts a check using the relevant Stat for the action. If the check is successful, the character has pushed his or her Attribute beyond his or her normal limits (increased an Attribute's Level by 1; accomplished a new, yet related action with an Attribute; or whatever else the GM deems acceptable). At the GM's discretion, the character may spend more than one Advancement Point to push an Attribute even further, such as by 2 Levels or even more. The spent Advancement Point counts toward the cost of purchasing the new Attribute. For example, if a bio-cyborg uses Speed to vibrate through a wall, it will assign the Advancement Point to the future acquisition of the Insubstantial Attribute. If the check fails, the character fails in the attempt and may suffer some sort of mishap, such as taking some damage — pushing yourself can be risky. Even if the character fails to push an Attribute, the Advancement Point is still allocated to increasing the Attribute Level or gaining a new Attribute; even a failure can teach a character something, if only what not to do the next time. Though characters can normally only push their Attributes, under special circumstances, GMs may allow characters to push their Stats.

CHARACTER ADVANCEMENT

Character advancement is unnecessary in a short adventure, but during a lengthy campaign, players may wish to improve the Stats, Skills, and Attributes of their characters. Advancement is not a requirement, but it can reflect the characters' learned knowledge through conflicts with the environment, with other characters or NPCs, or even with themselves.

The GM is encouraged to award all characters one-quarter X (round up) Advancement Character Points and Advancement Skill Points every two to five role-playing sessions. Each player can assign these Character Points to Stats or Attributes immediately (GM's discretion) or accumulate them for future use.

The Point cost for increasing a Stat, Attribute, or Skill is identical to the cost during character creation. Players are encouraged to assign Advancement Points to Stats, Attributes, or Skills their characters use often. Alternatively, players can rationalise their decision to the GM should their characters acquire a new Attribute or Skill. The GM may require a character to perform certain activities to rationalise the acquisition of a new Attribute. In particular, the GM should not allow characters to acquire any Attributes that would disrupt the balance of the game. At the GM's option, players can also use Advancement Points to remove Defects that are no longer appropriate to their characters' concepts.

The GM may allow characters with the Item of Power or Gadgets Attributes to "swap" existing items for other items of similar Point value during or between sessions if a good story rationale exists. For example, a technological inventor who uses a suit of power armour to fight crime may make some modifications to his suit between adventures, swapping Points in Flight to increase the armour's Special Attack Level — the Point cost for the suit of armour remains the same but the character has simply designed the Mark II version. Swapping Points requires the expenditure of in-game resources (favours, money, time, captured enemy gear, etc.) and (often several) Mechanics Skill checks before this can be completed. Additionally, this exchange is a time consuming process that can take several days or weeks of work, depending on the extent of the change attempted (though the Gadgeteer Attribute can reduce this time considerably).

GMs can award Points more frequently for faster character advancement as they desire. The GM also has the option of rewarding exceptionally talented or active players with an extra Advancement Point. Finally, players that complete contributions for the game should receive additional Bonus Points as well (page 58).

EQUIPPING THE CHARACTER

What would a campaign be without the sleek vehicles and high-tech toys that so many of the characters wield in their adventures? It would be incomplete.

The following section provides quick and simple rules that help players and Game Masters create a plethora of weapons and vehicles with which to outfit characters. The equipment created with the following rules is intended for use with the Gadgets Attribute (page 21). If a character requires a more powerful item, such as power armour or a magical ring, it should be created using the Item of Power Attribute (page 24). Item of Power reflects magical or supertech items that are exceedingly difficult to create. Gadgets, however, may be high-tech or incredibly expensive, but are within the ability of modern science. While a character's vehicle may be the best car on the road, anyone with enough funding and skill could build one. The power armour worn by cyberknights, however, requires far more than money and skill to create. Ensure that the desired item is, in fact, a Gadget before attempting to build it with the rules herein.

WEAPONS

Table 9-2: Weapons lists the damage values and other characteristics of common weapons. If a weapon is not listed, the GM should assign a damage value based on one that is similar in form and function.

Some weapons possess Abilities and Disabilities to reflect their unique capabilities. Full descriptions of these modifiers are on pages 32-36. Note that special or magical weapons might cause additional damage or possess unique abilities beyond those listed here.

The Armour Ratings and Health Points of operation weapons, such as firearms, are indicated in the table as well (page 75).

IMPROVISED WEAPONS

In combat, it is not uncommon for an exceptionally strong character to pick up a nearby object and wield it is a weapon. It is impossible to account for every conceivable weapon that the player characters may decide to throw at their opponents, but Table 9-1: Improvised Weapons provides commonly encountered examples of improvised weapons and their statistics. GMs are encouraged to use this table as a guideline should their players decide to grab something in the middle of combat that is not listed. Naturally, most weapons have the Melee Disability (page 36) as well, though they can be thrown in combat if necessary.

CUSTOMISING FIREARMS

Sometimes, nothing gets the trick done like a reliable firearm. The following options can be added to different types of weapons to enhance performance or otherwise alter them. Each accessory or feature normally counts as a minor Gadget. Some options are considered "mundane" (their advantages and disadvantages cancel), and do not cost Points.

Options for weapons are classed as either accessories or features. A feature is a change to the basic weapon template that reflects a particular factory model, or extensive after-market customisation. This requires the Mechanics (Gunsmith) Skill to install, and may require several hours or more. An accessory is something that can be easily attached or removed from the weapon within a few seconds to several minutes. Weapon options are available for any class of weapon unless otherwise noted.

ACCURISED

Modification Type: Feature

The weapon has been specially modified (custom grips, improved sights, polygonal rifling, heavier barrel, etc.) to improve its accuracy. This is typical of target pistols and competition or sniper rifles. This modification grants a +1 bonus to any attack check when firing single shots, but no bonus if used with Auto-Fire. An accurised weapon must be in excellent condition with its sights precisely aligned — it will lose its bonus if knocked about, dropped, or otherwise mistreated.

BAYONET

Modification Type: Accessory

The weapon is fitted with a lug to accept a bayonet (included with this option). When attached, the weapon is a bit more awkward, but it can be used in melee combat as a spear. When detached (requires one round), the bayonet is also usable as a knife. A bayonet is available for any rifle.

BIPOD ATTACHMENT

Modification Type: Accessory

When the bipod is unfolded, the weapon is treated as if it is Accurate (cumulative with any other Accurate bonuses) and Static. The weapon must be fired at rest with the shooter lying prone behind it. Folding or unfolding the bipod requires one round. A bipod is available for any rifle.

BRASS CATCHER

Modification Type: Accessory

This attachment collects cartridges as they are fired out of the weapon, and thus either saves them for hand loading or prevents any incriminating ballistics evidence from being left behind. A brass catcher is available for any rifle or assault weapon.

BRIEFCASE-FIRING

Modification Type: Accessory

The weapon is designed to be concealed in and fired from a briefcase or attaché case without removing it, using a hidden trigger in the case handle. The weapon must be an auto-loading pistol, machine pistol, or a submachine gun. The weapon suffers a -4 penalty to the attack check when fired from within a brief case. The gun can usually be unclamped from the case and used normally (takes one round). GMs may use similar rules for umbrella guns or other disguised weaponry.

CARBINE-FORMAT

Modification Type: Mundane Feature

The weapon has a shorter barrel and stock. A carbine format subtracts 1 damage but allows the weapon to be concealed under a long coat (see Concealable Ability, page 33) as if it were a submachine gun. A carbine-format weapon is available for any rifle.

FLASH SUPPRESSOR

Modification Type: Accessory

The hot gasses produced when a bullet is fired are quite visible at night. A flash suppressor is a long device that can be attached to the end of a weapon, masking this signature. A weapon with a flash suppressor attached is easier to detect if hidden (+1 bonus). A flash suppressor is not available for a grenade launcher, LAW, taser, or minigun.

FLASHLIGHT ATTACHMENT

Modification Type: Accessory

This attachment allows any weapon to be used with a flashlight, and permits illumination of targets at short range so that attackers can target them without any penalties for darkness. Of course, someone using a flashlight at night can also be detected at a greater distance.

FOLDING OR TELESCOPING STOCK

Modification Type: Feature

The stock on the weapon can be folded or telescoped down, making it handier and more concealable. Unfortunately, a weapon with this feature also suffers from the Inaccurate Disability (-2 penalty) when firing at targets at over half its effective range. It requires one round (one attack if the character has the Extra Attacks Attribute) to fold or unfold the stock. If the weapon is also carbine-format, sawed-off, or a submachine gun, there is an extra -1 penalty to any check to spot the weapon while concealed, which is cumulative with other modifiers. This feature can be assigned to any rifle, shotgun, or assault weapon.

LASER SIGHT

Modification Type: Accessory

A laser sight projects a small, bright dot of laser light exactly where the weapon is pointing, which helps the attacker determine whether or not he or she is on target. In game terms, the attacker receives a +1 bonus to their appropriate attack check in situations where they can see the laser dot on the target (usually up to Short Range unless combined with a scope). Laser sights with an infrared beam (visible only to people with night vision scopes or goggles) are also available.

NIGHT VISION SCOPE

Modification Type: Accessory (counts as 2 minor Gadgets)

This scope uses thermal imaging or light intensification technology to "turn night into day." This functions exactly like a regular scope, except that it also eliminates any penalties for darkness.

SAWED-OFF BARREL

Modification Type: Feature

This modification is for shotguns only. Sawing off the barrel of a shotgun means that it is easier to conceal, but is also shorter ranged. A sawed-off shotgun can be concealed under a long coat (see Concealable weapon Ability, page 33) as if it were a submachine gun. At up to Melee Range (5 metres or less) it has a wider spread of pellets (+1 bonus on attack checks), but suffers -4 penalty to damage at ranges beyond Melee Range.

SNUB-NOSE

Modification Type: Mundane Feature

A snub-nose is a shorter-barrel versions of any auto-loading pistol, revolver, or machine pistol. The weapon suffers a -2 attack check penalty at any range greater than 5 metres and delivers less damage (-1 to damage), but is substantially easier to conceal (-1 penalty to spot the hidden weapon, cumulative with other bonuses or penalties of the weapon).

Table 9-1: Improvised Weapons

Object	Damage	Abilities	Disabilities	Strength Requirement
Bus	30	Area Effect	Inaccurate Low Penetration	Superstrength Level 4
Car	24	Area Effect	Inaccurate Low Penetration	Superstrength Level 2
Dumpster	18	-	Inaccurate Low Penetration	Superstrength Level 2
Manhole Cover	24	-	Low Penetration	Body 16
Park Bench	8	-	Low Penetration	Superstrength Level 1
Steel Girder	30	Spreading	Inaccurate	Superstrength Level 3
Stop Sign	6	-	-	Body 10
Telephone Pole	20	Spreading	Inaccurate	Superstrength Level 2

Weapon Table Notes

"Damage" is how much punishment the weapon inflicts (the damage of the attack).

"Abilities" or "Disabilities" are any special capabilities or limitations the weapon possesses. See pages 32-36. Unless noted otherwise, a weapon has Medium range. All Improvised Weapons have the Muscle-Powered Ability.

"Skill" is the Skill and Specialisation that provides a bonus when firing the weapon.

* Requires two hands to wield properly; delivers +4 damage when wielded two-handed.

** Some shotguns are "double-barrelled" and can fire both barrels at once. If so, an additional 8 damage is delivered. Double Barrelled shotguns have the Limited Shots (2) Disability.

"Strength Requirement" indicates the minimum Body Stat or Superstrength Level required to wield the object as a weapon effectively. If any improvised weapon is thrown, it is treated as a Short Range weapon. The range increases by one category every 3 Levels of Superstrength above the Strength requirement. For example, if a supervillain character who has Superstrength Level 6, threw a manhole cover, it would be treated as a Long Range weapon (Short increased to Medium for 3 Levels above the minimum Strength Requirement and then to Long for an additional 3 Levels above the Requirement). Conversely, if the character throws a car, which requires Superstrength Level 2, it would be treated as a Medium Range weapon. If he wished to throw a bus at an opponent, it would be treated as a short-range weapon because he is only 2 Levels above the Superstrength Requirement to wield a bus as a weapon.

SCOPE

Modification Type: Accessory

A telescopic sight mounted atop the weapon gives the shooter an extra +1 bonus to his or her attack check when taking an entire turn to aim at a target (page 64). This bonus only applies to targets further away than Melee Range (over 5 metres). Scopes are available for all guns.

SILENCER

Modification Type: Accessory

A silencer, or more technically, a sound-suppressor, is a tube that attaches to the weapons barrel and reduces the noise the weapon makes while firing. A silenced weapon cannot be heard at a range of greater than 5 metres unless a nearby character makes a successful Body Stat check. The GM should modify this distance/check for conditions such as ambient noise, range, and Heightened Senses. Auto-loading pistols, machine pistols, submachine guns, and rifles may be fitted with silencers. A silenced weapon cannot be concealed or holstered until the silencer is removed, which requires one round.

Table 9-2: Weapons

Melee Weapons

Weapon	Damage	Abilities	Disabilities	Skill
Bladed Weapons				
Axe	10	Muscle-Powered	Inaccurate, Melee	Melee (Axe)
Broadsword	12	Muscle-Powered	Melee	Melee (Sword)
Knife or Dagger	6	Concealable, Muscle-Powered	Melee	Melee (Knife)
Long Sword	12*	Muscle-Powered	Melee	Melee (Sword)
Short Sword	8	Concealable, Muscle-Powered	Melee	Melee (Sword)
Spear	10	Muscle-Powered	Melee	Melee (Polearm)
Blunt Weapons				
Bo, Staff, or Pipe	6*	Knockback, Muscle-Powered	Melee	Melee (Polearm)
Club, Baseball Bat	6	Knockback, Muscle-Powered	Melee	Melee (Club)
Nunchuku or Chain	6	Flexible, Muscle-Powered	Melee	Melee (Whips/Chains)
Whip, Rope, or Belt	4	Concealable, Flexible, Muscle-Powered	Low Penetration, Melee	Melee (Whips)

Bows (2 Armour, 20 Health Points)

Weapon	Damage	Abilities	Disabilities	Skill
Crossbow	12	none	Slow, Limited Shots (1)	Archery (Crossbow)
Long Bow	10	none	Limited Shots (1)	Archery (Bow)

Guns

Pistols (4 Armour, 30 Health Points)

Weapon	Damage	Abilities	Disabilities	Skill
Light Pistol	8	Concealable	Low Penetration, Short Range	Gun Combat (Pistol)
Heavy Pistol	12	Concealable	Short Range	Gun Combat (Pistol)
Machine Pistol	10	Auto-Fire, Concealable, Spreading	Inaccurate, Limited Shots (6), Short Range	Gun Combat (Auto-fire)
Magnum Revolver	14	Concealable	Limited Shots (6), Short Range	Gun Combat (Pistol)
Medium Pistol	10	Concealable	Short Range	Gun Combat (Pistol)
Revolver	8	Concealable	Limited Shots (6), Short Range	Gun Combat (Pistol)

Rifles (5 Armour, 35 Health Points)

Weapon	Damage	Abilities	Disabilities	Skill
Assault Rifle	14	Auto-Fire, Spreading	Limited Shots (6)	Gun Combat (Auto-fire)
Heavy Assault Rifle	18	Auto-Fire, Spreading	Inaccurate, Limited Shots (6)	Gun Combat (Auto-Fire)
Hunting Rifle	14	none	none	Gun Combat (Rifle)
Light Rifle	8	none	none	Gun Combat (Rifle)
Sniper Rifle	20	Accurate	Limited Shots (6)	Gun Combat (Rifle)

Shotguns (5 Armour, 35 Health Points)

Weapon	Damage	Abilities	Disabilities	Skill
Shotgun	18**	Spreading	Limited Shots (6), Low Penetration, Short Range	Gun Combat (Rifle)
Heavy Shotgun	22**	Spreading	Limited Shots (6), Low Penetration, Short Range	Gun Combat (Rifle)

Assault Weapons (5 Armour, 35 Health Points)

Weapon	Damage	Abilities	Disabilities	Skill
Light Mini-Gun	12	Accurate, Auto-Fire, Spreading	Limited Shots (6), Static	Gun Combat (Auto-fire)
Heavy Mini-Gun	22	Auto-Fire, Spreading	Limited Shots (6), Static	Gun Combat (Auto-fire)
Machine Gun	20	Auto-Fire, Spreading	Static	Heavy Weapons (Machine Gun)
Submachine Gun	10	Auto-Fire, Spreading	Limited Shots (6), Short Range	Gun Combat (Auto-fire)

Heavy Weapons (4 Armour, 30 Health)

Weapon	Damage	Abilities	Disabilities	Skill
66 mm LAW Light Anti-Tank Weapon	40	Area Effect, Penetrating	Inaccurate, Burning, Self-Destruct, Slow, Static	Heavy Weapons (Launcher), Limited Shots (1)

Thrown Weapons

Weapon	Damage	Abilities	Disabilities	Skill
Concussion Grenade	30	Area Effect x3, Concealable	Limited Shots (1), Self-Destruct, Short Range	Thrown Weapons (Grenades)
Thrown Knife	4	Concealable	Limited Shots (1), Short Range	Thrown Weapons (Blades)

Non Lethal Ranged Weapons (3 Armour, 25 Health)

Weapon	Damage	Abilities	Disabilities	Skill
Tear Gas Grenade	30	Area Effect x2, Enduring	Inaccurate, Limited Shots (1), Self-Destruct, Slow, Stun, Toxic	Heavy Weapons (Grenades)
Taser	12	Stun	Low Penetration, Short Range, Slow	Gun Combat (Pistol)
Pepper Spray	12	Concealable, Irritant, Stun	Melee Range, Limited Shots (6), Toxic	none

Ordnance (15 Armour, 85 Health)

Weapon	Damage	Abilities	Disabilities	Skill
120 mm Heat	80	Area Effect, Burning, Long Range, Penetrating	Limited Shots (1)	Heavy Weapons (Launcher)
120 mm Sabot	100	Accurate, Long Range, Penetrating x2	Limited Shots (1)	Heavy Weapons (Launcher)
Stinger Missile	60	Area Effect, Homing, Long Range, Penetrating	Backblast, Limited Shots (1), Only Air Targets, Self-Destruct, Slow, Static	Heavy Weapons (Launcher)
Tomahawk Missile	140	Accurate x4, Area Effect x3, Long Range x8, Penetrating x2	Limited Shots (1), Self Destruct, Slow, Static, Stoppable	Heavy Weapons (Launcher)

Speed Loader

Modification Type: Accessory

A speed loader is a device that holds a number of revolver cartridges and permits them to be rapidly inserted into a cylinder. If a character has this minor Gadget, he or she can ignore the Limited Shots Disability of any revolver.

Trigger Lock

Modification Type: Mundane Feature

An integral lock that prevents the gun from being used without the right key or combination. It takes an extra round to unlock the gun before it can be ready to fire. In some areas, the law may require trigger locks on some or all firearms.

Types of Ammunition

It is assumed that characters have access to ammunition of whatever type they need for their standard weapons. Standard ammunition for auto-loading pistols, revolvers, rifles, and machine guns is a lead bullet; this type of bullet is called "ball" in military parlance. Standard ammunition for shotguns is shot. If characters have more than one type of ammunition, each extra type that is carried counts as a minor Gadget.

Armour Piercing (AP)

This is a bullet specifically designed to punch through Armour, using a steel or tungsten core rather than jacketed lead. Some brands of Armour-piercing ammunition are Teflon-coated, but contrary to myth, the coating on AP bullets has nothing to do with the Armour-piercing qualities — it simply helps protect the rifling inside the gun from the tougher material from which the bullet is made. Weapons using AP bullets are assigned the Penetrating (Armour) Ability (page 34). AP bullets are somewhat less lethal against flesh, and thus the actual damage is always halved (round up) after the effects of Armour are considered. These bullets are available for auto-loading pistols, machine guns, shotguns, revolvers, and rifles. AP pistol or revolver ammunition ("cop killer bullets") is usually illegal.

Bird Shot

The statistics given for shotguns assume they are using buckshot, which is the usual combat load. If using birdshot (with a greater number of smaller pellets) damage is reduced by 5 (minimum 1 damage) but the attacker gains a +1 bonus to his or her attack check. Bird shot is only available for shotguns.

Blanks

A blank is a cartridge without the bullet that also has a reduced powder load. A blank normally does not deliver any damage when fired, but if the gun's muzzle is directly in contact with someone, the hot gasses expelled can still be dangerous or fatal. When a character is using a blank-firing gun in combat, the gun is treated as if it is firing a rubber bullet, but range is limited to Melee Range. Blanks are available for auto-loading pistols, machine guns, revolvers, rifles, and shotguns.

Hollow Point (HP)

This is a bullet designed to expand after entering a target, therefore doing greater damage. Hollow Point bullets are known by various trade names, and include bullets described as "expanding," "dumdum," or pre-fragmented rounds such as "safety slugs." HP ammo is standard issue in many police departments, since the rounds are better man-stoppers and are less likely to pierce walls and injure bystanders on the other side. The Hague Convention prohibits HP bullets for military use in international conflicts. Hollow Point bullets have less Armour-penetrating power: Armour protection is doubled against the bullets. These disadvantages are cumulative with any Low Penetration modifiers. If even 1 damage succeeds in penetrating Armour, however, or if the target was unarmoured, 5 bonus damage is added to the damage that a living target suffers (the bullets "mushroom" inside living tissue), but only if the base damage penetrates the target's Armour. No extra damage is inflicted on machines or structures by HP bullets. HP bullets are available for auto-loading pistols, machine guns, revolvers, and rifles.

Rubber

These are bullets encased in rubber or plastic, which are designed to be "less lethal." A weapon using rubber bullets automatically suffers from the Low Penetration Disability (page 36) and delivers 5 less damage (minimum 1 damage). Rubber bullets are available for auto-loading pistols, machine guns, revolvers and rifles, and for shotguns firing slug ammunition.

Shotgun Slugs

A shotgun can fire big bullets instead of shot. Police will often use slugs to stop cars or blow open barricades. When using slugs, a shotgun loses both the Spreading Ability (page 34) and the Low Penetrating Disability (page 36). Slugs are available for shotguns only.

Incendiary Shells

Special shells are also available for shotguns; these shells contain phosphorous chemicals that convert the shotgun into an improvised flamethrower. Damage is reduced by 5 (minimum 1), but if any damage penetrates Armour, the target receives fire damage, and suffers one quarter (round up) the basic damage per round for the next five rounds. This damage is also very painful, imposing a -2 penalty on all checks. The ammunition tends to foul the gun after use, however. Any further shots fired before the gun can be carefully cleaned suffer a -2 attack check penalty, and the gun will jam on any roll of 1 or 2 (requiring cleaning before the gun can be reused). These shells are available for shotguns only.

Grenades and Explosives

The user throws these hand-held explosive weapons at a target. Their use uses the Thrown Weapons (Grenade) Skill. All of these explosives count as minor Gadgets except a satchel charge, which is treated as a major Gadget.

Concussion Grenade

This grenade is filled with high explosives. 30 damage is delivered to everyone in a six-metre radius who fails a defence check. Even if characters make the defence check, they still may suffer some blast damage (see Area Effect, page 32) unless there is sufficient cover (GM's option).

Tear Gas Grenade

This grenade bursts to fill a room-sized area (three-metre radius) with (usually) non-lethal irritant gas. Damage is the same as concussion grenade (30 damage), but is "stun only" — it wears off after a few minutes, and it does not affect non-living things or anyone wearing a gas mask. Anyone exposed to the gas also suffers a -2 penalty on all checks due to irritation if they fail a Body Stat check. This penalty lasts for a number of rounds equal to the amount by which the check was failed. Tear gas grenades also release a lot of smoke and may occasionally (GM's option) start fires if they explode next to paper or other flammable substances.

Flash-Bang Grenade

These special grenades produce a brilliant firecracker effect, stunning people with sound and light. This weapon is a favourite of hostage-rescue teams. No physical damage will be suffered, but the victims must make a Body Stat check or be blinded and deafened for a number of combat rounds equal to the difference between the Check Value and the roll. The character suffers a -1 Check Value penalty if he or she is right next to the grenade when it explodes. Characters wearing anti-flare goggles (such as a welding mask) and ear protectors will receive a +6 bonus to their check to avoid the grenade's effects.

Smoke Grenade

This grenade fills a room-sized area (three-metre radius) with non-toxic chemical smoke for 3 to 8 rounds (depending on wind). Anyone without night vision goggles or a night vision scope will suffer a -4 attack check penalty when attacking a target obscured by smoke.

Dynamite Stick

This explosive functions like a concussion grenade, except the blast covers only a three-metre radius, and it delivers 20 damage.

Satchel Charge

This is a knapsack full of plastic explosive or multiple dynamite sticks. The explosion is treated as a concussion grenade, but the blast covers an eight-metre radius and the maximum damage is 40. Unlike a grenade, a satchel charge is too heavy to throw far, so its range is limited to melee range for average humans — the attacker will be caught in the charge's blast unless it has a timer.

TIMED OR REMOTE DETONATOR

This device is used to explode a satchel charge (or other bomb) from a distance, either at a specific time or in response to an electrical or radio signal. Attaching the detonator to the explosive and properly setting it requires a Demolitions Skill check, with failure indicating a late or premature blast.

VEHICLES

Along with their specialised weaponry, many modern era characters use rigged and modified vehicles. Additionally, many international organisations use high-tech vehicles in their quests to keep their interests safe.

This section describes the standard vehicles likely to appear in a modern-day game. Some vehicles are suitable for use as personal vehicles by characters, while a desperate individual may commandeer others (such as a city bus) when no better transportation is available. This section concentrates on general types that are in common use, rather than providing individual statistics for specific models. All costs are approximate US dollar (USD) values, which can vary greatly.

Each vehicle counts as a major Gadget, with the exception of the motor scooter and ultra-light (minor Gadget). These basic templates can be modified using the Customising Vehicles guidelines (pages 79). Using the customisation options, the vehicle can be further modified to match the character's personal vision (adding options such as supercharged engines or armoured glass windows) with each option normally considered to be as a minor Gadget.

AUTOMOBILE

The basic motor vehicle of the 20th century. Automobiles have four wheels and are normally powered by a gasoline internal combustion engine. Standard features on modern vehicles include headlights, seat belts, air bags, and air conditioning.

PASSENGER CAR

An ordinary compact or mid-sized automobile. Cars are available in coupe (two doors, often with a hatch back and extra cargo space), sedan (four door), or station wagon (extra room in back, but reduced rear visibility for driver) body styles. Year 2003 cost: $12,000+ USD. For an expensive luxury car, add custom options such as Big Engine and Luxury Interior.

SUB-COMPACT CAR

A small, somewhat cramped passenger car. It seats four, but with a lot less comfort than a comparable mid-sized vehicle. It is easier to park, but not as robust. Year 2003 cost: $10,000+ USD.

PICKUP TRUCK OR SPORT/UTILITY VEHICLE

A light truck with cab seating (2-3 people), off-road suspension, and four-wheel drive and either an open cargo bed (pickup truck) or extra passenger capacity (sport/utility vehicle). Year 2003 cost: $20,000+ USD.

RACE CAR

A dedicated race car (such as a Formula 1 racer or funny car) with an aerodynamic body, a single seat, and very powerful engine. Such a vehicle is not "street legal." Race cars are "hangar queens" that require periodic maintenance every few hours just to keep their finely tuned engines and transmissions in working order. Year 2003 cost: $100,000+ USD.

SPORTS CAR

A car with good aerodynamics, a powerful engine, and superior transmission and suspension. Some sports cars carry two people, while others sacrifice already-meagre cargo space to carry an extra person or two in cramped back seats. Year 2003 cost: $50,000+ USD.

STRETCHED LIMOUSINE

An oversized passenger car. It will usually have a number of posh features, such as a luxury interior. Year 2003 cost: $50,000+ USD.

VAN

A light panel truck or mini-van, with one or two big rear doors and sliding side doors. Use this template with appropriate customisation for ambulances. Year 2003 cost: $15,000+ USD.

MOTORCYCLE

A two-wheeled bike powered by a gasoline engine. Standard features include headlights and rear-view mirrors.

MOTORBIKE

A big bike with a reasonably powerful engine. A second person can usually be carried without much difficulty. Year 2003 cost: $3,000+ USD.

SCOOTER

A small bike with an anaemic engine. Scooters are suitable for a single rider only. A minor gadget. Year 2003 cost: $2,000+ USD.

DIRT BIKE

A motorbike designed for off-road operations. Dirt bikes include the Off-Road Suspension option (page 80) at no extra cost. Year 2003 cost: $4,000+ USD.

OVERSIZED VEHICLE

A big ground vehicle with six or more wheels, usually powered by a diesel engine rather than gasoline engine (diesel fuel is cheaper, and less flammable). Standard features include headlights, seat belts, airbags, and air conditioning.

BIG RIG

An 18-wheel tractor-trailer combination, with a powerful tractor cab designed to tow a big trailer. With trailer, a big rig may be 20 metres long. Pick one of these options for the cargo area: flat bed (open cargo), van (enclosed cargo), refrigerated ("reefer"), tanker. If the trailer is unhooked from the "fifth wheel" (this takes at least two rounds outside the vehicle to do this), the rig's speed can increase by 10-20 kph. Year 2003 cost: $60,000+ USD.

BUS

A city, school, or excursion bus. In action series, these usually make their appearance when someone hijacks or plants a bomb on them. A typical bus seats 35-45 people (with plenty of standing and cargo room) and is about 10-15 metres long. Year 2003 cost: $50,000+ USD.

HEAVY TRUCK

A large truck, bigger than an ordinary van. Pick one of these options for the cargo area: flat bed (open cargo), van (enclosed cargo), refrigerated ("reefer"), tanker. A heavy truck may also be a cement mixer, dump truck, street cleaner, fire engine, etc. Year 2003 cost: $30,000+ USD.

HELICOPTER

A rotary winged vehicle. Modern helicopters are usually powered by a gas turbine engine, and require a pilot's license to operate. They have a horizontal main rotor that provides lift and (by tilting the helicopter) propulsion, and a small vertical tail rotor to act as a stabiliser. A helicopter is capable of executing vertical takeoffs or landings, and hovering. Standard features include landing lights (treat as headlights), seat belts, and often air conditioning.

COMBAT HELICOPTER

A devastatingly offensive helicopter (such as the AH-1W Super Cobra), typically used in battle against combat forces and either very powerful or very large monster threats. A combat helicopter counts as three major Gadgets. Year 2003 cost: $10,000,000+ USD.

LIGHT HELICOPTER

A small helicopter that can carry a couple of people. This is a typical news or police helicopter. Year 2003 cost: $100,000+ USD.

Table 9-3:Vehicles

Vehicle	Speed	MB	Size	People	Cargo	Armour	Health Points	Skill
Automobiles								
Compact Car	160	-	2	4	100 kg	4	50	Driving (Car)
Passenger Car	160	-	2	5	200 kg	5	60	Driving (Car)
Pickup Truck	160	-	2	3	1 tonne	6	70	Driving (Car)
Race Car	300	+1	1	1	-	5	60	Driving (Car)
Sports Car	200	-	2	2	200 kg	4	50	Driving (Car)
Sport/Utility	160	-	2	6	200 kg	6	70	Driving (Car)
Stretched Limousine	160	-1	2	6	500 kg	5	60	Driving (Car)
Van	150	-1	3	2	1 tonne **	7	80	Driving (Van)
Motorcycles								
Dirt Bike	140	+1	1	2	-	3*	40	Driving (Motorcycle)
Scooter	120	+1	0	1	25 kg	2*	30	Driving (Motorcycle)
Motorbike	180	+1	1	2	50 kg	3*	40	Driving (Motorcycle)
Oversized Vehicles								
Big Rig	150	-2	4	2	10 tonnes	10	110	Driving (Big Rig)
Bus	120	-2	4	30-50	1 tonne	9	100	Driving (Big Rig)
Heavy Truck	150	-1	3	2	5 tonnes	8	90	Driving (Van)
Helicopters								
Combat Helicopter	300	+1	4	2	2 tonnes	10	80	Piloting (Helicopter)
Light Helicopter	200	+1	2	3	250 kg	4	50	Piloting (Helicopter)
Utility Helicopter	200	-	3	2	2 tonnes **	7	80	Piloting (Helicopter)
Airplanes								
Combat Jet	2,500	+1	4	2	5 tonnes	16	100	Piloting (Jet Fighter)
Light Airplane	350	+1	2	4	250 kg	4	50	Piloting (Light Airplane)
Heavy Airplane	300	-3	5	4	40 tonnes **	11	120	Piloting (Heavy Airplane)
Ultra-Light	100	+1	1	1	-	2*	30	Piloting (Light Airplane)
Speed Boats								
Off-shore Racer	180	-	3	6	500 kg	7	80	Boating (Small Boat)
Recreational Boat	80	+1	2	3-4	100 kg	4	50	Boating (Small Boat)
Military Ground Vehicles								
Armoured Personnel Carrier	70	-	4	13	2 tonnes	20	120	Driving (Tank)
Heavy Tank	80	-2	4	4	2 tonnes	30	200	Driving (Tank)

Vehicle Table Notes

Speed is the top speed in kilometres per hour. Pickup trucks, sport/utility vehicles, and dirt bikes move at half speed off-road. Other non-military ground vehicles are road-bound and can move a maximum of one-quarter speed off road.

MB is the Manoeuvre Bonus. +1 means a +1 bonus to Initiative rolls (only), while a -1 or -2 means that penalty is applied to both Initiative rolls and to Driving Skill checks.

Size is a relative measure of the vehicle's mass and volume. "1" means the vehicle is about the size of a motorcycle — you could drive it through a house's door, or stow it in the back of a van (masses up to 500 kg). "2" means it is about the size of a car or pickup truck, and you can park it in a normal garage (masses 1-5 tonnes). "3" means it is the size of a large truck (uses multiple parking spaces, often masses 6-10+ tonnes when loaded). "4" means it is even larger, such as a big tractor-trailer combination that might haul 20+ tonnes. "5" is exceptionally large (50 metres plus).

People is how many people the vehicle will seat, including the driver or pilot.

Cargo is how many tonnes or kilograms of cargo the vehicle can typically carry without suffering movement penalties. An ** indicates that the cargo area can be converted into passenger space at a ratio of 5 people per tonne.

Armour is the number of damage points that the Armour stops. An * indicates that the Armour only protects the vehicle, not the driver or passengers.

Health Points indicate how much damage the vehicle can sustain before it ceases to function. The vehicle is not necessarily destroyed when its Health Points are reduced to zero — it has merely sustained enough damage to shut the engine down, hinder the control systems, or in some other way prevent the vehicle from working. For rules on destroying a vehicle, see Breaking Objects, page 82.

No range is listed, since all vehicles except the ultra-light can operate for 3-10 hours before requiring refuelling. The ultra-light's endurance is under one hour. Oversized vehicles (trucks, big rigs, busses) usually burn diesel fuel, while most other vehicles use gasoline.

UTILITY HELICOPTER

A larger helicopter that is often a civilian version of a military troop-carrying model. These choppers are designed to carry a dozen people or a decent cargo load. Helicopters of this sort are often used as air ambulances. Year 2003 cost: $1,000,000+ USD.

AIRPLANE

An airplane relies on wings for lift and a propeller or jet engine for propulsion. It requires a smooth, flat runway for takeoffs and landings. While airborne it must maintain a minimum speed (usually about 1/10 its maximum speed) to avoid stalling. Standard features include landing lights (treat as headlights), seatbelts, emergency parachutes, and often air conditioning.

Combat Jet

Military jets and bombers (such as the F/A-18 Hornet or B-2 Spirit) are incredibly powerful machines used to assist ground assaults or carry out missions alone. A combat jet counts as four major Gadgets. Year 2003 cost: $50,000,000+ USD (sometimes exceeding $1 Billion USD).

Light Airplane

A single-engine propeller-driven passenger airplane, capable of operating out of grass strips or landing on a smooth stretch of highway if necessary. Light aircraft are a favourite of drug runners. Use Pilot (Light Plane) Skill. Year 2003 cost: $100,000+ USD.

Heavy Airplane

A large plane, often with two or four engines, which is used primarily to transport large numbers of people or cargo. Heavy airplanes often require longer runways in order to take off or land. A heavy airplane counts as two major Gadgets. Year 2003 cost: $10,000,000+ USD.

Ultra-Light

A small one-man powered hang-glider that is used mainly for recreation. Counts as a minor Gadget. Year 2003 cost: $10,000+ USD.

Speed Boat

Boat designs come in a variety of shapes, depending on their desired function. Speed boats have sleek hull designs and powerful engines in order to travel at high speeds. Standard features include a VHF radio (treat as a CB radio), convertible tops, running lights, and lifejackets.

Recreational Speed Boat

A medium-sized powerboat, usually with an outboard engine. These boats are often used for water-skiing. Year 2003 cost: $10,000+ USD.

Offshore Racer

These large race boats, usually measuring between 10 and 18 metres in length, are used in offshore racing. Smugglers often utilise these sleek, fast boats to transport illegal goods. Year 2003 cost: $80,000+ USD.

Military Ground Vehicles

When battling against foreign incursions or giant monsters, the army will come to the rescue with their awesome firepower. Unfortunately, sometimes even that is not enough.

Armoured Personnel Carrier (APC)

A lightly armoured, full-tracked, air-transportable personnel carrier designed to carry and protect personnel and certain types of cargo. Year 2003 cost: $500,000+ USD.

Heavy Tank

Heavy tanks (such as the M1 Abrams) are the backbone of military forces. They provide strong mobile firepower while providing heavy protection for its crew in almost any environment. A heavy tank counts as three major Gadgets. Year 2003 cost: $4,000,000+ USD.

Customising Vehicles

Options can be added to different types of vehicles to enhance performance or give them additional capabilities. Unless otherwise noted, each accessory counts as one minor Gadget and can only be taken once.

Note that Engine Rebuild, Turbocharger, and Big Engine have approximately the same effect in game terms. A fast vehicle may have all three options assigned, however.

Some vehicles possess supertechnology, which grants them abilities beyond those outlined below. These abilities are covered using the Item of Power Attribute (page 24). Creating a vehicle such as this not only requires minor and major Gadgets for the base abilities of the vehicle plus any modifications but also requires a Level in Item of Power sufficient to purchase the Attribute(s) granted by the supertechnology.

Table 9-4: Vehicle Customisations

Airfoils	Manual Transmission
Armour	Nitrous Oxide Tank
Artificial Intelligence (A.I.)	Off-Road Suspension
Big Engine	Police-Band Radio
Burglar Alarm	Pontoons
Citizen's Band (CB) Radio	Radar Detector
Consumer Electronics	Rocket Engine
Convertible Top	Rotating License Plate
Door Mount	Sidecar
Electronic Countermeasures	Slick Tires
Engine Rebuild	Smoke Screen/Oil Slick
Extra Capacity	Special Tires or Puncture-Resistant
Extra Endurance	Stretchers and Medical Equipment
Furnishings	Stripped
Global Positioning System (GPS)	Sun Roof
Hidden Cargo Space	Supercharger
Improved Brakes	Tow Winch
Improved Shocks	Trailer
Lights and Siren	Turbocharger
Luxury Interior	Weapon Mount — Light
Manoeuvrable	Weapon Mount — Heavy

Airfoils

An aerodynamic feature (airdams, spoilers, etc.) that improves traction by increasing the downward force on a car. Gives a +1 bonus to any Drive (Car) Skill check at speeds over 100 kph. Airfoils are available for any automobile and some exceptionally fast boats.

Armour

The vehicle is retro-fitted with armoured panels, Kevlar inserts, and bullet proof glass on the windows. Each time the armour is assigned, the extra weight reduces top speed by 10 kph but increases the vehicle's Armour Rating by 5. Armour is available for any vehicle except an ultra-light aircraft, and counts as two minor Gadgets.

Artificial Intelligence (A.I.)

This can be assigned more than once. For one major Gadget, a vehicle can be given one Stat Value in Mind or Soul to a recommended maximum of 10 for each Stat. The A.I. customisation enables a vehicular computer to achieve a limited form of self-operation and eventually self-awareness. For these purposes, the Mind Stat represents processing power and database/knowledge access while the Soul Stat represents consciousness, self-determination, and free will. If an A.I. assists a character in the completion of a task, one-half the A.I.'s relevant Stat is added as a bonus to his or her Skill check (or Stat check).

Big Engine

An upgraded engine, such as a big V8 in a passenger car, or a V12 in a sports car. The engine often differentiates an ordinary passenger car from a luxury model, or a basic sports car from a racer. A big engine adds 20 kph to the top speed of any vehicle.

Burglar Alarm

If a door, trunk, or window is opened without the proper key, an alarm will sound to alert (and annoy) everyone in the vicinity. Defeating the alarm requires a Mind-Based Electronics (Security) Skill check. Marginal failure means the thief realises he or she cannot disarm it while a worse failure means will trigger the alarm.

Citizen's Band (CB) Radio

With a range of a few miles, truckers favour CBs for exchanging information on road conditions, speed traps, and general gossip. Unlike a personal cell phone, a CB broadcasts to everyone in the area — it is not useful for private communication, but is great for distress calls. A similar option can be taken for taxi dispatcher radios. A CB radio can be installed in any vehicle.

Consumer Electronics

These electronic gadgets include small TV sets, a vehicular computer, fax machines, etc. A CD or MP3 player in a car can be considered a fairly mundane item. Electronics can be added to any vehicle, provided the size seems reasonable.

Convertible Top

The vehicle with this option has a removable or retractable plastic, fibreglass, or fabric top. Removing the top gives a better view and nice breeze, but also means that the driver and passengers are now "partially exposed," and are at the mercy of the weather. Exposed occupants are also completely unprotected from overhead attacks and can be attacked (bypassing vehicle Armour/Health Points) more easily from the side or rear (-4 attack check penalty to ignore the car's Armour). On the plus side, those occupants can also fire out of the vehicle without any difficulty, and jump in or out more easily. This feature is available for automobiles; recreational speed boats and most offshore racers automatically possess this option.

Door Mount

This option is a post and bracket for mounting a light or heavy machine gun out a helicopter's or van's open side door.

Electronic Countermeasures

This advanced defence system enables the vehicle to avoid detection by radar and other sensors. Any attempt to mechanically detect the vehicle (except through the basic senses such as sight or hearing) incurs a -6 penalty.

Engine Rebuild

A rebuild is major custom upgrade to the engine, rather than just simply increasing its size. In a car, this may involve removing and completely cleaning the existing system (including "hot tanking" the engine block in a chemical bath to remove grime), then adding various modifications (known as "blueprinting"). Other engine "buzz-words" include forged dome pistons, tuneable fuel injection, strengthened rods and bearings, adjustable or hot cam socket, tubular headers, custom intake manifolds, big valves, and a bored-out throttle body. This option adds 20 kph to the top speed of any vehicle.

Extra Capacity

Some vehicles are customised to contain more cargo or passenger capacity. Each time this option is assigned, the capacity of the vehicle is doubled. Capacity for one passenger is approximately equivalent to a quarter-tonne of cargo space.

Extra Endurance

Most vehicles can operate for 3-10 hours before requiring refuelling (one hour for an ultra-light). Each time this option is assigned, the maximum time between refuelling is doubled.

Furnishings

Furnishings include a mini-bar, mini-fridge, kitchenette, chemical toilet, bunk bed, etc. For larger furnishings (kitchenette, bunks, etc.) each one added also requires replacing one or two seats, depending on the size. Furnishings can be added to any vehicle with Size 2 or more.

Global Positioning System (GPS)

This option uses satellite systems to provide precise navigational co-ordinators, which prevents the driver from becoming lost. Naturally, it is still possible to miss a turn through human error. A GPS can be added to any vehicle.

Hidden Cargo Space

This space is often used in vehicles that are designed to smuggle goods across borders or past highway patrols. Up to 10% of the vehicle's cargo capacity can be considered "hidden" under fake panels and bogus fixtures. Hidden space can be added to any vehicle with cargo capacity.

Improved Brakes

This option includes high quality brakes, drag chutes, or spiked tires that allow the vehicle to stop faster than normal. Those breaks provide a +2 bonus to Drive Skill checks on any manoeuvre where sudden, sharp deceleration is important. Improved breaks can be added to any ground-based vehicle.

Improved Shocks

Some vehicles have high quality or adjustable shock absorbers or springs, which provide an extra +1 bonus to Drive Skill checks in any circumstance where the suspension would be important (such as crossing over obstacles).

Lights and Siren

Any vehicle can be fitted with a noisy siren and flashing lights. This option can also provide a powerful spot search light.

Luxury Interior

Leather upholstery, lots of chrome, extra head room, or other items on a vehicle are a sure way to impress someone special. A plethora of luxury options are available for most vehicles.

Manoeuvrable

A vehicle with Manoeuvrable has superior handling characteristics that give it a bonus of +1 to Initiative each time it is assigned. This bonus is cumulative with the vehicle's Manoeuvre Bonus (see Table 9-3: Vehicles).

Manual Transmission

There are two types of transmissions: manual and automatic. An automatic transmission is assumed to be standard issue for automobiles (but not other vehicles), and means that the gear mechanism changes by itself. In a manual transmission, the driver must shift the gears on his or her own, usually with a stick and the clutch pedal. In the case of automobiles, a manual transmission gives an additional -1 penalty to characters who are trying to do something else while they drive, such as shoot a gun. If, however, a vehicle with an automatic transmission and one with a manual transmission are competing in a race, the GM should give any driver who has both the Drive Skill and a manual transmission an extra +1 bonus to reflect the greater speed control the manual transmission provides. This is a mundane option for automobiles.

Nitrous Oxide Tank

This option adds a nitrous oxide tank and push-button injection system. Nitrous oxide ("laughing gas") can be injected into the engine, which releases more free oxygen and improves cylinder pressures and engine temperature. This action allows extra fuel to be burned in a more controlled fashion, resulting in a quick power boost for a short sprint. A single injection adds 30 kph to speed and +2 to Initiative on any round it is used. A tank can be used for up to five rounds before depleting the nitrous oxide bottle. This performance enhancer is available for any vehicle except helicopters.

Off-Road Suspension

A raised suspension and special tires allow the vehicle to drive cross-country at two-thirds of the on-road top speed. The extra suspension weight also means -5 kph to road speed. For airplanes, this option corresponds to Rough-Field Landing Gear that lets the aircraft land without a proper runway. Off-road suspension is available for any ground vehicle or light aircraft.

Police-Band Radio

This radio allows the driver to listen to, and communicate on, police and emergency frequencies. If the cops find one of these in a vehicle, they may be a little suspicious, however. This radio is available for any vehicle.

Pontoons

Pontoons allow an aircraft to land in, or take off from, water. The extra air drag reduces the aircraft's top speed by 5 kph. Pontoons are available for any helicopter or light airplane.

Radar Detector

A detector can warn the driver if a police radar trap is within a few miles. Recent models also detect police laser scanners.

Rocket Engine

The vehicle is outfitted with a rocket engine (either replacing propellers for an airplane or as a booster rocket for ground vehicles). The engine drastically increases the speed of the vehicle by an additional 100 kph but the expensive modification counts as a major Gadget. Additionally, for ground based vehicles, the driver incurs a -2 penalty on all Drive Skill checks while the rocket booster is activated.

Rotating License Plate

With a flick of a switch, the license plate can flip to reveal an alternative identity for a vehicle. This illegal modification is available for any automobile or oversized ground vehicle.

Sidecar

Sidecars are attached to motorcycles, allowing an extra person to ride. This option reduces the top speed by 10 kph. A motorbike sidecar requires three rounds to attach or detach.

Slick Tires

A vehicle may be outfitted with flat racing tires (no grooves) for better traction. Slicks give a +1 bonus to any Drive checks on smooth, dry tracks, but unfortunately have a poor grip on wet roads: an additional -2 penalty is assigned to any penalties suffered by a vehicle for the weather conditions. Slicks are available for any ground vehicle.

Smoke Screen/Oil Slick

This option releases smoke behind the vehicle, obscuring view in a cloud about 10 metres in diameter. The screen will last for 1-6 rounds depending on the wind. Alternatively, it could act as an oil slick, which creates a slippery area that hampers the control of any vehicle driving through it. A driver may avoid the oil slick if he or she spots it in time. At GM's option, a character caught in a smoke screen/oil slick might be required to make a successful Driving Skill check to avoid an accident. A fully charged smoke screen/oil slick is good for three rounds of use, and is available for any automobile or oversized ground vehicle.

Special Tires or Puncture-Resistant

Tires may be designed with various special abilities. These include solid puncture-resistant tires that run while flat (halve penalties for losing a tire) or special snow tires (reduce or negate any penalties that the GM may assign for manoeuvring on snow or ice). Any ground based vehicle can be equipped with special tires.

Stretchers and Medical Equipment

This option differentiates ambulances from regular vehicles. Each stretcher replaces two seats for passenger capacity purposes. Medical equipment can be added to any van or utility helicopter.

Stripped

These vehicles are carefully stripped down to improve their power to weight ratio. In a car, this might mean removing glass from side windows (replacing them with nets), taking out the headlights, stripping out the doors (the driver will now climb through the window), modifying the seats, and otherwise removing items that are required for regular driving but unnecessary or unsafe for a high-speed race. Stripping a vehicle will add 20 kph to top speed if the vehicle is still "street legal" or 30 kph if enough stuff is removed so that the vehicle no longer meets minimum safety standards. All vehicles, except an ultra-light, can be stripped.

Sun Roof

A sun roof is an open hatch in the top of the vehicle, which can be added to any car or van. Characters who lean out the opening can be attacked, but receive a benefit for partial cover (-4 penalty to the attacker's check). A sun roof is available for any automobile or oversized ground vehicle.

Supercharger

A supercharger is designed to increase an engine's power. The supercharger uses a belt-and-pulley mechanism linked to an engine's crankshaft. It functions by forcing extra air and fuel into the engine's combustion chambers. A supercharger adds 20 kph to top speed and the extra acceleration gives a +2 Initiative bonus. Superchargers count as two minor Gadgets, and are available for any vehicle except a helicopter or ultra-light.

Tow Winch

A winch allows the vehicle to tow other vehicles of equal or smaller size (similar to pulling a trailer — see Trailer below). A winch is available for any pickup truck or oversized ground vehicle.

Trailer

A trailer lets the vehicle tow extra cargo. A typical trailer is designed for a car or van and can hold a half-tonne (for a car-sized trailer) or 1-2 tonnes (for a larger trailer). The vehicle's top speed will be reduced by 25 kphInitiative penalty while towing the trailer. Trailers can be added to any automobile or oversized vehicle.

Turbocharger

This device uses the engine's exhaust stream to drive an air compressor, which increases the engine's power output. This extra power adds 20 kph to top speed, but there is no extra initiative bonus, due to "turbo lag" — the delay it takes for the turbocharger to respond. Tuberchargers are available for any vehicle except a helicopter or ultra-light.

Weapon Mount — Light

A weapon mount is a bracket or pintle for mounting a light or heavy machine gun on the vehicle's roof, deck, or the underside of a wing.

Weapon Mount — Heavy

This mount is used for mounting heavy weapons such as rockets.

Body Armour and Protective Devices

Most armour only covers some of the body, leaving the face and often other extremities unprotected. An attacker can aim for an unprotected spot in exchange for suffering a penalty on his or her attack check (see Called Shot to Partial Armour, page 64). The Armour values listed in this section represent average-quality construction and materials. Shoddy workmanship, poor construction techniques, or weak materials can penalise the given Armour values by -1 to -4. Exceptional workmanship, advanced construction techniques, or resilient materials can increase the given Armour values by +1 to +4.

Table 9-5: Armour and Protective Devices

Armour Type	Armour Value	Penalties
Ancient Armour		
Light Mail	6	-2 on Body-related checks
Partial Metal Armour	10	-4 on Body-related checks
Full Metal Armour	12 to 16	-6 on Body-related checks
Modern Armour		
Leather Jacket	2	None
Soft Body Armour	8	-2 on Body-related checks
Tactical	16	-4 on Body-related checks
Shields		
Buckler	8	None
Standard Shield	12	Requires one free hand to use
Heavy Shield	16	Requires one free hand to use, -4 on Body-related checks
Tactical Shield	20	Requires one free hand to use, -2 on Body-related checks

Ancient Armour

Light Mail

A light shirt of fine metal links that can be hidden under a normal jacket and stops 6 damage. Due to the armour's weight, the character suffers a -2 penalty on physically-oriented Skill checks. Minor Gadget.

Partial Metal Armour

A mail hauberk or cuirass, open helmet, and arm or leg protection. It stops 10 damage. Due to the armour's weight, the character suffers a -4 penalty on Body-related checks. Minor Gadget.

FULL METAL ARMOUR

A complete head-to-foot suit of metal armour, similar to those worn by medieval knights in battle. It stops 12 to 16 damage. Due to the armour's bulk, the character makes Body-related and combat checks at a -6 penalty. Major Gadget.

MODERN ARMOUR

LEATHER JACKET OR RIDING SUIT

This mundane item stops 2 damage from melee attacks or concussion damage.

SOFT BODY ARMOUR

This armour is a light-weight ballistic-fibre "flak jacket" or "bullet proof vest." The armour works by catching the bullet in fibres and rapidly distributing the impact energy, often turning a potentially lethal penetration into a bruising blow. Armour is usually made of poly-aramid plastic fibres (Kevlar or Twaron) or extended-chain polyethylene (Spectra). A typical vest subtracts 8 from the damage inflicted on the character, but can be worn concealed under a jacket or coat. It is cumbersome, however, and penalises the wearer with a -2 penalty on Body-related checks. Spotting the armour requires a Mind Stat check; it will be obvious if anyone does a pat-down search. Minor Gadget.

TACTICAL ARMOUR

This armour is a heavy armoured outfit (with a helmet) of the sort worn by SWAT teams and soldiers. It consists of a rigid ballistic jacket, usually made of composite material such as Spectra Shield (Spectra fibres held in a special Kraton resin), sometimes with ceramic or metal plate inserts. The armour is resistant to nearly all pistol fire and some less powerful rifle rounds. Tactical armour cannot be concealed — everyone seeing the character will know he or she is wearing body armour. Tactical armour is uncomfortable to wear all the time, and characters will not be able to rest and relax while wearing it. Someone who wears the armour for several hours on a hot day may have to make Body Stat checks to avoid passing out from heat stroke. Tactical armour subtracts 16 from the damage inflicted to the wearer. The armour requires at least three rounds to strap on or take off, and is sufficiently heavy that physically-oriented Skill checks suffer a -4 penalty. Major Gadget.

SHIELDS

Shields stop a significant amount of damage if they are interposed between an attack and the target with a successful Block Defence (page 67). If the damage exceeds the Armour rating, the remaining damage is delivered to the intended target. This damage can reflect several events: penetration of the weapon through the shield; damage delivered to the target's arm through a forceful impact; the shield slamming against the head or body of the target; a piece of the shield splintering away into the target; a target's physical exhaustion after successive shield impacts; etc. The reason why the target receives the excess damage is best determined by the combat situation.

BUCKLER

This small shield can be strapped to a character's arm and be used to block attacks. Since it is strapped to the character's arm, it does not require a free hand to use. Stops 8 damage. Minor Gadget.

STANDARD SHIELD

This shield is approximately 1 metre in diameter and provides excellent protection for the character. Due to its size, however, the character must have one free hand with which to wield the shield. Stops 12 damage. Minor Gadget.

HEAVY SHIELD

This shield is approximately one to two metres in height and acts as a virtual wall, protecting the character from damage. Not only does it require a free hand for use, but its large size also makes it difficult for the character to accomplish Body-related checks, imposing a -4 penalty. Stops 16 damage. Minor Gadget.

TACTICAL SHIELD

This modern version of a Heavy Shield is built from light-weight materials. Due to its advanced construction, it not only provides greater protection but also is easier to wield, imposing only a -2 penalty on Body-related checks. Stops 20 damage. Major Gadget.

SPECIAL PROTECTIVE DEVICES

GOGGLES AND EAR PROTECTORS

This gear provides a +6 Check Value bonus to resist the stunning effects of flash-bang grenades, but prevents the character from hearing any normal conversations. They require one round to put on or remove. Minor Gadget.

GAS MASK

A gas mask protects against tear gas and similar attacks, but imposes a -4 penalty on all Check Values for actions requiring peripheral vision. It requires one round to put on or remove. Minor Gadget.

BREAKING OBJECTS

Battles between powerful foes often result in a great deal of collateral damage. How effective is a manhole cover as a shield? How much damage can a telephone pole deliver before it breaks?

Objects are divided into two main categories: static and operational. Static objects are those that exist without working parts, such as most melee weapons, furniture, buildings, etc. Operational objects are things that have moving parts that work together in some way to accomplish a task. Examples include firearms, vehicles, computers, and other similar objects.

STATIC OBJECTS

Static objects possess an Armour Rating. This is an amount of damage that the object is capable of stopping. If the object is hit with more damage than this, it suffers damage up to its Armour Rating and any remaining damage passes through it (possibly injuring characters behind it). Though the object is damaged, it still maintains its structure but will require repairs later. If an object suffers repeated damage, roughly 5 to 10 times within a short period of time (GM discretion), it has suffered sufficient damage to break. If the object suffers five times its Armour Rating in damage in one attack, it is completely destroyed — it is beyond repair and must be completely rebuilt or replaced.

OPERATIONAL OBJECTS

Operational objects have both an Armour Rating and Health Points. If the object suffers more damage than its Armour Rating, the excess damage is deducted from its Health Points. If its Health Points are ever reduced to zero, it ceases to function in its given task; a car will no longer run, a gun will no longer fire, etc. The object is not destroyed — it is simply rendered non-functional. It can be repaired later and returned to normal. Additionally, as with Static objects, if the item suffers five times its Armour Rating in damage in one attack, regardless of how many Health Points it has remaining, it is completely destroyed — it is beyond repair and must be completely rebuilt or replaced.

PENETRATING (ARMOUR) VS. OBJECTS

When a character uses a Special Attack with the Penetrating (Armour) Ability (page 34), the attack is more likely to destroy an object. Each assignment of Penetrating (Armour) reduces the multiplier required to destroy an object by 1. For example, if a character attacks a steel girder, he or she must inflict over 75 damage (Armour Rating of 15 times 5) to destroy it. If the character had special claws with Penetrating (Armour) assigned three times, however, the character only needs to inflict over 30 damage (Armour Rating of 15 times [5 minus 3 due to three assignments of Penetrating: Armour = 2] = 30).

ARMOUR RATINGS OF OBJECTS

The Armour Rating of an object indicates how much damage the object can stop and it is dependent on the material from which the object is made, the size of the object, and how well it is constructed. A hollow, aluminium pole will be far weaker than a solid aluminium pole of the same size. Table 9-6: Static Object Armour Ratings provides rough Armour Ratings for common Static objects. GMs are encouraged to use this chart as a basis when determining the Armour Rating of other objects encountered in their games, adjusting for the material from which the object is made, the thickness of the material, the quality of construction, and other similar factors. The Armour Ratings and Health Points for common operational objects are listed in Tables 9-2: Weapons and 9-3: Vehicles. In most cases, the Health Points of an operational object is equal to 10 plus five times the object's Armour Rating.

Table 9-6: Static Object Armour Ratings

Object	Armour Rating	Object	Armour Rating
Bench/Table, Metal	8	Steel Cables	8
Bench/Table, Wood	4	Steel Girder	30
Cement Barrier	30	Stop Sign	6
Door, Wooden	8	Telephone Pole, Metal	20
Door, Vault	50	Telephone Pole, Wood	16
Dumpster, Metal	18	Tree, Giant	40
Furniture, Wood	6	Tree, Large	30
Ladder, Metal	8	Tree, Medium	20
Manhole Cover	24	Tree, Small	10
Melee Weapons	Equal to the weapon's maximum damage, see Table 9-2: Weapons		
Buildings	See Table 9-7: Building Armour Ratings		
Planetary Objects	See Table 9-8: Planetoid Armour Ratings		

DAMAGE TO WEAPONS

When a character uses a melee weapon against an armoured foe, there is a risk of the attack's force breaking the object. The damage from an attack must either be delivered to the target, or (if the target is armoured) delivered to the weapon itself. If the target's Armour prevents damage equal to five times the weapon's Armour Rating in one attack, the weapon breaks, snapping under the strain. When a character scores a critical hit (page 69), his or her weapon will not break, regardless of any damage prevented.

BREAKING ITEMS OF POWER

Items of Power are treated as if they possess an additional 5 Armour per Level of the Item of Power when determining whether or not they break.

For example, a character with a long sword that is a Level 4 Item of Power attacks a dragon. The character strikes a fantastic blow, delivering 42 damage. The dragon has 45 Armour. Under normal circumstances, a typical long sword, which can inflict a maximum of 8 damage, would break if 40 damage was prevented (5 times it's Armour Rating of its maximum damage value of 8). Since the character's sword is an Item of Power, however, it will only break if 140 damage is stopped by an attack (8 Armour Rating + 5 damage per Level of Item of Power = 28; 28 x 5 = 140).

DESTROYING BUILDINGS

Characters usually gain automatic successes when they target a building in a melee or ranged attack. Most buildings, whether they are mainly comprised of stone, brick, wood, or steel, have 5 Armour for each size ranking. If a building suffers more damage than its Armour rating, it has suffered structural damage; there will be holes in walls and/or floors, powered systems begin to cease working, etc. If the building ever suffers five times its armour rating in damage in one attack, some or all of the building will collapse. For example, a mid-sized office building partially collapses if it suffers 125 damage in one attack. Characters within or adjacent to a collapsing building may suffer damage equal to half the building's original Health Points total, unless they can reach safety (GM's discretion). As with normal Static objects, repeated damage may eventually destroy a building (page 82).

Weapons without the Area Effect or Spreading Abilities are much less effective against large structures such as buildings: any damage that penetrates the building's Armour is halved, representing the attack only damaging a small area of the structure.

Table 9-7: Building Armour Ratings

Type of Building	Size Ranking	Armour Rating
Phone Booth	1	5
Wood Shed	2	10
Three-Bedroom House	3	15
Small Office Building (6 Floors)	4	20
Mid-Sized Office Building (12 Floors)	5	25
Large Office Building (24 Floors)	6	30
Skyscraper (50 Floors)	7	35

BLOWING UP WORLDS

Really large and dense objects like an asteroid, moon, or planet has an exceptionally high Armour rating (15 Points for each size ranking) representing the massive thickness of rock or gas that surrounds its core. In order to do any significant damage to the planet itself (rather than just blowing away cities, vegetation, or other surface features) this Armour value must also be penetrated. Only weapons with Area Effect assigned multiple times are useful — all other attacks simply do not affect a large enough section of the object to be noticeable. Table 9-8: Planetoid Armour Ratings shows the armour rating of planetoids. If an attack delivers more damage than this value, the object has suffered damage necessary to blow away its atmosphere, cause massive earthquakes and (if it has oceans) tsunamis, and other similar disasters. If an attack inflicts five times this value in one blast, it will actually destroy the world, blasting it into smaller chunks or an asteroid belt. As with normal Static objects, repeated damage may eventually destroy a planetoid (page 82).

Table 9-8: Planetoid Armour Ratings

Size of Object	Awkward Size	Armour Rating
Meteor (100 metre radius)	6	90
Small asteroid (1 km radius)	9	135
Medium asteroid (10 km radius)	13	195
Big asteroid (100 km radius)	16	240
The Moon or Mercury	21	315
Mars	23	345
Earth or Venus	24	360

STRIPPED TO THE CORE:
THE HEART OF TRI-STAT dX

Tri-Stat dX is a flexible and easy-to-learn rules-light RPG system. It is also exceptionally comprehensive, with character creation options that can handle any character you can imagine. But at what point do options move a game from comprehensive to complex?

We believe that Tri-Stat presents a nearly transparent rules system that spotlights the role-playing, rather than the gaming, process. Once you understand the basics of its modular components, the rest falls into place. Players looking for a "fast and loose" system may be overwhelmed by the many pages of options presented, however, without recognizing that this book contains exactly what they are looking for. A sort of "can't see the forest for the trees" scenario.

The suggestions presented herein outline alternative ways of viewing Tri-Stat dX that may clarify our design focus.

Stats

The process of assigning Stats (Body, Mind, and Soul) to a character (page 8) is both straightforward and intuitive.

Attributes

Attributes present the widest range of options in this book, since they are the basis of character powers. Although each Attribute presents its own description and Level progression, they all follow the same basic pattern: low Levels are weak; high Levels are powerful.

You can summarize the entirety of pages 9-41 by pairing the Attribute names and Level costs listed in Table 3-3: Attributes to the effects summary in the chart below (intermediate and higher Levels can be interpolated as necessary). As the GM, you get to decide what a character can accomplish with "Moderate (Level 4) Mind Control," "Extreme (Level 8) Speed," or "Primal (Level 10) Teleportation." The Character Point cost remains equal to the Level times the cost/Level.

LEVEL 2 The Attribute has a minor character or game effect.
LEVEL 4 The Attribute has a moderate character or game effect.
LEVEL 6 The Attribute has a major character or game effect.
LEVEL 8 The Attribute has an extreme character or game effect.
LEVEL 10 The Attribute has a primal character or game effect.

PMVs

The Power Modifier Values are a useful option to differentiate different characters with the same Attribute, but they are not necessary for play. The Area, Duration, Range, and number of Targets affected by a Attribute are qualitatively subsumed by the Attribute Level; the higher the Level, the more powerful or far-reaching the effect.

As a more specific alternative, you could assign values to the Area, Duration, Range, and Target variables approximating equivalent PMV Ranks given in Table 3-1: Power Modifier Values (page 10). For example, Level 6 Environmental Influence (a major game effect) could affect an Area with a 10 km radius (Area 6) up to 1,000 km away (Range 6). Similarly, Level 10 Healing (a primal game effect) could instantly heal the injuries of 10 million targets (Targets 10) anywhere on the planet (Area 10).

Special Attack

Under normal game mechanics, the Special Attack Attribute (page 32) inflicts a base damage of 20 per Attribute Level. Damage decreases by 20 each time you assign an Attack Ability; conversely, damage increases by 20 each time you assign an Attack Disability.

A less mechanistic approach moves the Special Attack's effectiveness, and thus Level, up or down depending on the number of other advantages (up) and disadvantages (down) it provides. For example, an attack that simply inflicts 120 damage has a major effect (Level 6). If it can also track its target, partially penetrate armour, strike at great distances, and affect insubstantial characters, the attack has increased from a major effect (Level 6) to a primal effect (Level 10): Level 6 + 4 advantages = Level 10. Restricting the attack with inaccurate targeting and unreliable firing mechanisms reduces it back to an extreme effect (Level 8).

Skills

Skill Groups (page 46) indicate general knowledge within an area of expertise, and can be preferable to the full Skill system.

Defects

Like Attributes, the Defect descriptions on pages 50-57 can be summarized in the chart below. You can select the Defect names from Table 6-1: Defects, assign the appropriate number of Bonus Points, and determine the game effects.

1 BP The Defect occurs infrequently, and/or has a slight effect on the character.
2 BP The Defect occurs frequently, and/or has a moderate effect on the character.
3 BP The Defect occurs constantly, and/or has a severe effect on the character.

Initiative

To reduce the number of dice rolls, participants can roll once at the beginning of a combat to determine their characters' Initiatives for the entire battle (i.e. they act on the same Initiatives each round).

Delivering Damage

For faster combat resolution, all attacks can inflict 100% of their normal damage values (i.e. do not roll on Table 8-6: Damage Percentage). Critical hits can still deliver double damage.

GAME MASTERING INTRODUCTION

The greatest responsibility in a role-playing game is the job of Game Master (or GM). As Game Master, you create the opponents, plots, and situations that challenge the player characters. You take on the roles of all of the other characters in the story, resolve actions using the game rules and adjudicate rules questions that arise during play. This chapter provides brief Game Mastering suggestions and guidelines to help you run dynamic and exciting games of your own.

GAME MASTERING BASICS

You, as Game Master, fill many roles, handling all the parts of the game that the players do not. These roles can be broken down into four main areas: creator, actor, narrator, and referee.

CREATOR

You are responsible for creating the world in which the heroes have adventures, from the supporting characters to history, geography, and current events. It requires great effort, but many game worlds are similar to our own, and so a lot of the setting information already exists.

ACTOR

You play the roles of the various non-player characters (or NPCs) in the game, including the player characters' major opponents and allies. Keep the NPCs' goals and motivations in mind, but also focus on keeping the game fun for everyone.

NARRATOR

You also narrate events in the game, describing to the players everything that their characters see, hear, touch, taste, and smell. A good GM provides players with enough descriptive information for them to understand their characters' surroundings, but not so much that it slows down the game and turns it into a droning monologue of "flavour text." For example, you might say to one player:

"Your nightly patrol has been uneventful. The city is peaceful, its glittering lights shining downtown. You pause at the park for a moment in your squad cars, watching the city skyline. Suddenly, an alarm rings out and you hear the distant sound of gunshots coming from several blocks away!"

You have explained to the players where they are, what they are doing, and placed them in an active situation. The players may ask for clarification about your description, such as how many gunshots do they hear? Answer their questions to the best of your ability, while encouraging them to take action.

While providing narration for the players, try to avoid assuming actions or feelings on the part of their characters. For example, in the above description, do not end with "... the sound fills you with anticipation, so you speed away toward the commotion!" Each player must decide their own character's actions. Similarly, do not tell players how their characters feel about a particular NPC unless there is some outside force imposing those feelings. Rather than saying, "you take an instant dislike to him," when a character is dealing with an unpleasant NPC, you might try "he just does not seem very likeable." Better yet, simply play the NPC as unpleasant and rude, and the characters will start to dislike him naturally, without any prompting from you.

REFEREE

Finally, you apply and interpret the game rules and answer any rules questions that arise during play. You make the necessary rolls for NPCs, apply the effects of characters' Attributes and actions, and use the game rules given to resolve conflicts during the game.

KEEPING THE PLAYERS INTERESTED

One of your key GM roles involves keeping the players interested and involved. If you and the players are not having fun, your game needs to adapt quickly.

KNOW YOUR PLAYERS

Do you know what your players want to accomplish in the game? Discover their interests, likes, and dislikes, and cater to them. In some cases, players may be interested in story elements or plot ideas that do not inspire you, or you may want to run a type of game in which the players are not particularly interested. Negotiate something that is agreeable to, and enjoyable for, everyone.

Players have different styles. Some players like to immerse themselves in detailed characters, role-playing interactions with NPCs and the other heroes. Others like lots of action and the opportunity to blow off steam at the gaming table. There are those who want to play ultra-competent characters who are the best in the world at what they do and those who enjoy flawed or tragic heroes who make mistakes and suffer misfortune. Some are thinkers, enjoying puzzles and mysteries, while others are builders, always coming up with new characters and ideas. It is possible to satisfy all of these different types of players by understanding what gives each of them the most enjoyment in the game.

There may also be certain elements your players do not want to see in the game. Try and respect this as much as possible. It is difficult to fulfil the player preference of "I never want my character to lose," but it is easier to accommodate "I want my character to be truly unique. I never want to see a main NPC with the same Attribute focus as him," or "I really hate having my character framed or set-up," or "Violence and sex should not mix in any of our adventures."

LISTEN TO THE PLAYERS

Once your campaign is underway, pay attention to what your players are telling you. Most of the time, players make it clear when they are enjoying themselves and when they are not. They often like to speculate or think out loud, saying, "I think that the people behind the plot are ..." or "wouldn't it be cool if...." Use these discussions as insights into the minds of your players.

If the players speculate about a particular mystery or possibility, perhaps they might like to see the plot proceed in that direction. You can always change a mystery to fit the players' ideas behind the scenes — a tool called "retroactive Game Mastering" — so long as it does not interrupt the flow of the game.

Be sure you get feedback from your players. At the end of each session or adventure, ask them if they enjoyed themselves and what they liked. If they have criticism, accept it gracefully and use it to make your next story even better. If it seems that a player is not having fun, ask why and see what you can do to correct the situation. Sometimes players have bad days or just do not care for a particular adventure, but other times their expectations for the game are not being met.

SPOTLIGHT THE CHARACTERS

The focus of attention in your campaign should be on the player characters and their actions. This advice might seem like common sense, but a campaign can easily get caught up in events over which the characters have little control, taking the focus away from them and putting it on the plans and actions of NPCs. If you have created a detailed and interesting setting, you are going to want to show it off, but do not do so at the expense of the player characters. The story is supposed to be about them.

Likewise, be careful not to allow a particular player or character to dominate the plot. Some players may be more forceful than others, but try to give everyone equal time. In particular, include the specialities of the various characters in the adventure. There should be objects for the strong characters to lift and break, shadows in which the skulkers can hide, mysteries for the detectives to solve, etc.

If you are finding a particular character dull or uninteresting, mention this to the player and work together to develop his or her story further. Find hooks that make for interesting adventures or build a subplot around that hero to inject some more life and colour.

TAKE A BREAK

If you find yourself "burning out" because of stress, the demands of everyday life, or simply because you have run the game for too long, you only have one clear choice: take a break. Put the campaign "on hiatus" for a while and run something else or, better yet, let a player run a new game and give you a chance to play! When you feel like your creative batteries have been recharged, come back to the game with renewed energy. This solution is much better than allowing the campaign to drag and become a chore.

HANDLING THE RULES

Part of the Game Master's job is handling and interpreting the various game rules. Tri-Stat dX is of the "rules light" variety, but players have a way of putting their characters in situations the game's designers did not contemplate. No rules system can take every possible situation into account; Tri-Stat dX purposely leaves many aspects of the rules open for interpretation. You, as GM, ultimately must make the calls.

Designer's Note

Cheating: Just Do It!

If you want your players to think you are the best Game Master in the world, you only have one option: cheat, and cheat often. Never make a single dice roll without thinking to yourself, "Hmmm ... if I cheat and change the result of this roll, will I make it a better game?" In the games of Game Mastering and role-playing, there are no rules about "being fair," "sticking to the dice roll," or "being honest with the players." There is only one rule: make your game the best it can be. Gott würfelt nicht: "God does not play dice," said Einstein, and neither should you. Dice are only a tool to suggest how you should make up your mind. You make the decisions, not the dice.

Whether you ask your players to also follow this advice is up to you....

RULES QUESTIONS

Questions about the rules will arise during games and you must resolve them. They may be questions about how a rule works, what rule applies in a particular situation, or how to handle an unusual situation or application of a rule.

Become as familiar with the rules of the game as you can. Do not commit them to memory, although they may find their own way there the more frequently you play and run the game. Read through the rules thoroughly at least once before running the game, however. If you can, run a couple of solo test combats using the characters in this book or ones of your own creation to better understand how the game plays.

When a rules question arises, take a moment to handle it and make your answer as clear as possible to the players. When you first play the game, you are likely going to need to consult the rules more often, until you and the players understand the Tri-Stat System dX and its nuances. You may prefer to ask one of the players to look up rules for you during the game so you can focus on the story.

Most situations can be adjudicated without dice, or with a simple Stat or Skill check with an appropriate modifier. When in doubt, ask a player to make a Stat check for the character and apply a modifier (bonus or penalty) that suits the situation. See Check Value Difficulty Modifiers and Should I Make My Players Roll Dice? on pages 60 and 59 for additional guidelines.

Sometimes during the game you will make a "GM's call," where you say, "this is how I want to handle it for now." Ask the players to respect your ruling and move on with the game. If necessary, you can talk after the game about the ruling and how to best handle similar situations when they arise in the future.

HOUSE RULES

Every gaming group tends to develop its own set of "house rules" over time. These are modifications (or clarifications) of the game's rules or specific rules about conduct at the gaming table. House rules should make the game a more pleasant and enjoyable experience for everyone, and the players and the Game Master should agree upon them in advance.

Let the players know if you have changed any of the game's rules or if you are using any of the optional rules in your campaign. If the players have any concerns about these rules changes, discuss them and come to a compromise, if necessary. Record any rule changes and make a handout for the players, so everyone knows the rules; this will minimize disputes.

Rules of conduct, or "table rules" as they are sometimes known, vary from group to group. Some groups prefer to limit side conversations, inappropriate movie and television quotes, or jokes while the game is in progress. Others have no such rules. Use whatever works best for your group.

CHANGING THE RULES

On occasion, gaming groups may want to change the rules provided in this book to better suit their own games and style of play. If you find that a particular rule does not work for you then change it! Of course, you may want to consider carefully how any changes will affect point balance and other rules in the game. Test a rules change for a session or two and see how it works. You can always change it back or modify it further as necessary.

A particular opening in the rules does not necessarily require a rules change, but rather discussion and agreement among the players. In many genres, characters can have tremendous powers, and those powers can be abused by inexperienced players (see Power Abuse). Rather than changing the rules to restrict the characters, consider talking to the players and asking them to voluntarily modify their characters' behaviours to eliminate the abuse.

Never change the rules arbitrarily or without informing the players in advance of the change, and your reasons for it. This ensures there will be fewer rules disputes and confusion during the game.

TROUBLESHOOTING

Even the best gaming groups (and Game Masters) encounter difficult situations. When problems arise, you must resolve them. The following are some of the more common troubleshooting techniques you can use to help keep your campaign running smoothly.

MAKING MISTAKES

Sometimes you may make a mistake, whether it is misinterpreting a rule or not recalling an important fact about an NPC. If the mistake occurs during the game, own up to it, do what you can to correct it, and move on. It is much better to tell your players, "oops, I made a mistake," than to try and cover it up or, even worse, refuse to admit it and allow the game to suffer because of it.

Most mistakes are not likely to make much difference in the game. If a mistake does result in serious consequences (such as the death of a player character), you can either choose to reverse the problem — changing history and saying it never happened — or you can redress it in a future adventure. Perhaps the heroes get an opportunity to fix the mistake, or even to travel back in time and change history themselves, in order to "right the cosmic balance" by preventing an event that should not have happened.

CONFLICT BETWEEN PLAYERS

Although most campaigns are about teamwork and co-operation, conflict may arise between players in your group. Note this is not conflict between characters, which can be interesting and fun, but a conflict between the players that threatens to spoil everyone's enjoyment of the game.

If a conflict develops between two or more of your players, discover what it is and settle it through some mutually agreeable compromise. Make it clear to the players that they should keep their personal disputes out of the game. If they are incapable of doing so, or settling matters, then ask one or more of the difficult players to leave the game. Most problems can be solved long before that becomes necessary, however.

In the case of conflicts over events happening in the game, remind the players that it is just a game and the goal is for everyone to have fun. If an in-game conflict is not enjoyable for a player, try modifying or eliminating it. If there is conflict in the group about the game, find out what it is and settle it by changing the campaign's plot or adding some house rules that address the issue.

POWER ABUSE

The player characters may have tremendous powers. Perhaps they can literally move mountains, or change the course of history. Sooner or later, someone will decide to see just how far he or she can go with their character's powers.

While you should encourage player creativity, there are some uses of powers that are either inappropriate to the campaign genre or likely to ruin everyone's enjoyment of the game, if they are permitted. In those cases, you need to step in and politely, but firmly, refuse to allow them. For example, it is certainly possible to create a character able to control the minds of everyone on Earth with sufficient Levels of the Mind Control Attribute and the Area, Range, and Targets PMVs. Does that mean you have to allow such a character in your game? No. In fact, you probably should not. Tell the player "I do not think that idea works for our game" or "I do not think that your character would really do something like that, do you?" A gentle reminder is usually enough to dissuade most players, especially if it is for the good of the campaign as a whole.

In cases where players create abusive powers or characters, you can simply ask them to drop or redesign them to fit the campaign. There is nothing wrong with saying, "your interpretation of that Attribute is simply too powerful for this game" and setting limits on what the characters are capable of accomplishing. Alternatively, when an abuse of power happens in the game, you can surprise the players with the consequences of their actions in a later session.

GETTING BACK ON TRACK

No adventure plan survives unchanged after contact with the players, who do the most unexpected things ... some of which can derail a planned adventure. Sometimes all you can do is go with the flow and follow where the players lead you. If you have a good grasp of the setting and characters for your game, you should be able to improvise and deal with most digressions from your plot. The players may even provide you with some ideas and opportunities you had not originally considered.

Other times, when an adventure is diverting wildly from the story, you may need to nudge things towards the best direction. The trick is to do this without the players realizing, since the ideal adventure leads the players as little as possible. Fortunately, there are a number of ways to guide wayward players back in the right direction.

Give Them a Clue

Villains are notorious for taunting heroes with clues about their fiendish master plans. If the heroes wander away from the plot, have the villain drop them a hint like a riddle, a sudden attack, or a threatening message. A decent clue can put the heroes hot on the villain's trail again.

Sudden Insight

Provide a more direct clue using the heroes' abilities. A psychic or mystic hero might have a vision or flash of insight, or a skilled detective might piece together certain clues. Heroes with enhanced senses may pick up on clues others failed to notice, while a telepathic hero might sense a stray thought or "psychic impression."

NPCs

If all else fails, you can have an NPC guide the characters in the right direction. The best way to enact this is to have the characters come to the NPC's rescue, rather than the supporting character solving the problem.

Creating a Campaign

Creating a campaign may be as simple as running one adventure after another. There is an almost limitless number of different stories you can tell with Tri-Stat dX, and some campaigns are better suited to some gaming groups than others. This section looks at the major choices that go into building a successful adventure series.

Player Input

The first thing to do when planning your campaign is to ask your players what sort of game they would like to play. If you want to run a occult campaign featuring the world's greatest psychics battling against the evil undead forces, and your players want to play a far future space opera game, you are both going to end up disappointed. Negotiate with the players as necessary until you have a concept that everyone will enjoy.

Once you have established the kind of campaign type, ask the players what kinds of characters they would like to play, since that can affect decisions about the campaign as well. Some character concepts may not be appropriate for your campaign, and it is better to deal with that up front than have a player get set on a particular character idea that does not suit the game.

Campaigns, Mini-Campaigns, and One-Shots

A role-playing game can range from a brief one-shot adventure that takes a few hours to play to a lengthy campaign that can run over many sessions for a period of months or years. The story pacing and plot depth of a campaign is different from that of a mini-campaign, which in turn differs from that of a one-shot adventure.

Campaigns

A campaign usually has a vast or epic scope with a number of shorter plot arcs that weave together to reveal the greater story. The characters have time to develop unique personalities as they are faced with challenges to their bodies, minds, and souls. The characters can also learn new Skills and Attributes and establish lasting relationships with NPCs. In a campaign, the players have ample time to explore the various aspects of the world that the GM has created. Additionally, antagonists will come and go over the course of a campaign as they are defeated, destroyed, or reformed by the characters. The GM should establish the outline of a plot for the beginning of the campaign before play begins, but the middle and the end of the story will be largely determined by the interests and actions of the characters.

Mini-Campaigns

A mini-campaign is a single story arc that usually takes place over 4-8 gaming sessions. The characters may not develop much over the course of a mini-campaign since the plot only spans a few days to a few weeks. The antagonists are often present in every session with the major villain, if any, usually surviving at least until the final climactic conclusion to the story arc. Mini-campaigns require a greater plot structure than an open-ended campaign, and thus the players are required to focus more on the story and less on their own characters. The GM should know where the characters will start (the beginning) and where they should go (the middle), but the closure at the end of the story is heavily dependent on the choices made by the player characters during the game.

One-Shot Adventures

A one-shot adventure covers one single story idea in a 3-8 hour gaming session. These adventures are frequently run at conventions and for demonstrations at game stores. The characters are unlikely to develop much during an adventure because the story only spans a few hours to a few days. To maintain a high level of intensity during the game, the role-playing of character personalities is often sacrificed for dramatic action and conflict. In order to finish the adventure in one session, one-shots are often highly structured and only offer the characters a limited number of choices for each dilemma that they face. Most GMs usually script the plot to establish the beginning and middle of the story, and have a rough outline of the story ending that can be influenced by the players' actions (for example, will the villain win, lose, or escape?)

Using Attributes Unexpectedly

Sometimes, players will want to use their Attributes in ways that are not covered by the rules. Consider the following three solutions to this problem:

Use the Pushing Your Attributes Rules

On page 72 you will find useful guidelines about Attribute pushing. Players spend Advancements Points to push their characters' Attributes in specific ways. This method creates a mechanic to circumvent the rules for each Attribute, and is a great technique to keep a balanced game.

Low Levels of Dynamic Powers

Suggesting that all players assign low Levels of the Dynamic Powers Attribute (page 17) to their character during creation offers you a safety net when players want to do the unexpected. Since Dynamic Powers is such an open-ended Attribute, players can explore their characters themes — speed, combat, magic, strength, etc. — within the rules.

Just Fake It

When in doubt, make it up. If a character uses an Attribute in an unexpected way, adjudicate on its use and move on with the game. This technique avoids the rules completely, and does not impede the flow of your game session.

Sources of Inspiration

Sources of ideas for adventures are everywhere in the real world. Game Masters looking to feed their creative fires should consider the following:

Books

You can get many story ideas from reading both fiction and non-fiction books — mystery, fantasy, SF, biographies, real science, true crime, history, comic books, etc. When you come across a particularly interesting character or idea, ask yourself, "how would this work in my campaign?"

Internet

The internet is a source for nearly every type of information. You can find websites dedicated to various fictional characters (some of them astoundingly detailed) as well as sites devoted to role-playing in general, or Tri-Stat dX role-playing specifically.

Real Life

You can also draw inspiration from everyday life. Take inspiration from current events and news items, or turn your last vacation or visit to a museum into an adventure idea.

RPGs

Other role-playing games can provide ideas and inspiration for your campaign. Superhero RPGs are full of ideas that are easy to use; just change the game stats to work with Tri-Stat dX. You can also grab ideas from other games. A space station from a sci-fi RPG may be the ideal secret orbital base for a hero or villain team. A monster from a fantasy RPG may be unleashed on an unsuspecting city. Alien races can visit Earth, gadgets can show up in a character's arsenal, etc.

Television and Movies

TV shows and movies can give you ideas for characters and plots. They are useful for plots because they tend to have simple, self-contained stories that can be told in a short period of time. Many of your favourites may be available on video or DVD to rent or buy.

Technology and Gaming: A Changing Landscape

The face of role-playing today is drastically different from that of the '70s and '80s. Technology has had a significant impact on gaming, broadening the definitions of "campaign" and "game" to include a plethora of options available to households with computers and internet connections. Even if you are a traditionalist and prefer keeping role-playing as weekly face-to-face interactions with your local group of friends, computers can still augment your gaming experience in unobtrusive ways. You can greatly enrich your Tri-Stat dX campaign by taking advantage of even a small fraction of what computers can offer to you and your players.

WWW.YOUR-CAMPAIGN.COM

Establishing a website for your campaign showcases your creativity to the gaming public and is an ideal way to keep players up to date between sessions. Additionally, by posting important documents on the site, you can ensure the players always have access to vital gaming records — session logs, character backgrounds, world history and timeline, cast of NPCs, maps, and perhaps even their own character sheets and advancements. Documents posted on your webpage have several advantages over printed paper ones as well: they saves on photocopy/printing costs, they can be updated frequently without reprinting, and the players can access your website from any computer (even while on vacation).

If you do not have your own website already, one of your players or friends may be willing to host it for you. Perhaps a player will even design and programme your site in exchange for Background Points! If you don't have these options, many companies will host your webpages for a small fee, or even for free. Search the internet for "web hosting" for more information.

Private Emails

Email provides you with a fast and easy method to communicate with your players between sessions concerning campaign meta-issues: where and when the next game will be held, who is responsible for bringing munchies, social events you plan to do before or after the session, etc. It is also a great medium for one-on-one role-playing between sessions, for both player-GM and player-player interactions. A player's character might wish to pursue a lone thread from your campaign, but since no other character is involved, you may decide there is not enough time to role-play it during the normal session. Solo email role-playing, while not as dynamic or exciting as face-to-face interactions, can supplement your campaign by giving that player a chance to pursue his or her goals. This method of role-playing is also useful to further develop the backgrounds of the players' characters, rather than simply treating them as historical footnotes.

With your approval, email can also keep your players' characters connected between sessions. Players can discuss strategy and tactics, develop bonds that cannot be role-played during the sessions due to time constraints, or simply get to know one another's characters better. If the players copy you on the emails, you can comment on the players' messages when required or desired.

Email Lists

Email lists (also known as listserves) are similar to private emails, but all people on the list receive each and every message. This communication method is useful for game announcements and document distribution, especially if you don't have a website. Your internet service provider (ISP) might offer listserve creation as a feature (often handled by a programme called "majordomo"), or you can use one of the many free mailing list services offered by companies on the web. One of the best free services is Yahoo Groups (http://www.yahoogroups.com), which has an intuitive interface and many customizable options. You can set up your email list to allow only approved members (i.e. your players) to join, or open your list to allow anyone to sign up. This latter option is not usually a good idea for a closed campaign, since only a small group of people are involved in the game.

Guardians Of Order hosts many email lists for our fans, including one for the Tri-Stat System. To subscribe, send a message to tristat-subscribe@yahoogroups.com.

Play-by-Email

While a traditional gaming group of one Game Master and handful of players that meets weekly or biweekly to play is perhaps the best way to enjoy a role-playing campaign, forming and maintaining such a group is not always possible (or desired). An alternative to this is a game played over email with players across the city, or even around the world. Play-by-email games trace their roots to the '70s and '80s when play-by-mail games — people playing scenarios by sending messages and role-playing through the postal system — were popular. Although the face-to-face interaction is lost in an email game, it allows friends (or perhaps strangers) from vastly different locations to game together over cyberspace. As the GM, you send messages to all players, describing the events taking place in your superhero world. In turn, the players send you and the other players emails describing their actions and reactions. You adjudicate their responses, and continue the process by letting the players know how their actions transpired.

One main difference between traditional role-playing and an email RPG involves the game system. Frequently, the Game Master does not roll dice to resolve conflicts, but rather decides what would be best for the players and campaign and describes the results through email. Email games usually grant you more control over the story and plot than a standard campaign.

Cyberchatting

Online chatting is a great way to supplement both traditional campaigns and play by email games. If you and your players can find a chat room (preferably a private one) somewhere on the internet, you can meet there at scheduled times between sessions to discuss issues in real-time. A chat is similar to email communication, except the messages and responses can often be sent much more quickly and efficiently to everyone participating in the chat. A telephone conference call is a good analogy to an internet chat, except the chat is naturally slower but there are no long distance charges. Some chat rooms have an archive feature, which allows you to capture a text document of the chat transcript and post it on your campaign website; players who were unable to attend the chat can then catch up on what was said.

One popular form of cyberchatting is organized on-line campaigns known by many names: MUD, MUSH, MUX, MU, MOO, and others (derivations of "MU," which stands for "Multi-User"). These games are usually free to play to anyone on the internet (thousands of them are available), and might be a great way to meet other like-minded players and form a play-by-email game.

Shared Worlds

Although an entire book could be written on the concept of shared worlds, this treatment will be brief. A shared role-playing world is akin to a game setting controlled and directed by multiple Game Masters (and perhaps players). Each GM contributes his or her ideas to the direction and destiny of the world, while considering the input of the other participants. Each GM then uses the co-operatively created setting in his or her respective campaign. Feedback from the results of each role-playing session is then contributed to further develop the world. The process yields a living campaign world that is vast, intricate, and dynamic, shared by all those who participated. The creation of a shared world is perhaps best facilitated though an email list with an archive function, or a website message board.

NETWORKING DURING PLAY

If your entire gaming group is tech savvy and equipped, perhaps all players could bring their portable computers to each session and network them together. This decadent set-up can be used to send instant messages between players and the GM, distribute maps and illustrations of places and people, and even generate random numbers for everyone to see (a sort of public dice rolling). Computer networks may have an important place in the future of face-to-face role-playing.

TECH AND THE ONGOING GAME

If you can use a computer to supplement your campaign, why not other forms of technology? Cellular phones offer a wide range of services, such as paging and instant messaging, that may assist you expand your game into an engrossing 24/7 campaign. In-character phone calls are a fast and easy way to inject adventure into your normal sessions, especially if they are made to one of your players by a mysterious third party! Consider how some of the following can be used to turn your weekly game into a daily event for your players: faxes, custom burned CDs or DVD, camcorders, postcards from exotic locations mailed to your players, cryptic notes in school lockers or on the radio, classified ads to the player characters in the school or local newspaper, etc. The options are limitless.

Remember to tell your players about some of your ideas in advance, though, so you don't freak them out when they receive phone calls from some guy named Orpheus telling them that they are the ones that will save the world from destruction!

CONVENTION GAMING

Each year, hundreds of thousands of gamers worldwide spend one or more weekends playing games with complete strangers at game conventions. The largest in the world is probably Spiel (held in Essen, Germany), which hosts over 150,000 gamers each year (although much of the focus is on board games). In the Americas, both GenCon (25,000+ gamers) and Origins (10,000+ gamers) are well attended, attracting people from all over the world. Large regional cons may have attendance in the high 100s to low 1,000s, while the small ones may only have a few dozen participants. Regardless of size, the format is the same: show up at the con, pay your registration fee, sign up for games as a player or GM, and have a great time!

CONSTRUCTING ADVENTURES

Role-playing games run at conventions are called a variety of names: one-shots, adventures, modules, demos, scenarios, tournaments, and many others. Usually, you would design a short scenario (2-6 hours) for a small group of players (5-8 perhaps), focusing on a single idea. While the stories behind adventures vary greatly, you may wish to follow a traditional formula.

LEVEL OF DIFFICULTY

The first question you need to ask yourself is: "How much knowledge of Tri-Stat dX do the players need?" If you run a novice or beginner game, you will probably have some people sign up who have never played the system before. If you indicate that the game is for advanced or experienced players only, a player could show up who knows the rulebook inside and out. Let the convention organizers know the experience level you expect from the players so everyone can be better prepared.

PRE-GENERATED OR CREATED?

When running a convention one-shot, you might ask each player to create a new character with restrictions specific to the game. This may be your best option, but it can also pose some problems as well. If some players have never played a Tri-Stat System game before, you will need to provide them with a copy of the rules and help them create characters. Additionally, character creation may steal precious minutes from your game time, since most games have a fixed duration.

Instead of having players create characters, you can construct a handful of custom-built characters, with attached background history, for the game before the convention begins. These pre-generated characters are given to the players, allowing you to start the game right away. One major drawback, however, might arise from one player's desire to have a different character. For example, if you give a Roman senator character to a player who wants to play a gladiator instead, you have a problem.

Between the previous two option lies a third: a partly pre-generated, partly created character. You may give the players characters with half of their points allocated, for instance, and ask them to add more Points to develop and customize the designs. This method can save valuable time compared to players creating characters from scratch, but still provides flexibility in character concepts.

BE PREPARED

You should assume that the players will show up to your game completely unprepared, and consequently make preparations for them. Be sure to have enough dice, paper, character sheets, and pens for each player, in case they forget to bring their own. Wear a watch so you can keep track of time. If you can manage it, bring one or more extra copies of the Tri-Stat dX core rulebook for players to reference before/during the game. Purchase all the drinks and snacks you will need during the game early, to avoid disturbing the flow of the story later. Encourage players to do the same. If it's important, ensure your gaming friends know where you are during the adventure should they need to reach you.

PROPS

Props can greatly add to the atmosphere of your game adventure if you use them effectively and sparingly. Since you only have a limited time to play, and you might not have met any of the players before the game, using props can convey your ideas more intensely than words alone.

Consider how you can use the following props in your convention scenario: deluxe character sheets in specially designed folders, short history documents for the setting, city maps, headquarter floor plans, illustrations of NPC heroes and villains, trinkets that players will find during the game, pre-recorded sounds or discussions and a portable stereo so you can play them, costumes, and miniatures and a battle map if your adventure is more tactical in nature.

K.I.S.

Keep It Simple. Your one-shot adventures should have a single, clear focus, with a linear plot and clearly defined endgame outline — the exact opposite of a well-rounded campaign. You must ensure that your players do not have too much to accomplish; it will take them time to adjust to the game and consequently they will not be as quick to resolve the plot conflicts as your normal gaming group. After all, the players are interacting with a group of people they have never met before and may be a little uneasy. You must ensure the players do not get distracted chasing unimportant plot tangents if you want them to finish the adventure.

FOUR SHORT HOURS

Players arrive 10 minutes late (3:50). Introduce yourself and hand out character sheets and other information (3:40). Answer questions (3:25). Wait until Joe Gamer returns from the men's room (3:20). Answer more questions (3:10). Set the scene (3:00). Now you only have three hours left to play the game and it hasn't even started yet! Knock off another 30 minutes minimum if you want players to create new characters. 2:30 and time's wasting....

Oh yeah — don't forget that half the players will be leaving 15 minutes early so they can grab a bite to eat before their next game begins.

SOMETHING FOR EVERYONE

Perhaps one of the most difficult parts of running a con game is balancing time and action amongst the players. In your home campaign, you can fix the mistake of giving one player less time during one session by giving him or her additional role-playing opportunities the next time the group meets. At a convention, you do not have that support and consequently must get it right the first time.

Players want you to present them with opposition where their strengths can shine: players with strong or combat-oriented characters want to fight enemies; players with smart characters want to solve mysteries; and players with spiritual characters want to explore funky, non-traditional occurrences. Take a close look at the composition of your player characters and ensure the plot has something for each character to accomplish, both as a group and as individuals.

WRAPPING UP

By keeping an eye on your watch, you can predict whether your scenario will finish during the "correct" scene or not. If it looks like the adventure will be unfinished at the end of the scheduled time, you must adjust the action slightly to draw the plot to a conclusion before times runs out. Perhaps that means skipping a planned encounter, or having the enemy leave additional clues that direct the group to the climax of the story. The players will be very unsatisfied if you run out of time in the middle of battle, with the conclusion no where in sight.

If you can manage it, finish the game a few minutes early so you can gather your belongings and answer questions that the players might have. They will likely want to know what really happened, who was really behind the plot, and what will happen to their characters after the adventure.

DID I WIN?

Role-playing games are not competitive by nature, but you can establish a scenario where some players are considered to have done better than others (i.e. "won"). This is prevalent in tournament-type scenarios, where the top players from one event advance to the sequel event where they play with others who advance under similar circumstances. It is also important to determine the winners if prizes are provided by the convention.

You know better than anyone else who did the best. "Best" might mean "defeated the most enemies," but it could also mean "solved the most riddles," "saved the most people," or simply "role-played the character most accurately and intelligently." You can decide who won by yourself, but polling all the players in secret (get them to write a name or two on a piece of paper and give it to you) can give you additional insight.

SHARED GAME MASTERING

If you are attending the convention with some of your local gaming friends, you might consider asking one of them to share the Game Mastering with you. Although this is perhaps best suited for games with large numbers of players (12 and up), sharing the responsibility can also benefit the pacing and intensity of an adventure for 4-8 people. If you want to really demonstrate your creative talents, try running a con scenario for 24 players, with 4 Game Masters: you serve as the head GM, while your friends help as assistant GMs. Aside from possible logistical nightmares, the main problem with shared Game Mastering involves the GMs' different styles of play and task resolution. If you decide to run an adventure co-operatively, talk to the other GMs an hour before play begins to set some ground rules — how specific events should be adjudicated, how the Mastering duties will be divided, how the strengths of each individual GM can best be used, etc.

CROSSOVER GAMES

The crossover game is one of the best character creation alternatives for a convention scenario. For these games, players bring their characters from their home campaigns to the convention and play them in your crossover adventure. Obviously, the players will need to know this in advance so they remember to bring their characters, and thus it is vital that you give the convention organizers a suitable description of the game for their pre-registration booklet. Crossover games ensure that each player assumes a role with which he or she is comfortable and familiar, and allows you to jump into the action of the scenario right away.

You need to decide whether the characters can be played in the adventure as they are — with any number of Character Points and no restriction on Attributes and Defects — or whether each character needs to be slightly retooled to fit certain specifications (for example, all 100 Point characters, with no Mind Control Attribute allowed). Either choice will work, although the first method is perhaps best suited for more advanced or experienced players who will not be distracted by a Character Point spread amongst the group.

FREEFORM GAMING

Freeform gaming emphasises the role-playing aspect of an RPG more than the game aspect. The game environment is quite different; rather than sitting at a table and mixing player talk with character talk, freeform games encourage players to walk around, making use of the entire room (or perhaps even building), and remain in-character for nearly the entire game. The players — and for much of the time, the Game Masters — take the roles of actors, playing their parts in an improvisational theatre. You, as head Game Master, also undertake the director's position, using NPCs to loosely guide the characters through the events of the scenario.

A freeform scenario obviously requires more forethought than a regular adventure and often features a more restrictive plot and setting. For example, the adventure could focus on the events of a supernatural murder or grand theft, set in a posh hotel or on a small island. Some Game Masters take freeform gaming in a slightly different direction known as a LARP, or Live-Action Role-Playing. LARP participants frequently wear costumes appropriate for their characters. The most ambitious LARPs at the Origins and GenCon conventions are played over the entire weekend and support hundreds of participants.

Freeform games work best with a large group of players and multiple Game Masters. They also benefit from an environment away from the gaming tables that are standard at many game conventions. Consider hosting your game in more comfortable surroundings, such as the convention's hotel lobby or university lounge. You must also set specific ground rules before the game starts, stating very clearly to the participants that:

- no real or replica weapon props are allowed in the game;

- combat will be resolved using the game rules, and not acted out;

- no one should grab, hold, hug, or make physical contact with another participant; and

- everyone should stop what they are doing when a GM says, "freeze."

MOVING BEYOND TRI-STAT dX

Once you have perfected the art of Game Mastering Tri-Stat dX, what do you do next? Move beyond the confines of the system presented in this book.

Remember back to your childhood when you played "House," "Cops and Robbers," (and perhaps even "Doctor") with your friends. There were no Character Points, no rules, no dice, and no character sheets at that time. All that mattered was the role-playing. Capturing the essence of those games you played long ago should be your ultimate goal: just role-playing, and nothing else.

We believe that you are holding the best universal system ever created, but that doesn't mean we believe using the system is the best way to actually role-play. We have outlined some brief suggestions below how you can move beyond the game.

REMOVE THE SKILLS

The main purpose of a Skill system in an RPG is to help define a character's knowledge, most often used to differentiate low-powered characters from each other. The same result can be achieved by defining a character's background and history during creation, however. When a question arises during a game session that is not covered by a descriptive element, such as "can Dr. Jones swim?" or "does Xon-233 speak Cantonese?" the player can simply answer with "yes," "no," "a little," or "depends on the circumstances."

REMOVE THE ATTRIBUTE LEVELS

Rather than assigning Speed Level 5 and Superstrength Level 3 to their characters, players could indicate that their creations are superfast and superstrong. The same applies to PMVs and Defects: let the players define them how they want. When confronted with a situation in which a character's Superstrength is opposing an enemy's Superstrength, you should resolve the conflict in a way that best benefits the story.

REMOVE THE DICE AND THE RULES

Why use any rules at all? Since the story is the most important element, do you need to contain it within numbers, dice rolls, and charts? Dumping the rules moves the role-playing into the realm of improvisational theatre, where you and the players work off each other as the adventure progresses. If you feel this is a little too radical and want the safety net of randomness that only dice can provide, consider having the players roll two dice any time the result of an action is in question: the higher the roll, the better the outcome.

REMOVE THE GAME MASTER

Yes, you can cut yourself out of the game — as the GM — but continue on as a player. Co-operatively weaving an adventure without the moderation of a Game Master is a challenging process for traditional role-players, but millions of children around the world do it daily in the Land of Make-Believe.

Magnum OPUS

Publishing your own game really can be this much fun!

Read on to discover how GUARDIANS OF ORDER's creator-owned publishing imprint can help make your "great work" a reality.

MAGNUM OPUS OVERVIEW

Magnum Opus is GUARDIANS OF ORDER's creator-owned role-playing game publishing imprint. This line, which GUARDIANS OF ORDER will publish, distribute, and administer on behalf of our creative partners, is tailored for core games, accessory rule books, and campaign supplements developed under license for the critically acclaimed Tri-Stat System and our point-based redefinition of the d20 System Open Gaming License.

What Is A "Creator-Owned Imprint?"

This imprint is a publishing line where you, the creator, retain all copyright, trademark, and development rights to your work. Although we publish the Magnum Opus titles on your behalf, you retain control. The model used by one of the big players in the comic industry is a reasonable analogy to the Magnum Opus imprint.

Why Did You Choose The Name "Magnum Opus"?

"Magnum Opus" is Latin for "great work" — your great work.

Why Shouldn't I Just Publish On My Own?

While self-publishing is a great option for individuals with business experience and savvy, it's not for everyone. The adventure gaming industry has a very low bar for entry — almost anyone can publish their own products inexpensively, especially as PDFs — but it is very difficult to be profitable unless you are familiar with the inner workings of the distribution and retailer network. The Magnum Opus imprint allows you to concentrate on what you do best (create game books), while we use our established industry relationships to handle the rest (printing, distribution, shipping, and sales). Your Magnum Opus product will be sold as an actual hardcopy book — not merely a PDF on a website.

What Type Of Books Can I Publish Under Magnum Opus?

The Magnum Opus imprint is ideal for all Tri-Stat System products, as well as d20 System books produced under the Open Gaming License that use GUARDIANS OF ORDER's point-based variation (for more information about the OGL, see http://www.opengamingfoundation.org/). This includes:

- Core Tri-Stat dX role-playing games
- Tri-Stat dX supplements — rule books, new settings and genres, campaign worlds, adventures, etc.
- Supplements for *Big Eyes, Small Mouth* or *Silver Age Sentinels*
- Supplements for *BESM d20* or *d20 Mecha*
- General d20 System supplements that use the point-based variation presented in *BESM d20*

How Do I Sign On To Magnum Opus?

First, you decide if your product will be a Tri-Stat System product, a d20 System product, or a dual-statted producct. Then you contact us for a trademark license and Magnum Opus distribution contract. During the creation of your product we will work together on additional details.

The contact for Magnum Opus is GUARDIANS OF ORDER's President, Mark C. MacKinnon. You can reach him preferably through his email address (mark@guardiansorder.com).

Tell Me More About A Tri-Stat System License

Since the Tri-Stat System is not part of an open gaming license, you will require a Tri-Stat System license There are three versions of this ten-year license.

The first is for a brand-independent Tri-Stat dX supplement, which means that the product will carry the Tri-Stat dX logo, but not any of GUARDIANS OF ORDER's brand licenses (*BESM* or *SAS*). This license is ideal for game supplements that are not closely connected to anime or superhero gaming, but rather can be beneficial to nearly any Tri-Stat dX game. The fee for this ten-year logo trademark license is $200 USD, which includes the right to print the Tri-Stat dX logo on your product.

The second license is for supplements of one of our Tri-Stat System core brand lines, either *Big Eyes, Small Mouth* or *Silver Age Sentinels*. The fee for this ten-year brand trademark license is $700 USD, which includes the right to print the Tri-Stat System logo and the particular brand logo on your product. You also have the right to indicate that your product is compatible with, or a supplement for, the particular brand.

Finally, the third license is intended for products that are stand-alone Tri-Stat dX core games. These products, like our core RPGs, do not require your customers to own any other book to play the game for they are complete games and not supplements. The fee for this ten-year trademark and reprint license is $1000 USD, which includes the right to print the Tri-Stat dX logo on your product, and access the Tri-Stat System Reference Document (SRD). This SRD is approximately 80,000 words in length. Your license allows you to reprint any of the text, in part or in whole, in your product, and to alter the text to your specifications.

Tell Me More About A d20 System License

The core aspects of the d20 System, as well as significant portions of *BESM d20* and *d20 Mecha*, are part of Wizards of the Coast's Open Gaming License (see http://www.wizards.com/d20 for more information). Consequently, you do not require a license from us to publish a product under the OGL, but this license does not allow you to indicate compatibility with any of our products. To distribute your product under the Magnum Opus imprint, it must indicate compatibility with our d20 line, and thus you are required to obtain a trademark license from us. The fee for this ten-year license is $500 USD, which includes the right to print the particular brand logo on your product and indicate that your product is compatible with, or a supplement for, the particular brand. Your product must still adhere to the requirements of Wizards of the Coast's OGL and trademark licenses.

Tell Me More About A Dual-Stat License

If you wish to include both Tri-Stat System and d20 System game information in your product, you will require a ten-year license similar to the $700 Tri-Stat brand supplement license. This includes the right to print the Tri-Stat System logo and the particular brand logo(s) on your product and indicate that your product is compatible with, or a supplement for, the particular brand under both game systems.

Can I Re-Print Parts Of Your Text That Are Not Included In Your SRD?

Yes, although there is a reprint fee of 2¢ USD for each word of our text that you wish to include in your product. We can provide you with an electronic copy of the required text.

When Are The License Fees Due?

All license fees are due in advance upon the signing of the license agreements. The costs associated with the distribution and sales of your Magnum Opus products are withdrawn from your sales income, and thus there are no up-front costs to you.

Is There An Approval Process?

A brief one. All products must meet GUARDIANS OF ORDER's reasonable standards for quality and decency.

What Are My Responsibilities?

As the creator, you are solely responsible for final manuscript production. This means that you must find people to write, edit, illustrate, and layout the book in its entirety. You could do it all yourself, possibly with business partners, or hire freelancers instead. Contact us if you need some assistance with these matters and would like to hire our company to perform some of your production functions (such as editing, layout, or graphic design). We will provide you with the book's ISBN and barcode, but you must set the product's retail price (we can provide guidance for this, of course).

You are also responsible for advertising, marketing, and promoting the product outside our normal solicitation efforts. We will certainly provide some additional exposure for your products on our website and at conventions, without extra cost to you.

What Do I Do When The Book Is Complete?

You provide us with an electronic copy of the book and at least one printout. We can then check it for completeness and formatting errors. If you provide the files in a format compatible with our operating systems (recommended), we can ensure the files are correctly formatted for our printer as well.

How Does The Book Get To Retail Shelves?

Once we have the manuscript, we solicit it to distributors and retailers as a Magnum Opus imprint product, for release five months later. This window is necessary to gather enough pre-orders to cover the printing costs immediately in the first month of sales. We then print the books on our account, ship them to our warehouse, and deliver them to the distributors. Days later, your books are on retail shelves around the world!

How Much Do I Get Paid, And When?

Once a month, you will receive payment for sales of your product during the previous month from us (40% of retail value), less actual costs and our imprint fee. Monies are withdrawn from sales income to cover printing costs (variable), shipping costs (typically about 3% of retail value), warehousing/handling costs (about $0.35 USD for each book shipped), and our imprint fee (4% of retail value).

Can You Give Me An Example?

Let's assume you create a book with a retail price of $25 USD. The product will bring in approximately $7.90 USD (31.6% of retail value) for each unit sold, after all printing costs have been paid:

- $25 USD book sold to distributors at 40% of retail = $10 USD invoice value
- Shipping charge of approximately $0.75 USD
- Warehousing/handling cost of $0.35 USD
- Our imprint fee of $1.00 USD

Sounds Great! How Do I Get More Info?

Contact Mark C. MacKinnon at mark@guardiansorder.com.